RUGBY
REVEALED

RUGBY REVEALED

REACHING YOUR RUGBY POTENTIAL

Featuring advice from over 100 of the world's top players and coaches

Gavin Hickie and Eilidh Donaldson

BLOOMSBURY

Bloomsbury Sport
An imprint of Bloomsbury Publishing Plc

50 Bedford Square   1385 Broadway
London   New York
WC1B 3DP   NY 10018
UK   USA

www.bloomsbury.com

BLOOMSBURY and the Diana logo are
trademarks of Bloomsbury Publishing Plc

First published 2015

© Gavin Hickie & Eilidh Donaldson, 2015
Illustrations © Tom Croft, 2015

Gavin Hickie & Eilidh Donaldson have
asserted their right under the Copyright,
Designs and Patents Act, 1988, to be
identified as Authors of this work.

British Library Cataloguing-in-
Publication Data

A catalogue record for this book is
available from the British Library.

ISBN: Print: 978-1-4729-1618-1
        ePDF: 978-1-4729-1619-8
        ePub: 978-1-4729-1620-4

2 4 6 8 10 9 7 5 3 1

Designed by Austin Taylor
Printed and bound in China
by C&C Offset Printing Co.

Bloomsbury Publishing Plc makes
every effort to ensure that the papers
used in the manufacture of our books
are natural, recyclable products made
from wood grown in well-managed
forests. Our manufacturing processes
conform to the environmental
regulations of the country of origin.

To find out more about our authors and
books visit www.bloomsbury.com. Here
you will find extracts, author interviews,
details of forthcoming events and the
option to sign up for our newsletters.

CONTENTS

CONTRIBUTORS

■ PROPS

Cian Healy (Ireland & Leinster)
Dan Cole
(England & Leicester Tigers)
Jack McGrath (Ireland &
Leinster)
Marcos Ayerza
(Argentina & Leicester Tigers)
Martin Castrogiovanni
(Italy & Toulon)
Mike Ross (Ireland & Leinster)
Owen Franks
(New Zealand & Crusaders)

■ HOOKERS

Ben Kayser
(France & Clermont Auvergne)
Bismarck du Plessis
(Springboks & Sharks)
Corey Flynn
(New Zealand & Toulouse)
Keven Mealamu
(New Zealand & Blues)
Schalk Brits
(Springboks & Saracens)

■ LOCKS

Devin Toner
(Ireland & Leinster)
Eben Etzebeth
(Springboks & Stormers)
Geoff Parling (England & Exeter)
George Robson
(England & Harlequins)
Jamie Cudmore
(Canada & Clermont Auvergne)
Jim Hamilton
(Scotland & Saracens)
Joe Launchbury
(England & Wasps)
Marco Bortolami (Italy & Zebre)

■ FLANKERS

Jacques Burger
(Namibia & Saracens)
Kelly Brown
(Scotland & Saracens)
Sam Warburton
(Wales & Cardiff Blues)
Scott LaValla
(USA & Stade Français)
Sean O'Brien (Ireland & Leinster)
Shane Jennings
(Ireland & Leinster)
Steffon Armitage
(England & Toulon)
Tom Wood (England
& Northampton Saints)

■ NO. 8s

David Denton
(Scotland & Edinburgh)
Duane Vermeulen
(Springboks & Stormers)
Juan Leguizamon
(Argentina & Lyon)
Jerome Kaino
(New Zealand & Blues)
Todd Clever (USA & OMBAC)
Tyler Ardron (Canada & Ospreys)

■ SCRUM HALVES

Aaron Smith
(New Zealand & Highlanders)
Ben Youngs
(England & Leicester Tigers)
Mike Blair
(Scotland & Newcastle
Falcons)
Rory Kockott
(France & Castres)
Ruan Pienaar
(Springboks & Ulster)

■ FLY HALVES

Andy Goode (England & Wasps)
Beauden Barrett
(New Zealand & Hurricanes)
Felipe Contepomi
(Argentina & Club Newman)
George Ford (England & Bath)
Handré Pollard
(Springboks & The Bulls)
Ian Madigan (Ireland & Leinster)
Johnny Sexton (Ireland & Leinster)
Ruaridh Jackson (Scotland
& Wasps)

■ CENTRES

Conrad Smith
(New Zealand & Hurricanes)
Gordon D'Arcy (Ireland
& Leinster)
Jamie Roberts
(Wales & Racing Metro)
Ma'a Nonu
(New Zealand & Hurricanes)
Manu Tuilagi
(England & Leicester Tigers)
Nemani Nadolo
(Fiji & Crusaders)
Rene Ranger
(New Zealand & Montpellier)

■ WINGS

Blaine Scully
(USA & Leicester Tigers)
Brett Thompson
(USA & Edinburgh)
George North
(Wales & Northampton Saints)
Horacio Agulla (Argentina & Bath)
Marland Yarde
(England & Harlequins)
Tommy Bowe (Ireland & Ulster)

■ FULL BACKS

Andrea Masi (Italy & Wasps)
Chris Wyles (USA & Saracens)
Rob Kearney (Ireland & Leinster)
Willie Le Roux
(Springboks & The Cheetahs)

■ KICKERS

Leigh Halfpenny
(Wales & Toulon)

■ COACHES

Aaron Mauger (Leicester Tigers)
Alex King (Northampton Saints)
Alex Magleby
(USA & Dartmouth College)
Ben Herring
(Forwards & Defence Coach)
Brendan Venter (Sharks)
Conor O'Shea
(Harlequins Director of Rugby)
Daryl Gibson (NSW Waratahs)
Dave Hewett (Crusaders)
Eddie Jones (Japan Head Coach)
Gary Gold
(Sharks Director of Rugby)
Geordan Murphy
(Leicester Tigers)
Graham Rowntree
(England Forwards Coach)
Gregor Townsend
(Glasgow Warriors Head Coach)
Les Kiss (Ireland Assistant Coach)
Mark McCall
(Saracens Head Coach)
Mike Catt
(England Attacking Skills Coach)
Mike Cron
(New Zealand Forwards Coach)
Mike Ford (Bath Director of Rugby)
Mike Tolkin (USA Head Coach)

Paul Burke (Backs Coach)
Rob Hoadley (Defence Coach)
Rob Howley (Wales Back Coach)
Scott Lawrence (Life University)
Sir John Kirwan
(Blues Head Coach)
Stuart Lancaster
(England Head Coach)

SPECIALIST COACHES

■ KICKING

Dr Dave Alred
(Elite Performance Coach)
Greg Hechter
(Stormers' Kicking Coach)

■ PERFORMANCE

Billy Millard (Cardiff Blues)
Isa Nacewa (Blues)

■ STRENGTH & CONDITIONING

Ollie Richardson (S&C Coach)
Stephan Du Toit (Stormers)

■ SKILLS

Mick Byrne
(All Blacks Skills Coach)
Nick White
(Blues Set Piece Coach)
Simon Hardy
(RFU Specialist Coach)

PLEASE NOTE: **bold** typeface
has been used at first
mention of each contributor
throughout this book

PREFACE

> *We have been humbled and overwhelmed by the positive reaction of all those involved in rugby and their outstanding support, honesty and generosity. Their passion for the sport has been truly inspiring. To see the idea of the rugby family put to the test and pass with flying colours has been the most satisfying part of writing this book Thank you all for sharing your experiences of the game we love.*

Gavin HICKIE & Eilidh DONALDSON

CRED T: TIGER IMAGES

>> **The rugby pitch is a very honest place.** If you put the work in, you will get the rewards.' My lifelong friend and regular teammate Shane Jennings told me that and it's true.

I have spoken to some of the best in the game, over 100 players and coaches from around the world, and one message is loud and clear. There is no magic formula to reach your potential in rugby; it's about hard work. You must have that mindset, that ethos to fulfil your potential.

What this book reveals should be highly satisfying for young players. With guidance, time and effort the skills are all attainable and your ambitions are within your reach if you give 100 per cent every time you put on your boots.

In my professional playing career I was fortunate enough to play with and against some of the world's best players and was able to learn from them. Just one example was the work I did with **Simon Hardy** on my lineout throwing. The transformation in my throw from getting his expert insights on my technique and adopting some of his principles was incredible. It changed my game.

Providing access to the knowledge of the top names in the sport, such as Simon, is what I hope this book will do for others. The shared wish of

my fellow author Eilidh Donaldson and I is that a player reading this book takes its advice on to the field and sees an improvement. They should feel that with time and effort they can attack like **Johnny Sexton**, pass like **Aaron Smith**, tackle like **Tom Wood** or run lines like **Jamie Roberts** because they know what those players do and the work needed to get there.

As a player, I benefited from listening to the lessons of others and I feel very strongly that I am a significantly better coach now than I was before we started this book for the same reasons. The process has been a very practical reminder to me that you never stop learning the game, you never stop working, and you never stop aspiring to get better.

With the growth of the sport globally opening up more opportunities to compete, it is an incredibly exciting time to be a young rugby player. We hope this book helps you take your opportunities and reach your rugby potential.

Gavin HICKIE & Eilidh DONALDSON

▸▸ How this book can help you play rugby

Rugby is a race ... to get more points on the scoreboard, to beat your opponent to the ball on the ground or in the air, to think and act faster than the defence can react and to get fitter and stronger so you can outlast the opposition. It's also a race to stay ahead of the players challenging for your position, a race to improve your skills and a race to stay ahead in this constantly evolving sport. Whatever your goal or ambition, this book combines the voices of over 100 of the top players and coaches in the modern game to help explain how you can win your race.

Told by those who are at the forefront of the sport, this book can help find the right position for you, explain the skills required for that position in detail, improve your understanding of your role in attack and defence, and how to play the game.

THE POSITIONS

Rugby is often referred to as the 'game for everyone'. This is true both physically and mentally – there is a role for you whatever strengths and qualities you can bring to the team. Outlining the key skills for each position, this book features the insights of top professionals, delving into the individual roles and discovering what makes the good players great.

THE SKILLS

Everything flows from your ability to catch, pass, run and tackle, and core skills are rightly front and centre in this chapter. The players and coaches featured break down the mechanics of each individual skill and offer advice on how to improve.

TEN WAYS TO BECOME A BETTER PLAYER

We asked all contributors to give one piece of advice for young players and what emerged were ten points that any player could use to develop their game. From picking your position, through focusing on key aspects of your game to what you do away from the field, their advice outlines a blueprint for reaching your rugby potential.

Whether you are just starting to learn the game or you are already an established player looking for some insight to improve in your position, this book is a game changer. Get ready to play the best game in the world.

THE TEAM consists of 8 **Forwards** (bigger players who contest the set piece) and 7 **Backs** (faster players who run the ball). Within the Forwards players can be grouped into; the **Front Row** (1-3), **Second Row** (4, 5), the **Front Five** (1-5) and the **Back Row** (6-8).

RUGBY NUMBERS

- **100m** long x **70m** wide field of play
- **15** players, **8** Forwards and **7** Backs
- **8** substitutes
- **2** teams
- **3** officials
- **1** ball
- **80** minutes of action, **40** minutes per half
- **5** points for a try, **2** for a conversion and **3** for a penalty kick
- **10** minutes in the sin bin for a yellow card, **off** for a red

THE SCRUM A method of restarting the game following a minor infringement, such as a knock-on. The scrum involves both teams' sets of Forwards binding together before engaging in a pushing contest for the ball. The referee signals to the scrum-half to throw the ball into the middle of the scrum, known as the **tunnel** and the Packs can then push which is known as **scrummaging**.

THE LINEOUT A method of restarting the game after the ball has gone into **touch** (out of the field of play). Each team's Forwards form a line and the hooker for the attacking team throws the ball down the middle of the lineout. The aim is for the throwing team to win possession of the ball by throwing to a jumper, aided by two lifters.

TEAM NICKNAMES Some teams have alternative names for their national sides: **All Blacks** (New Zealand), **Eagles** (USA), **Los Pumas** (Argentina), **Springboks** (South Africa) and **Wallabies** (Australia).

RUCK AND MAUL

A ruck is two players, from opposite teams, on their feet and in contact with each other, contesting for the ball. Rucks can also be referred to as "the breakdown" and usually form following a tackle.

A maul must consist of at least 3 players; the ball carrier, defender and another player on the attacking team, binding on the ball carrier. All players must be on their feet to form a maul.

SCORING POINTS A **try** (5pts) can be scored by any player on the team who crosses the opposition's **try line** and grounds the ball. A **conversion kick**, which follows a try (2pts), and a **penalty kick** which follows an infringement (3pts), are both scored from the tee while play is stopped. A **dropped goal** (3pts) is kicked from the hand during open play.

KICKING FOR TERRITORY The ball cannot be passed forward but teams can kick the ball forward to gain field position or ease pressure. There are a range of kicks like a **grubber** (low flat kick), a **spiral** (a ball that spins through the air), a **chip kick** (short kick over defending player), or an **up and under** also known as a **Garryowen** (a high kick to test the opposition).

1.THE
POSIT

IONS

THE TEAM

The positions on a rugby team each have a specific role to play. Different physical attributes are required for each position, although strength and speed are key right across the team.

As a young player it's important to try out different positions as you learn the game and develop physically. This not only helps you gain an understanding of the different roles but also helps you find the position that makes best use of your skills and size.

All 15 players are on the field at all times and play in attack or defence based on possession. The team is notionally split into two groups, forwards and backs, who work collectively in different elements of the game:

Forwards (Pack) (Nos. 1–8)

The forwards pack is involved in all set piece plays and contests the lineouts and scrums. Larger and more powerful than the backs, they aim to win or retain the ball and drive the team up the field.

Backs (Nos. 9–15)

The backs tend to be smaller than their forward brothers as they need speed and agility to run the ball into space. They have to maximise the possession provided and get points on the board.

> *Keep everything as broad as possible in terms of your development and don't pigeonhole yourself into a position unless it's clear and obvious.*

Stuart LANCASTER, England Head Coach

While all positions have their skills and roles to perform individually, they also have close relationships with other players at set pieces and in open play. Understanding between these players is key if a team is to function fully, as they work together in critical elements of attack and defence.

- Front row (loose-head, hooker, tight-head)
- Second row (locks)
- Tight five (loose-head, hooker, tight-head, locks)
- Back row (flankers, No. 8)
- Scrum half and fly half
- Centre partnership
- Back 3 (wings, full back)

↓ Position of players on the rugby pitch

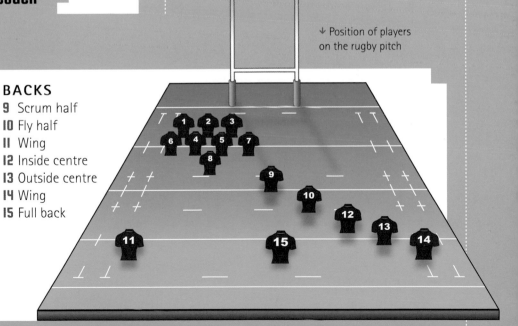

FORWARDS
1 Loose-head prop
2 Hooker
3 Tight-head prop
4 Lock
5 Lock
6 Blind-side flanker
7 Open-side flanker
8 No. 8

BACKS
9 Scrum half
10 Fly half
11 Wing
12 Inside centre
13 Outside centre
14 Wing
15 Full back

FORWARDS

We are looking for our tight five to set a solid platform. It's one of the tenets for us that they have to be the 'engine room', to win the ball at scrums and lineouts. That is first and foremost their responsibility, so making sure they are doing the fundamentals of those jobs is critical for the team.

Mike TOLKIN, USA Head Coach

A forward must be prepared to work tirelessly for his team and provide a strong attacking platform and clean, quick ball for the backs from set pieces. While the primary focus should be on their role in the scrum, lineout and at restarts, Nos. 1 to 8 are also expected to carry the ball, provide support and make tackles to benefit their team in attack and defence.

FORWARDS NEED TO BE:

■ Technically able to master the specialist skills for the set piece while still maintaining strong levels of core skills for general play. England coach **Stuart Lancaster** is clear on this point, 'One of the big challenges for coaches is to develop forwards technically in the set piece but also maintain that development of core skills – passing, catching, running lines, change of tempo/pace/direction – all those factors you need in a modern forward'.

■ Physically capable of performing the challenging roles required at set piece and have the stamina to give 100 per cent in general play for the full 80 minutes. All Blacks forwards head coach **Mike Cron** explains how fine the line is, 'Physically, a forward needs to be heavy enough to get the job done, but not one kilo heavier. If you want to play a fast attacking game this is a priority. Being strong is important, but being able to stay strong with movement is the key'.

■ Mentally strong enough to 'tough it' out against their opponents and gain dominance in the set piece. Natal Sharks head coach **Gary Gold** is under no illusion how hard the world's top players have to work, 'Mentally they need to be really strong to understand that it's going to be a tough environment. When you are playing against quality individuals week in and week out it is pretty hard'.

PROP

‘ *I moved between prop and hooker for a while, but when I left school the decision to play loose-head prop was nailed down. It is probably the one position in the game where you have to be physically dominant over your opponent, and there is a level of enjoyment in that. There is also a level of not enjoying it when you are going backwards in the scrum! But that means there is a big reason to work very hard; and you get to see direct rewards for the work you put in.* ’

Cian HEALY, Ireland & Leinster

»» As the engine of the team, props are strong, tough and technically sound rugby players who compete in the set piece where they are called upon to display core strength, excellent balance and explosive power. They should relish the one-on-one physical battle of the scrum and the technical manipulation of their opposite man, which can have a major impact on the success of the team.

Aside from the technical mastery of scrummaging, props must be strong ball carriers, be prepared to make the hard yards and to get their team on the front foot. They must move and tackle like a back row player without being exposed for pace in defence.

■ 'I was 18 when I started playing as a prop but I still played flanker too. I felt I was good as a prop and wanted to learn more about the position so I stuck with it and I love it now. One of the things I most enjoy is the profile of a front five player – humble, hard-working, low profile but really an important part of a team'.

Marcos AYERZA, Argentina & Leicester Tigers

■ 'In my first game of rugby, I played in the second row and I did not like it. I was sore and my scrummaging was terrible! After the game, my coach told me that I should play prop because I had the physical attributes of a prop of the future. It's a tough position but it is the best. Best thing about playing prop has always been the scrums!'

Martin CASTROGIOVANNI, Italy & Toulon

■ 'I played No. 8 when I was younger, then I started playing loose-head prop when I was 15, moving to tight-head full time at 18. It stuck because I wasn't athletic enough to be in the back row and I enjoyed the confrontation. It's probably the most physical position on the field and has the challenge of the competition at scrum time'.

Dan COLE, England & Leicester Tigers

■ 'Early on my body type fitted in with playing prop, but as I started to get older I leaned out a bit. That's when I started with the gym work and eating a lot so I could put on the muscle to keep playing. The feeling you get when you dominate someone is really high. Conversely, when you don't have a good day you take it really personally. That is why you work so hard in our position because you want to have more good days than bad days'.

Owen FRANKS, New Zealand & Crusaders

⊁⊁ Skills required to play prop

Set piece play dominates the prop's skill set. It is very important that props work hard to ensure they maximise their core skills but the focus should be on their set piece play.

'As a tight-head prop, your first job is to scrum, your second job is to perform your lineout duties, and every job after that is a bonus', explains **Dan Cole.** 'My coach at Leicester Tigers, Richard Cockerill, said that to me and it simplified my game and allowed me to focus on the job that was required. If you want to be a big ball carrier, get a job in the back row. Your job at tight-head is to push in the scrum. You won't get near the team if you go backwards in the scrum'.

Scrummaging

The primary role of a prop is at the set piece, i.e. scrums, lineouts and kick-off receipts. The most important is the scrum as this is where props can make the biggest contribution to their team. Ireland's **Mike Ross** stresses that the prop's role in the scrum takes priority over all others, 'You are there to scrummage. Not to run around, that's a bonus. Get that part [scrummaging] of your game right and you'll always be in demand'.

Developing the technical aspects of scrummaging – body profile, feet position and binds – is vital to being an effective scrummager. These areas are essential not only for generating maximum power but also to ensure safety, which is of paramount importance. Players new to the position should build up their understanding of this specialist aspect of the game under a coach's expert guidance. **Marcos Ayerza** is clear on this: 'A prop should develop their technique for the scrum and get a feel for it, for safety reasons but also to gain an understanding of the formation,

which is unique and so precise'. Dan Cole is even more precise, 'Your prime job as a prop is to keep the scrum up and move forward, or at least not move backwards, so it's about static exertion', he explains. 'You need knowledge and understanding of the technical aspects like force and body angles'.

It's a role you practise on the training field but only really learn through experience in games. It is important to use each scrum, good or bad, to make you a better player. It takes time, which can be frustrating, but with age comes experience. 'I do not know many props who dominate others from a young age,' says Italy's **Martin Castrogiovanni**. 'Props tend to get stronger as they get older and develop technique through experience.' Ireland's **Cian Healy** agrees, 'You learn through experience of being in tough positions over the years. You have to fight it out in bad places.'

» **Learn more about scrummaging** – *see pages 126-47*

↓ Loose-head and tight-head props bind with the hooker to form the Front Row of the scrum

Lifting in the lineout

In the lineout, props lift the jumpers into the air to contest for the ball. This skill requires speed across the ground and explosive strength to lift a jumper. Props need to be very strong to hold the jumper in position, before returning them safely to ground. Crusaders' coach **Dave Hewett** outlines the roles of props in attacking and defending lineouts, 'In attack your lifters are helping the jumpers secure the ball by providing that propulsion of lifting. The other side is they are trying to keep track of what the jumping guys are doing given the defensive lineout they are trying to operate.'

>> **Learn more about lifting in the lineout**
– see pages 151-2

Physical strength

You must have a very strong work ethic when it comes to your own physical development in the gym to play prop at the highest level. Playing prop requires dedication to build a body that can tolerate the intense pressure of the scrum. Focusing on exercises like squats and deadlifts will help to build strength in the lower body and core. While focusing

→ Props Marcus Ayerza and Owen Franks lift their jumpers in the lineout

on Olympic movements can be of functional benefit, as All Black's Owen Franks explains, 'Olympic movements, like push press, are really good for replicating lifting in the lineout. Any exercise where you are using full body movements and you are using your legs and your arms at the same time will help come game time.'

Cian Healy believes it is about maximising your flexibility and strength as a prop but also adding other aspects to your game, 'When you combine those two as well as working on speed work, running skills and evasion, which all add another dimension to a prop's game, it helps to set you apart as a prop.'

→ Props like Owen Franks can provide vital metres for their team with ball in hand

Stubborn mindset

Requiring a mixture of aggression, competition and a desire to dominate your opponent, prop is not just a position; it's a state of mind. The Stormers strength and conditioning coach, **Stephan Du Toit**, feels it is important young players understand that they need to be mentally and physically tough. 'Make sure you want to play there and don't get put in it against your will.'

You have to be single-minded in your desire to beat your opponent in the scrum or, as Dan Cole states, have the 'no quit' mindset.' Mike Ross backs up that point, 'You have to be stubborn; a lot of scrummaging contests come down to who blinks first when the pressure comes on.'

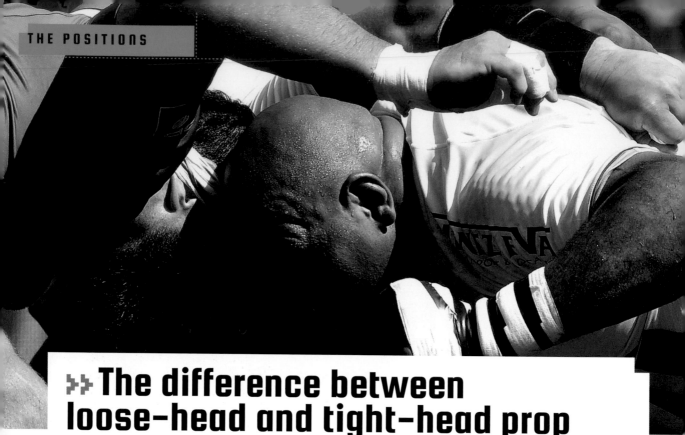

>> The difference between loose-head and tight-head prop

The naming of the props' positions refers to their different head placements when the scrum is engaged. The No. 1 is referred to as the loose-head prop, as the left-hand side of his head is free, while the right hand side of his head is against the opposition's tight-head prop. One side of his head is unrestricted, i.e. loose. The No. 3 is called the tight-head, as both sides of his head are restricted against the opposition hooker and loose-head prop.

Loose-head (No. 1)

The more attack-focused of the two props, the loose-head has a destructive role in the scrum and is tasked with disrupting the opposition tight-head by destabilising him and driving him backwards. Martin Castrogiovanni outlines the role, 'As a loose-head, you have a shoulder free and this allows you to work with a little more freedom.

You are looking to get under the opposing tight-head prop and drive him backwards.'

Tight-head (No. 3)

The tight-head is the anchor of the scrum, or as Cian Healy describes, 'the heavy timber who locks down the scrum.' The tight-head has the more physically demanding role in the scrum because a lot of the weight comes through them. They also have to defend against two opponents, as Martin Castrogiovanni explains, 'The tight-head has two people in front of him in the scrums, the opposite loose-head and hooker, and they are looking to attack you. A tight-head must be as strong as possible and be able to defend himself against these two opposite players.'

↑ Toulouse's South Africa prop Gurthro Steenkamp (R) faces Bayonne's French prop Aretz Iguiniz (L) in a scrum

✢✢ A prop's role

In attack

There is a lot of grind and very little glory in playing prop. Of course, set piece play and, in particular, scrummaging is the primary duty of the prop. It is their effort at these points in a game that secures possession for the team. Set piece play takes a huge physical toll. Owen Franks points out that 'people don't realise how hard it is to get up off the ground after a scrum or a driving maul to do the rest of the work that everybody else does'.

However, props also need to contribute to the attack, and thereby to the overall success of the team. Outside of their roles in the set piece, props perform a lot of the unseen work around the field, for example, ensuring their team maintains its momentum in attack at breakdowns. Props need to ensure they are incredibly strong while also possessing very high levels of fitness to be able to get around the pitch following the set piece. They are also required to possess all the necessary skills to catch, pass, run with the ball and get over the gain line.

As with any position, it is important for props to understand their role in attack, which usually means clearing out rucks. Mike Ross advises young props to work on their rucking skills, which will help them 'target any threats to the ball carrier and take them past the ruck, ensuring clean ball for the scrum half'.

But other skills are crucial too, 'Ball carrying is being able to break tackles and get over the gain line' says Ireland's **Jack McGrath**. While Mike Ross believes it is important that, when the opportunity does come 'you make sure you run hard and square and look after the ball at all costs'. Cian Healy, a prop noted for his ball

carrying skills, stresses how important it is that 'skilful props at international level can get around the pitch and influence open play'.

Perhaps Argentina's Marcos Ayerza description is the clearest, however, 'Lifting in lineouts, setting up mauls, clearing out rucks, running with the ball, being a good footballer – all those skills are part and parcel of what you need generically, but the prop's job all starts from the scrum'.

In defence

In defence, props are usually expected to make tackles around the ruck. Props must snuff out the opposition attack in this area by doing their utmost to stop the opposing team getting over the gain line. They must also keep a close eye on the opponents' scrum half who will look to drag props out of their defensive position by running themselves and using runners off them.

All Blacks forwards coach **Mike Cron** outlines why a prop has to be as fit as a flanker, 'In top-level modern day rugby props make a fifth to a quarter of your total team tackles. They also make a quarter of the team's misses as well, so you have to work on that. Modern day props are running 6 kilometres in a game where they play 55 to 60 minutes'.

It is important that props keep their place in the defensive line where they can be of most use to their team. Keeping your head up in defence and not getting isolated is important according to Ireland's No. 3 Mike Ross, as you will be targeted by the more agile members of the opposition in open play. 'Outside backs will be quicker and nimbler than you nine times out of ten, so if you're out in the midfield, make sure you stick with the defensive line and swap in closer to the ruck if there's time, as you'll be needed to stop any pick-and-goes around the side of the ruck or to smash any one out runners or if the scrum half tries to have a go'.

GOOD
V
GREAT

WHAT MAKES A GOOD PROP A GREAT PROP?

The ability to do everything that is required on a rugby field and not just be a one trick pony. The main thing is being able to scrum consistently well, get the job done nine times out of ten at scrum time every game. The best props are the ones that can do the whole package and do it well. *
Owen FRANKS, New Zealand & Crusaders

Having a good knowledge of the game, mental toughness, scrum work, lineout work, tackle technique, ball carrying ability and ruck work. To be a great prop you need to have all of the attributes. Cian Healy has all of these and has proved he is world class. *
Jack MCGRATH, Ireland & Leinster

A healthy disregard for their personal safety, great consistent scrum technique and a large dose of aggression. Cian Healy always goes into games full bore, and is very much the modern prop – freakishly strong, powerful, and very good with the ball in hand (for which he should be stripped of his membership of the front row union!). *
Mike ROSS, Ireland & Leinster

→ No prop averaged more metres made per match (14.8m) than Cian Healy in the Pro 12 in the 2013/14 Season. Graft. @OptaJonny

Good prop to great prop is just determination to keep going and learning from mistakes. Traditionally it's an older position because you learn your trade. You have to get your arse handed to you so you learn and come back stronger. Sometimes that happens in a game or it can be over a series of games, next time you play you keep going. Carl Hayman is what you want from a tight-head in regards to his scrummaging ability but also what he did on and off the field as well. **'**

Dan COLE, England & Leicester Tigers

Props will always judge props by how they scrum. What really makes a prop a good prop is a mentality to want to be the best, dominant in every game and a good asset for his team. His technique and detail of the things he does at scrum time make him the best. Carl Hayman has been an amazing prop and all-round player, breakdown intelligence, clearing rucks, one of the best tight-head at scrum, willing to play the scrum and test himself going forward. A good ball carrier if needed. **'**

Marcos AYERZA, Argentina & Leicester Tigers

Marcos Ayerza is the best loose-head in the world and doesn't get the recognition he deserves. Tony Woodcock has been up there for a long time and is a very tough opponent. **'**

Martin CASTROGIOVANNI, Italy & Toulon

→ Carl Hayman was the 1000th player to be capped for the All Blacks

Gethin Jenkins was one of the first to show that he could be a good scrummager and ball carrier and he showed a good bit of poke too. He played in a couple of Lions' series as well, and that shows how to be the best at something. Closer to home you have Jack McGrath who gets his scrum work done but also gets on the ball and enjoys having a run around. **'**

Cian HEALY, Ireland & Leinster

HOOKER

' One of my high school coaches thought it would be good for me to change position. I was playing No. 7 at the time and when he said change position I thought he meant a move to the blindside! Now that I have played hooker for a long time I really enjoy it. You are continuously in the game, a big part of the lineout, leader of the scrum and always involved around the pitch. It is a position that I love so much. '

Keven MEALAMU, New Zealand & Blues

▸▸ **A dynamic position on the team,** the No. 2 is a role that calls on a player to switch between the high intensity of contact and the isolated pressurised skill of lineout throwing. The mental challenge is matched with the diverse technical and physical challenge a hooker undertakes.

The No. 2 scrummages and hooks the ball, has to throw the lineout ball with pinpoint accuracy, and possess a huge appetite for work around the pitch in attack and in defence, effectively supplying the team with an extra back-row forward. Composed, confident and mentally tough, great hookers tend to be leaders within the team.

■ 'I used to play back row then my coach suggested I play hooker and it's probably the best decision I've ever made. At hooker I can add a different dimension. It's the best position on the pitch because I can do everything. I'm in the backfield catching the ball, I'm running a lot, I'm defending, I've got the scrum and the throwing at the lineout to deal with.'
Schalk BRITS, South Africa & Saracens

■ 'I played No. 8 and loose-head prop. One day the hooker got injured and I'd played a lot of basketball so the boys said "Ben can throw," and I did it and it went well. It was more the technicality of throwing and the fact I'd played forward that made me play hooker. It's about being good at the scrum with all the technical ability you'd expect from a back row. That's why it's so fascinating and exciting to play.'
Benjamin KAYSER, France & Clermont Auvergne

■ 'I actually started out at fly half and full back but our hooker was injured and I promoted myself to the No. 2 jersey where I've been playing ever since. The position has always appealed to me as you're always close to the action and part of most of the plays – scrums and lineouts.'
Bismarck DU PLESSIS, South Africa & The Sharks

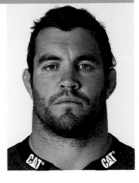

■ 'My coach at school said I probably wouldn't get picked to play my position of flanker, so if I wanted to play for the first XV I could play hooker, and I've played it ever since. I enjoy always being around the ball, be it scrum or lineout, and in the modern game you act as a fourth loose forward anyway.'
Corey FLYNN, New Zealand & Toulouse

▸▸ Skills required to play hooker

The hooker is a specialist position, requiring exclusive specialist skills. These skills are throwing the ball into the lineout and hooking for the ball in the scrum. In order to execute these skills at a consistently high level, while under immense pressure, the hooker must possess both a choleric and phlegmatic temperament.

England's forwards coach **Graham Rowntree** believes that 'a hooker is picked for his set piece, scrum and lineout at international level. Next on the checklist is a ball carrier, then his ruck and carry the same as other players.' RFU specialist coach **Simon Hardy** reels off a long list of requirements, which touch on all aspects of the player's character and skill set, 'Size, strength, game understanding, to be mentally and emotionally tough, to want to master key skills, to have good values in terms of work ethic, life skills and habits, to concentrate on the next action and not the last, to understand and manage yourself.'

Lineout throwing

Lineout throwing, one of the toughest skills in rugby, requires the hooker to display pinpoint accuracy and meticulous timing throughout the 80 minutes of the game, while under pressure from the opposition. Throwing has become harder, according to All Blacks forwards coach **Mike Cron**, because 'teams are competing more on opposition ball than they used to.'

The throw is only one part of the lineout. In order to ensure the team has a functioning and effective lineout, every player in the pack needs to work together. **Keven Mealamu** explains that feedback among the players on the field is vital to get the precise timing required,

↑ Bismarck Du Plessis gets ready to throw into the lineout

→ Corey Flynn scrums down in the front row for Top 14 team Toulouse

'Telling my locks at the lineout that I want them to get into position a little quicker or them telling me that they want the ball in quicker if my throw is too lobby is key. Making sure that you are having those little conversations makes a huge difference.'

Like the goal kicker of the team, the hooker has the responsibility of executing an isolated skill. His aim is to ensure his team claims possession of the ball. The responsibility of lineout throwing comes with pressure. That pressure is intensified if the lineout misfires, as **Corey Flynn** describes, 'It's a lonely job playing hooker because if the lineout isn't going well, you get the blame. It could be any one of three or four reasons why it's not going well: the lifting, jumping, wrong call, or it can be a bad throw. However, it's always the hooker's throw that seems to get blamed. You need to spend hours perfecting your throw and building confidence.'

» **Learn more about lineout throwing** –see pages 153-7

Scrummaging and hooking

As part of the front row, the hooker has the key role of being the leader in the scrum. This means that he sets the height of his pack's scrum and determines when the pack are ready to 'engage' with the opposition forwards. He also has the crucial responsibility of hooking the ball on his scrum. 'For scrummaging you have to be physically strong and have good technique,' explains Keven Mealamu, 'but you also need to do a lot of work with the people around you, your props, your locks and everyone in the scrum.'

The scrum is a dark place so it is important to build trust and understanding between the front row. Corey Flynn spent seven years as part of a front row consisting of props Wyatt Crockett and Owen Franks at Super Rugby team the Crusaders, 'We got to a point where it didn't matter if anyone had been injured or been away with the All Blacks, it was just like putting on a glove again,' he says. 'You learn people's traits over time and that's how you get trust because you are all working towards a common goal.'

South Africa's hooker **Bismarck du Plessis** has some very practical advice for young hookers on how to build strength and also develop their understanding of the role at the scrum, 'Start by making sure your neck and traps (the muscles on the top of your shoulders) are very strong. My dad made me a head harness, which I still use to this day, to keep those specific muscles very strong. If you move to hooker from another position, my suggestion would be to start out

at a lower level for a season or two. It's very important to learn how to fall when the scrum collapses, for instance.'

Hooking the ball requires flexibility and precise timing in order to win the ball and not destabilise/depower the scrum. As Mike Cron explains, 'you want the foot off the ground for the minimum amount of time. You want to get back into a strong pushing position to resist the power. Flexibility helps get you back into pushing position after you hook.'

» **Learn more about scrummaging and hooking** – *see pages 138-9*

↓ Schalk Brits loves the diversity of playing hooker including running in attack

Mental strength

Hookers must compose themselves before each lineout throw. This is a mental challenge, as the lineout may follow an intense scrum or multiple phases of play. Often suffering fatigue allied with a racing pulse, the hooker must display mental fortitude to deliver an accurate throw whenever required. French hooker **Benjamin Kayser** believes it's similar to the challenge faced by the kicker, 'You need to get fired up and, a split second later, be focused, cool-headed and technically good enough to throw into the lineout.'

Schalk Brits relishes what he refers to as the tricky part of being a hooker and says this variety is why he loves the position, 'As a hooker, you've got to scrum against the opposition where there's no hiding; it's a one-on-one battle. Then you have to run and tackle as many people as you can to get the ball. Then someone kicks the ball out and you have to throw the ball with pinpoint accuracy at the lineout.'

►► A hooker's role

In attack

Typically hookers are one of the main ball carriers within the pack of forwards. A strong core skill set along with pace, power and strength are required to be an effective hooker in attack. 'For England, we pick an aggressive carrying hooker and play a set piece that gets him to carry on second or third phase,' says Graham Rowntree. Corey Flynn, a former flanker, says that if you are 'a hooker looked upon as a fourth loose forward, you want to get your hands on the ball and be a ball-playing option.' 'A hooker isn't going to

> *You need to get fired up and, a split second later, be focused, cool-headed and technically good enough to throw into the lineout.*
>
> **Benjamin KAYSER**

have the footwork of a winger but he can still carry the ball and get go forward like a winger,' highlights Crusaders coach **Dave Hewett**.

South Africa's Schalk Brits has always enjoyed running with the ball and it's something he has done effectively from a young age, 'A lot of what I've learned to do I learnt playing 4 v 4 touch with some mates on a small patch of grass. It really helped with the biggest skill in the game – decision-making.'

In defence

The hooker's role in defence is similar to duties performed by the back row. This means making tackles and competing for the ball at the ruck by getting very low, with a wide base [legs wide, hips down] over the ball. Graham Rowntree believes that 'A hooker who is as good a tackler as a flanker has another string to his bow.'

USA Eagles head coach, **Mike Tolkin**, stresses the hooker's work around the ruck in defence. Like his flankers, he wants the hooker – indeed the whole front row – to 'get stuck in and slow down the ball by making it difficult to move them off the ball.'

GOOD V GREAT

WHAT MAKES A GOOD HOOKER A GREAT HOOKER?

A great hooker is somebody who does his core jobs very well and then applies himself around the pitch well too. '
Keven MEALAMU, New Zealand & Blues

Reliability and consistency in performance. You look for your hooker to be the key man who will never miss a tackle, be strong in the scrum, be a complete all round good player and be an accurate thrower even under pressure. I've always admired Keven Mealamu because he is relentless and has the whole package – very good tackler, leader in combat, very good scrummager, worked hard on his throwing to get more accurate through the years. For the French team William Servat ticked all the boxes. '
Benjamin KAYSER, France & Clermont Auvergne

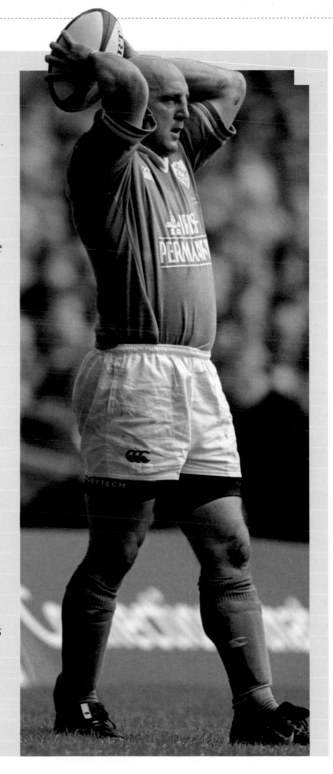

↙ Keven Mealamu was the third All Black to reach the 100 caps milestone

→ Ireland's Keith Wood has inspired many hookers, including author Gavin Hickie

❝ *You play against* different hookers and you can pick things from each one of them. Keven Mealamu who in close quarter running is next to impossible to stop. He is fantastic the way he can change his direction. Then you have Bismarck du Plessis who when he gets over the ball you can't move him. I've been lucky enough to play against some really good hookers and these two would be the ones I would think of as great for sure. ❞

Corey FLYNN, New Zealand & Toulouse

❝ *I had a few* I based my game upon – Keith Wood, Keven Mealamu, Andrew Hore, while Tatafu Polota-Nau is also a very good hooker. I learnt something from all of them. ❞

**Bismarck DU PLESSIS,
South Africa & The Sharks**

❝ *Keith Wood and Uli Schmidt* were both pioneers from a hooker's perspective, and responsible for modern hookers playing more like an extra loose forward. Ireland's Wood was a skilful guy but he got around the pitch a lot, as did South Africa's Schmidt, and they really inspired me and the way I wanted to play. ❞

Schalk BRITS, South Africa & Saracens

LOCK

> At high school, I played in the back line before former Springbok lock Hennie Bekker suggested I move to lock and I've not looked back. I enjoy the physicality, as well as competing in the lineouts and just mixing it up with the big boys.

Eben ETZEBETH, South Africa & The Stormers

»Traditionally the 'big fellas' of the team, modern-day locks are now tasked not just with securing the ball for their team at lineouts and kick-off and providing support in the scrum, but also acting as extra back rows.

Mobility and versatility are essential for a lock to be successful in open play where they need to be strong ball carriers. While their height is an asset in jumping, it is a distinct disadvantage in possession where their challenge is to get low to stop defenders getting under them or where they have to work harder than everyone else to effectively hit a ruck.

■ 'I started playing at No. 8, but then I hit 6 foot 4 and didn't stop growing until I was 6 foot 10! So naturally I was put into the second row. I love playing the position because it incorporates a lot of skills needed for rugby, catching high balls, lineout jumping and lifting, scrummaging. You also need to be proficient with ball in hand and in defence.'
Devin TONER, Ireland & Leinster

■ 'I played a lot at No. 8 when I was younger, but with my height second row was always going to be my position. I like the physical side of the game and I like the blend, there's a licence to be slightly freer and get your hands on the ball.'
Joe LAUNCHBURY, England & Wasps

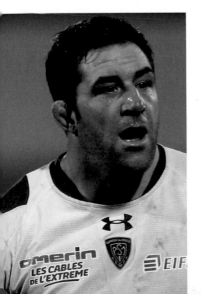

■ 'I started in the back row and then got pushed down into lock. For me it was body type – basically long arms, long legs and able to push quite well. The forwards seemed to be having the most fun, so that's where I wanted to be.'
Jamie CUDMORE, Canada & Clermont Auvergne

□ 'Locks act like an extra back row through a high work rate, and are usually among the top tacklers in the team. It's not a "glamorous" position. [Locks] work hard and do a lot of the "unseen" work so that other teammates can profit.'
Geoff PARLING, England & Exeter

▶▶ Skills required to play lock

The primary job of the locks [second row] is to win the ball at the lineout and kick-offs. Their next task is to support their props and push in the scrums. After their set piece responsibilities, locks are expected to be strong ball carriers and support players in attack. Defensively, locks must make tackles and lots of them.

To achieve their primary objective of winning the ball, locks need to work on their aerial and catching skills. 'The basics are so important and other parts of your game need to be built around these,' stresses Scotland lock **Jim Hamilton**. Ireland second row **Devin Toner** agrees that these skills are 'the bread and butter for a second row', but added, 'You can't forget the defensive responsibilities and work at the breakdown, securing possession at ruck time'.

Jumping at the lineout

Usually, one of the locks has the responsibility of calling the lineout, but both second rows are expected to be able to jump to contest for the ball. Explosive and powerful, a lock needs to work on their jump and timing with their lifters to ensure they are in the right place at the right time to catch the hooker's throw. Springboks' **Eben Etzebeth** breaks down the elements of the skills a lock needs to work on, 'Jumping in the lineouts entails working on your speed on the ground, explosiveness and "jumping power."'

▶▶ **Learn more about the lineout** – *see pages 148-59*

Kick-offs & restarts

In order to catch the ball at kick-offs and lineouts, it is very important that locks work on their catching skills in order to secure possession of the ball for their team. Practising catching the ball under pressure at training will help to build confidence in this area. 'I would tell a young player to first work on their aerial skills, catching high balls and to be comfortable doing it,' advises Devin Toner. 'This will help at restarts and also lineout time'. Canada's **Jamie Cudmore** highlights the attacking potential of catching the high ball in open play, 'A good kick receipt and setting up of a good platform [ruck or maul] to counter-attack the opposing team is a really important part of a second row's game'.

▶▶ **Learn about kick-offs & restarts** – *see pages 160-2*

Scrummaging

Locks are in the second row of the scrum, behind the props and the hooker. They contribute to the power of the scrum by optimising their pushing profile in support of the front row. Eben Etzebeth recommends that as a lock you should 'focus on your low body position, keep your feet back and then work forward in unison. Also, keep a strong bind on the prop in front of you and the lock next to you'.

▶▶ **Learn more about the scrum** – *see pages 126-47*

→ Locks like Devin Toner need to be good in the air to catch at the lineout and from kick-offs and restarts

✛ The difference between Nos. 4 and 5

Traditionally, there is a difference between the two locks. The No. 4 is usually bigger and heavier. At lineouts, he is commonly jumping at the front, and in scrums he is generally on the right-hand side, behind the tight-head prop. The No. 5 is typically slightly taller and more agile. He can ordinarily be found at the middle of the lineout and frequently is the team's lineout caller. In the scrum he is on the left-hand side, behind the loose-head prop.

For Jamie Cudmore, the ideal locks pairing sees players with a blend of skills that complement each other, 'The No. 4 is on the tight-head side of the scrum and he is a bit heavier, a grinder who pick and goes, getting over the gain line, a real rock behind the tight-head prop. The No. 5 is more of a rangey player, longer, with good lineout sense and good ball-handling skills.'

✛ A lock's role

In attack

Second rows have similar roles to the back rows in attack. Their main duties are to support the ball carrier and hit rucks low and hard, to clear out any threats from the opposition. Locks are also expected to be mobile ball carriers, helping their team get over the gain line. England forwards coach **Graham Rowntree** believes that second rows are at their best when utilised in this way, 'The team that will win the World Cup will have

← Jamie Cudmore clears the ball from the ruck for Clermont Auvergne

a back five [in the scrum] of back rowers. I want my locks to act like back rowers in terms of ball carrying, offloading and clearing out rucks.'

Devin Toner cited advice he received from Jono Gibbes [Leinster forwards coach and former All Black] as helping him understand his role, 'You can be the most skilful lock out there but if you can't secure possession at your own breakdown you're no use to anyone. You need to hit rucks with intensity and aggression and just be able to move people out of the way.'

A high work rate is required from all top players, but the range of responsibilities for the lock at set piece when coupled with their role in general play means athleticism and stamina are crucial. All Black forwards coach **Mike Cron** highlights two of his players as examples of the physical standards required, 'Brodie Retallick and Sam Whitelock have huge engines, high work rates and are athletic, big men that can get around the paddock quickly. The way the game is going means it's hard to leave a guy out there for 80 minutes if you want to play at high octane level the whole time.'

In defence

The locks' high work rate in attack is matched by their high tackle count. Eagles head coach **Mike Tolkin** looks to his USA second rows to be 'big impact tacklers'. Canada's Jamie Cudmore says, it's about 'stopping the opponents' big runners around the ruck.'

Devin Toner agrees that the main role is 'to slot into the defensive system and make your tackles. Come off the line hard and try and put pressure on the attack.'

WHAT MAKES A GOOD LOCK A GREAT LOCK?

Great second rows *are the ones who are able to run a really successful lineout on top of excelling at all their other duties. Victor Matfield and Paul O'Connell have been at the top of their game for so long and both are pretty much masters of the lineout, both offensively and defensively. You can tell that they put a lot of work in their analysis of the opposition and this tells because they disrupt so much of their opposition's ball.*

Devin TONER, Ireland & Leinster

A hard worker *for the team. They'll do a lot of the unglamorous work, they hit rucks, make tackles, jump in the lineouts – for me that's what makes a great lock. Somebody who epitomises that, and who I look up to is Paul O'Connell. He has been at the top of the game for a long, long time and he is rightfully getting the plaudits for that. For me, he is a great lock forward.*

Joe LAUNCHBURY, England & Wasps

→ Victor Matfield is one half of the successful Springbok Second Row pairing with Bakkies Botha

→ Ireland's Paul O'Connell captained his team to back-to-back RBS 6 Nations titles

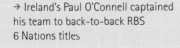 *Great players* are the ones who can perform under high pressure. Guys like Nathan Hines or Brad Thorn are able to perform consistently at a high level and under pressure. **᠊**

**Jamie CUDMORE,
Canada & Clermont Auvergne**

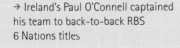 *For me, lineout ability* is paramount if you want to become a great lock. Hand-in-hand with the lineouts are physicality, a massive work rate and playing like an extra loose-forward on the field. The perfect lock would probably be a mould between Bakkies Botha and Victor Matfield. **᠊**

**Eben ETZEBETH,
South Africa & Stormers**

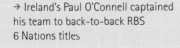 *Great players* have the physical attributes but also the skills levels to match. Second rows like Victor Matfield and Bakkies Botha are great examples. **᠊**

**George ROBSON,
England & Harlequins**

BACK ROW

'*No. 8 chose me. I initially started playing No. 6 and 7, but my build became the natural build to slot into a No. 8 ... You are a key link between the forwards and the backs and there are lots of opportunities when you can put yourself into the game. I love No. 6 as well because you are in a key leadership role. Defence is my favourite part of the game and as a No. 6 you are in a position to put your influence on the game defensively.*'

Jerome KAINO, New Zealand & Blues

>> **The workhorses of the team,** the back rows spend the game in search of the ball. From their role at set piece to their responsibilities in support and at the breakdown, Nos. 6, 7 and 8 are in constant motion, which explains their high tackle count and metres gained.

In addition to being big, athletic and quick ball carriers and support players, back rows need to be astute decision makers and fierce tacklers who are always on the lookout for an opportunity to steal the opposition ball in the contact area and force a turnover.

FLANKER

■ 'I like the physicality and it suited my size at the time when I was 16 or 17. I'd played a few positions up to then but I liked the idea of being a big back row forward. You are involved a lot and have a big influence on the game.'
**Sean O'BRIEN,
Ireland & Leinster**

■ 'I started as a centre and my old man, who was a big influence on me becoming a rugby player, said you know you are the same height as George Smith, you are playing centre and doing pretty much what he does. After that he took me to see George Smith play and it looked fun. You are always around the ball or getting your head stuck in there, and I liked it.'
Steffon ARMITAGE, England & Toulon

■ 'I played stand-off until the age of 13 and then I moved into the back row. It's got a lot of different aspects to it: tackling, passing, running, rucking, turning over the ball so you are constantly involved in the game. It's a position that really does test out all your basic skills.'
**Kelly BROWN,
Scotland &
Saracens**

■ 'I played lots of different positions, but the natural position for me was the back row because I wanted to be in the thick of it all the time. You can't hide in the back row; you are always working, always looking for the next job.'
**Tom WOOD, England
& Northampton Saints**

NO.8

■ 'When I started out, I played in the front row but then I got a bit taller and moved to lock and not long after that, we needed someone in the back row so I moved again and this time I stayed there. I like playing at No. 8 because you are a link between the forwards and the backs, you're always close to the ball, you get to steal, carry and tackle – it's like being in the heat of battle all the time.'
Duane VERMEULEN, South Africa & The Stormers

■ 'I played in every position of the back row: Nos. 6, 7, and 8. One of the reasons that I like the back row is being in contact with the ball as much as possible, and playing No. 8, you can have more opportunities to play with the ball, to attack and to make big decisions in a game.'
Juan LEGUIZAMON, Argentina & Lyon

■ 'When I first started playing rugby with my brother, I was the youngest and the smallest so they put me at wing and at full back. So back row wasn't my first choice, but it worked out well for me. You have to work hard, be fit and be physical and I enjoy all those aspects of the position.'
Todd CLEVER, USA & OMBAC

■ 'When I was younger I was in the backs, and as I started getting bigger I thought the back row was the area where you could get into the game the most. The back rows and centres tend to get through the most work in a game and it's nice to be central to that.'
David DENTON, Scotland & Edinburgh

⇥ Skills required to play in the back row

Back row players are part of the forwards pack and are involved in the set piece. However, their main contribution to the team is in open play, where the skills of the Nos. 6, 7 and 8 complement and combine to get the ball over the gain line and prevent the opposition achieving just that.

The key responsibilities for the back row are ball carrying and support play in attack, tackling and forcing turnovers [stealing the ball] in defence. To be able to execute these skills consistently, back rows must possess a very high level of fitness. They must know and understand all the forwards' and backs' calls and be able to predict where the next tackle or ruck will be so they can get there quickly.

The Springboks' No. 8 **Duane Vermuelen** outlines the skills he thinks a back row player must have, 'The key ingredients are determination and hard work. When it comes to specific skills, I rate the following important: vision, good handling skills and explosivity'.

Tackling

Tacking is a fundamental skill of the back row. You cannot be a poor tackler and play in the back row because you have so many tackles to make. Leinster flanker **Shane Jennings** describes this vital skill as being about 'technique backed up by a lot of confidence in your abilities'.

'It's not something that you can do half-hearted because that's when injuries happen', was the advice New Zealand's **Jerome Kaino** received as a young player from his father; 'If you go in

↑ 34 - The number of tackles by Saracens Jacques Burger v Exeter in 2013, the most recorded by Opta in an Aviva Premiership game in 10 previous seasons. Barrier. @OptaJonny

[to contact] with everything you've got, give it 100 per cent, more often than not he'll come off worse than you'.

⇥ **Learn more about tackling** – *see pages 108-21*

Support play

Whether in attack or defence, the back row is expected to be in close proximity to the ball carrier. USA's **Scott LaValla** thinks the role of a flanker is to be 'all over the field, winning and securing possession, taking off loads, and offering options for the playmakers'.

To be in the right place every time a player has to be able to read the game and predict what will happen next. USA Eagles captain **Todd Clever** believes this means the extra work of learning 'all the backline plays as well as the forwards' calls' if they are to be effective. Shane Jennings says knowing the calls 'allows the flanker to be able to predict where the next tackle contest or ruck will happen on the pitch. This, in turn, allows the flanker to run the most efficient line to the next perceived point of contact (ruck).'

Fitness

Playing in the back row is a physically demanding challenge with a high work rate in attack and defence, so a very high level of fitness is a prerequisite if you are to make a contribution throughout the full 80 minutes. No. 7s Shane Jennings and **Jacques Burger** are both keen to stress that fitness is an essential part of the open-side flanker's role if you are to cover the ground you need to in a game. 'Fitness is not something you can be taught. You will need a lot of self-discipline and hard work which is what the 7 shirt is all about' stresses Burger.

Strength and conditioning also play a vital role, but Duane Vermuelen argues that 'what you can do in the gym does not really count all that much – it's all about what you can do on the field. Preparation and conditioning are very important, but it's pointless if you can bench the most but you fall off tackles.' Wales and Lions captain **Sam Warburton** agrees, highlighting the need to be good in both areas, 'To play 7 you require a lot of physical attributes, strength, speed, endurance as well as being good in contact.'

→ David Denton claims the high ball for Scotland in an RBS 6 Nations game against England

Set piece

As part of the forward pack, back rows contribute to the lineout, scrum and kick-offs. Assistant coach for the Crusaders, **Dave Hewett**, sums up the back row's duties in the set piece as, 'jumping or lifting at the lineout and at scrum time, their primary role is providing power for the scrum so the No. 8 can launch at attack or provide good, clean ball for the 9.'

Argentina's Juan Leguizamon outlines the No. 8's responsibilities at the scrum, 'As an 8 you must control the scrum and the ball from the back, and then be able to manage the ball the best you can. You look to attack from the base or to leave it to your 9, who provides a clean and fast ball for the backs.' Scotland's **David Denton** advises working on your passing from the base of the scrum, 'particularly passing right to the left because that's where you are required to do it the most, but I work on both hands.'

>> **Learn more about the set piece** – *see pages 124-63*

Aerial skills

Often, the No. 8 remains in his own half if he feels the opposition are going to kick the ball. This means that the No. 8 effectively acts as a second full back at times, so he must possess the aerial skills to catch the ball before running it back into the opposition territory. The main reason the No. 8 is elected to catch these kicks is because the team's No. 8 is usually the main ball carrier within the forward pack.

Catching a high ball is something Scotland's David Denton practises every day, 'The thing I practise the most is aerial skills, it's a very central part of playing at 8.'

>> **Learn more about catching the high ball** – *see pages 183-4*

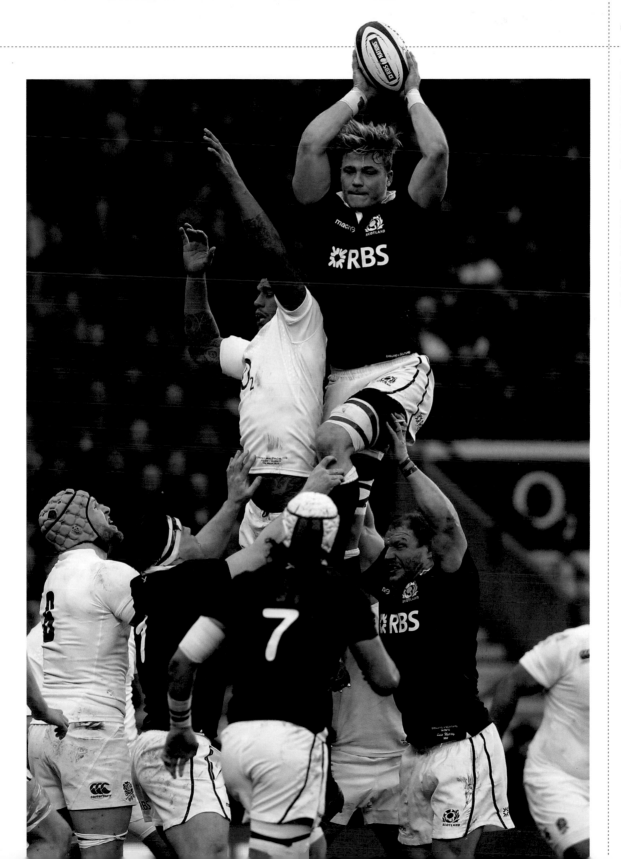

▶▶ The difference between Nos. 6, 7 and 8

The roles of the back row vary between teams, but ultimately a team wants a range of skills spread across the three players that provide options and balance in attack and defence. Players can be strong in a number of areas but they can't do everything. England's **Tom Wood** highlights the dilemma, 'My speciality is lineouts but I can't win the ball in the lineout and run off the back to win the kick chase at the same time.'

In broad terms a No. 6 tends to be a lineout jumper and a tackler. The No. 7 is the team's main tackler but also works on the ground. This means he is trying to poach [steal] the opposition ball or at least slow down their ball at the ruck. For both positions **Graham Rowntree** highlights 'tackle selection and post-tackle threat' as key features.

Back rows' defensive focus should be on their ability to read and react to the opposition's attack. They have to constantly communicate and organise teammates around them. 'You are dictating things, talking a lot, communicating different things to the backs outside you and your 8 inside you,' says **Sean O'Brien**.

The No. 8 is usually the main ball carrier within the forward pack, both in open play and off the set piece. Graham Rowntree explains that he is looking for 'horsepower from my No. 8, he has to be the main carrier for us. From scrums, short lineouts and in the backfield, receiving high balls and bringing them back for us.'

Tom Wood offers two ways to approach the role, 'The No. 8 is either big, strong and can carry the ball far or they are skilful and can put the ball through the hands and act like an extra back.'

▶▶ The back row's role

In attack

The back row provides continuity to a team's attack by supplying support options to the ball carrier and protecting the ball in the ruck. They need to 'be first everywhere', as **Steffon Armitage** puts it, first in support and first over the ball if someone goes to ground after being tackled.

To provide support you have to be in the right position at the right time and this takes

knowledge of the game, and reading and reacting to what plays out in front of you. USA captain Todd Clever speaks of the importance of thinking ahead, 'You have to have vision for the game and play the game in your head before it actually unfolds by knowing where the next breakdown is going to be. It takes time, and the more you play the game the more you find shortcuts, and this really helps your development.'

USA Eagles coach **Mike Tolkin** stresses the importance of having a back row who can act as effective ball carriers and support players, as 'the ability to perform both of these tasks, makes the back row become really valuable players.' From **Juan Leguizamon**'s perspective, back rows are all about adding pressure in a game, adding that in attack their role is about 'making the other team feel uncomfortable in defence through hard running'.

All Blacks forwards coach **Mike Cron** speaks of the value a great ball carrying No. 8 can bring to a team, 'All the great teams have a great No. 8. He should be an explosive athlete, great ball carrier, good in the lineout. They are like backs just a bit bigger. You want an athletic No. 8 because we get the ball in ours hands more and you need athletes that can make the right decisions.'

↑ Sam Warburton takes on Rory Best in the Wales v Ireland RBS 6 Nations clash

In defence

Relentless, ruthless and fearless, back row players look to expose any weakness in the opposition to slow down play and preferably turn over the ball. This means tackles and lots of them. USA head coach Mike Tolkin stresses that it's not just the number of tackles that is important, 'Lots of people focus on the amount of tackles as a measure of work rate, but if there are no dominant tackles in there, you really don't have the whole story.'

One of the top tacklers in the game, Namibia's Jacques Burger, prides himself on his defence and says he sets out to dominate every collision but emphasises the importance of tackle technique, 'I see it as my job to stop teams getting over that gain line, especially off first phase attacks. Yes, you need to be fearless but safety is very important, as you will have to make about 20 of these a game on average. Make sure your technique protects you when going into contact.'

Decision making at the breakdown is also a part of the flanker's game, 'When to attack a breakdown and when not to chase lost causes' is an important part of a flanker's skill set, explains Burger. 'You can dictate the speed of second phase ball, which buys your team some time to get set in defence.'

As a back row you have to disrupt the attack and contest the ruck. To be a 'destructive player' Shane Jennings highlights having 'good balance, good footwork and a low centre of gravity, so you are difficult to move at the ruck.'

Mike Tolkin feels that poaching the ball is not as important as the player's ability to add pressure over the ball and slow down the attack, 'If the back row can start making the opposition resource more players than they want to and make the ball sloppy and messy, turning it into a street fight, they have done their job.' This is a feature of the game that Steffon Armitage also highlights, 'If you can't make that tackle, you have to be the first one there to help out your No.10. or whoever is around you and get your hands on the ball. You want to be a nuisance and disrupt everything; your job is to slow the ball down.'

As a back row you have to have the ability to handle pressure, and cope physically and mentally with sustained attacks for long periods in a game. It's important not to panic or let frustration get the better of you and concede penalties. Discipline is key and Tom Wood reminds players of the consequences of getting impatient and diving into rucks, 'This either causes a penalty and an easy three points or, if you are in the ruck and you shouldn't be, there is probably space somewhere else where you should be. '

The back row have to know each other's jobs and constantly have an awareness of where each other is on the pitch if they are to be an effective unit. Communication on and off the field is key in achieving that trust and understanding. Sean O'Brien uses his own experience to explain the point, 'I know my job is to make the tackle and leave Jamie (Heaslip) to get the ball. I'm going to get out as quickly as I can or stand up in space or vice versa. It's the same for different combinations in the team; you can certainly work together as a unit and have that trust with one another.'

Steffon Armitage believes trust is about 'tackles and talking' and feeling sure that your teammate will make that tackle when it counts. 'If you go, you know your teammate has got the inside of you covered. If they haven't, they let you know so you can come back in. Just like everything in rugby, it's about talking to each other. Once you get that, the trust is going to come.'

WHAT MAKES A GOOD BACK ROW A GREAT BACK ROW?

GOOD V GREAT

FLANKER

Decision-making and game intelligence. George Smith reads the game very well and makes intelligent decisions. He's got good feet, and he's even a playmaker with ball in hand. In and around the rucks he's a complete nuisance, and he's got a vast array of tools from which to choose when he gets there. He's either pulling you over the ruck, pushing you off it, or beating you to the ball. He makes his tackles and gets people to ground quick, which is where he really thrives, but it's his decision making and game intelligence that sets him apart.'

**Scott LAVALLA,
USA & Stade Français**

George Smith's ball in hand decision-making was great. Jerry Collins is a hard man who always took it to the opposition. Those guys had the skills I wanted to combine.'

Todd CLEVER, USA & OMBAC

→ George Smith has over 100 caps for Australia and made over 140 appearances in Super Rugby for the Brumbies

(continued overleaf)

FLANKER (CONTINUED)

Consistency. There are a lot of players out there that are able to have one good game, or even one good game every few months, but it is players that are able to play well week in and week out that really show their world-class ability. Richie McCaw is the one that stands out the most with regards to this, simply because he has been doing what he does for so long and doing it well. *

Tyler ARDRON, Canada & Ospreys

Ball-poaching. As the game has got quicker there are more phases and more opportunities to get back into the game and Richie McCaw is still the best at that. He's a real natural ball-poaching 7. *

**Graham ROWNTREE,
England Forwards Coach**

Innovation. Richie McCaw has evolved his game faster than anyone else and stayed one step ahead of the curve in terms of what you can get away with on a rugby pitch and the rest of the world has copied him. Little subtle techniques he would base his game on and, as a back row player, those are the small margins you need to be successful. He always seems to have been innovating and influencing the game at the very highest level and that is what has kept him at the top so long. *

**Tom WOOD, England
& Northampton Saints**

Mental strength. Jacques Burger made 28 tackles in 70 minutes against Clermont in the 2014 Heineken semi-final, while only touching the ball twice, and he does that kind of stuff all the time. When he does carry, he goes forward and runs hard. That impressive physical commitment doesn't come from exceptional size and power either, it's mental strength and a willingness to put his body consistently on the line. *

Scott LAVALLA, USA & Stade Français

🖉 **Experience.** *It takes years to develop to a world-class standard. Players like David Pocock, George Smith and Richie McCaw have been studying and rehearsing these skills since they were kids. This has given them the ability to be destructive around the pitch and cause a lot of problems to the opposition.* 』
Shane JENNINGS, Ireland & Leinster

NO. 8

🖉 **Two things that stand out** *for me when you separate the good ones from the great ones are anticipation and knowledge of the game. Currently, I rate Kieran Read very highly – apart from all his superb skills, he is mentally very tough as well and reads the game brilliantly.* 』
Duane VERMEULEN, Springboks & Stormers

🖉 **Versatility.** *Having a little bit of every aspect in your armour is the difference. Being able to poach, being able to carry, be a smart defender, and be able to make smart decisions, having good feet – all those little bits and pieces. All the best back rows in the world have that. Kieran Read, Richie McCaw and David Pocock, they all have a bit of everything and that's what makes a world-class player.* 』
Sean O'BRIEN, Ireland & Leinster

🖉 **A great No. 8** *can read a game and take it to another level. There are lots of good No. 8s out there who have the skill set and play game-by-game but never take it to the next level.* 』
Jerome KAINO, New Zealand & Hurricanes

🖉 **Duane Vermeulen** *is a big ball carrier, works really hard on his aerial skills, and his skills are of a very high level, but he is always very physical and very aggressive. Kieran Read is very skilful but is a more mobile No. 8 who tends to play in the backs a lot more.* 』
David DENTON, Scotland & Edinburgh

🖉 **The thing with the back row** *is because there are so many different aspects to it you get guys that are stronger at different sides of the game, they may be strong in the breakdown, or better ball carriers. Kieran Reid does all aspects of the game exceptionally well and that's what makes him the best back row in the world.* 』
Kelly BROWN, Scotland & Saracens

🖉 **At 8 we want high tackle** *effectiveness and post tackle, i.e. nicking the ball. Best in the world is Kieran Read.* 』
Graham ROWNTREE, England Forwards Coach

🖉 **One player** *who inspired me was Zinzan Brooke who was a phenomenal No. 8 for New Zealand.* 』
Shane JENNINGS, Ireland & Leinster

← In the 2014 Rugby Championship Richie McCaw made 77 tackles and had a 91.7% tackle success rate. (Super Rugby & Opta Sports) No player made more offloads than Kieran Read. He also won more lineouts (27) than any other player in the tournament. @OptaJonny

> *Forwards win games,*
> *backs decide by how much.*

CKS

The aim of the backs is to receive the ball from the forwards and attack the space on the pitch with the aim of crossing the try line. Each position within the backline has positional specific duties and responsibilities. Speed of mind and body is a prerequisite for a back and Nos. 9–15 are usually the players who dictate the tempo of the game.

Wales backs coach Rob Howley lists what qualities he looks for from his backs
Physical: speed, agility, power and strength
Technical: ability to pass, kick and run
Mental: confidence, focus, concentration, composure, emotional control to cope with pressure

BACKS NEED TO BE:

■ Technically proficient in their core skills; with the ability to kick, run, or pass the ball consistently and accurately while making their tackles in defence. **Eddie Jones**, head coach of Japan is particularly clear on this, 'A technical base is important – good consistent core skills are vital.'

■ Physically quick and agile enough to evade opponents, backs combine their speed with the strength to break tackles to get over the gain line. Irish fly half **Johnny Sexton** outlines the preparation required in training for his position, 'I did speed work in the gym and worked with strength and conditioners. I worked on my tackling as well, in terms of strength, power and technique.'

■ Mentally strong under pressure, they are able to make decisions and are constantly scanning for opportunities. USA winger **Brett Thompson** explains how this develops, 'Backs constantly scan and communicate in practice so it becomes natural in the game.'

ALTERNATIVE NAMES FOR BACKS:

■ Scrum half = 9, half back
■ Fly half = 10, outside half, stand-off, first five-eighth
■ Centre 12 = Inside centre, second five-eighth
■ Centre 13
■ Wing = 11 winger, wing three-quarter
■ Full back 15

SCRUM HALF

' *I like being a linkman,* being a key cog in a game and being in control. Being vocal and telling people what to do – I can't lie; it's something I really enjoy doing. Being able to motivate people and deal with the reaction to that. As a small man being able to control big things is always pretty exciting.'

Aaron SMITH, New Zealand & The Highlanders

▶▶**The 'general' on the pitch,** a scrum half is the boss of the forwards and is clear and confident in his demands for the type and speed of ball he wants them to provide for the backs. Confident, vocal, a good communicator, proficient in his own skills – passing and kicking – he has to possess vision for the team, be self-assured and abrasive to work effectively as the link between the backs and forwards.

He has a close relationship and understanding with the fly half, which gives him the responsibility of ensuring the forwards are delivering on the game plan in attack and defence.

■ 'I was a No. 10 until I was 16, then the head academy coach at Leicester Tigers felt I would be a better scrum half. You are always in the game and you get more touches than any other position. You make key decisions all the time and I enjoy the pressure and the fun of trying to create scoring chances from in and around the breakdown.'
Ben YOUNGS, England & Leicester Tigers

■ 'It came naturally for me as I was one of the smallest players until 15 years old. I enjoyed being in the middle of the action all the time and was quick off the mark. There is a mindset and attitude that goes with playing scrum half, a never say die and resilience against big forwards and fast backs.'
Rory KOCKOTT, France & Castres

■ 'I played 10 up until the age of 14 then I tried scrum half and I really enjoyed the position. You are a crucial decision maker and are involved in most of the attacking play. The 9 and 10 are the two most important positions on the pitch in terms of making decisions, getting the team going forward and playing in the right areas of the pitch.'
Ruan PIENAAR, South Africa & Ulster

■ 'I chose scrum half purely and simply because my dad was a scrum half! We were asked in primary 5 who wanted to play prop, second row, etc. and I said, "I'll play 9, please". I love it because you get your hands on the ball the whole time and have an influence on every game that you play.'
Mike BLAIR, Scotland & Newcastle Falcons

▸▸ Skills required to play scrum half

Technically proficient and tactically astute, the scrum half constantly reads the game, making decisions under pressure and providing service for others. The scrum half is responsible for directing the forwards; the No. 9 supplies the No. 10 with the ball whenever they want it. **Rory Kockott** summed it up by saying, 'A No. 9 has to have accurate passing, consistent kicking and good vision for reading the play'.

Passing and kicking

The No. 9 has the most touches in a game and has to provide service for the team. Their core skill levels will influence the outcome of a game. They need to be able to select the right pass or kick and be able to deliver the ball accurately time and again if a team is to build momentum. **Ben Youngs** explains, 'You have to be able to pass and kick as [these skills] are key to putting your team in the right areas to attack or getting the ball out to enable an attack'.

   Aaron Smith believes passing is what playing scrum half is all about, 'Passing has got me to where I am. If you can't pass as a 9 then don't even worry about it. There are a lot of 9s who can run and kick but who can't pass and that's the key thing to our game. Passing is everything, anything else is a bonus'.

   When it comes to box kicking (a high over-the-shoulder kick, used mostly in tight attacking or defensive situations), the All Blacks No. 9 reminds young players that it's not just about the kick, it's also about the target, 'You want to get the ball so it's hitting land'.

▸▸ **Learn more about passing** – *see pages 101-3*
▸▸ **Learn more about kicking** – *see pages 207-13*

↑ Rory Kockott in action for France

Decision making under pressure

Confident in his analysis of the game, a scrum half has to quickly read the options and react to take full advantage. Constantly under pressure from the opposition, the scrum half has to remain assured, composed and keep communicating with those around them, 'For a 9, the speed of ball, scanning of the opposition defence and communication are all key for your decision making process,' suggests **Mike Blair**.

'You have to be a good decision maker as you have more decisions than anyone else in the team,' explains Ben Youngs. 'You develop this skill by reviewing your games. Use training to see what things work and what doesn't.' USA head coach **Mike Tolkin** agrees, saying that skilled decision making comes with 'constant practice, feedback and self-analysis.'

Ruan Pienaar highlights the impact a player's skills can have on the options they choose, 'You only have a split second to make good decisions and to provide your team with positive outcomes, so focus on your core skills. All the different aspects such as line breaks will come but passing, kicking and high levels of fitness are your main areas of focus.'

Organisation

Charged with marshalling the forwards, the scrum half has to ensure he has the players where he wants them at all times to allow his team to advance in attack or remain solid in defence. The scrum half has a busy game: organising the forwards to build momentum for the team, be ready to run himself, or deliver an accurate pass to the No. 10 when they want the ball. It's 'being in the middle of all the plays as well as being an organiser' that appeals to players like Ruan Pienaar.

›› A scrum half's role

In attack

As a playmaker for the team, the No. 9 needs to make decisions under pressure. The scrum half 'works in tandem with [the] 10 to decide what tactical choices are best,' says Rory Kockott, stressing that players 'need to be in agreement with what the tactical strategies are before and during the game.' Ben Youngs explains how other players help with that process, '[The scrum half] needs clear communication from the players outside so he knows if he should pass to the forwards or the backs.'

The scrum half evaluates the options by scanning the field and organises his teammates to get them into the best position. 'The ability to bring others into the game,' is a skill which Mike Blair highlights, is 'creating space and challenging the line through positive running.' Rory Kockott sees the scrum half's role as, 'running when defence is at its weakest or support running with others who have broken the defensive line.'

The No. 9 needs to think fast and react quickly to take advantage of any opportunities they see. Both their pass and kick need to be accurate. 'Defences are so good these days it's about putting teams under pressure,' says Aaron Smith. 'You can do that through speed of ball.' Mike Blair believes 'being able to scan in attack to see where the space is and passing quickly and accurately are key points for youngsters growing up.'

Ruan Pienaar lists some of the things young players need to look at before they get to the ruck, 'You check and see if there is space at the back, whether the forwards are on or whether there is space behind them out in the backs or if the blindside is open or if you can snipe [a term for scrum half deciding to run] yourself'. He stresses it is important to have that vision and clarity of what you are doing, 'Some games you will do well in those areas and some games you will struggle, but once you get going that is the key to making good decisions'.

When the scrum half decides the best option is for him to carry he needs to be confident in his ball carrying skills and commit fully. A scrum half should be a running threat so the defence has to pay attention to him. Ben Youngs reminds players that 'there is a balance to be struck with sniping, you can go too much or too little and it's key to get it right. What's important is seeing who you are sniping at. If it's a prop, you need to back yourself. If it's a winger they can be harder to catch out. Whatever you do, once you have made up your mind you have to go through with it'.

The Nos. 9 and 10 drive the attack, so the understanding between these two players is critical if a team is to maintain momentum in a game. Ruan Pienaar clicked with his Ulster teammate Ian Humphreys from the start and he explains how that helps on the pitch, 'Sometimes you get into a groove with a player and without him even saying anything, you know what he wants. It can take a while but once you get that relationship with your 10, it's just brilliant. It's about building that understanding in practice and making sure you communicate during games so you stay on the same page, 'Repetition in training and putting in the hard yards with your 10 is key', concludes Pienaar.

In defence

Scrum halves have a huge role in defence to organise the pack and to provide cover when required. Their organisational skills are called on to ensure the line remains strong against sustained attacks. 'Organising the defence depends on the defence philosophy, whether it is a drift defence, a rush defence or an outside in defence', explains Ruan Pienaar. He sees the scrum half's job as being 'to cover the chips over the defence and help the wings and full back out and cover the spaces'. Both Mike Blair and Aaron Smith agree a scrum half has an important role in filling the gaps. Mike Blair believes it's about 'covering people's backs where they have made mistakes or are too slow into position. So the skill of the read and the ability to tackle are key'.

'No. 9s are the glue, whenever there is a hole we have to fill in quickly', believes Aaron Smith. 'Off set piece we have a huge role, we are like another loosie or a 10 and be in that transition zone, which is probably the toughest zone to defend'.

For Rory Kockott, playing scrum half is about 'communication, and a lot of it'. They have to clearly communicate what they need at all times. Aaron Smith explains there is a huge emphasis on the No. 9 to communicate to the forwards, 'If they are pretty tired, they will put their heads down and all they want to know is where you want them to go and what position they are in. I am the guy that watches it all and respects what they do for us. If they don't fill the gap, I have to and I don't want that either'.

USA's Mike Tolkin outlines where he wants his scrum half to position himself behind the ruck when they are directing the defence in phase play, 'A lot of 9s stand right behind the ruck, but we want our guys 5–7 yards behind with good vision and directing traffic and organising'.

GOOD V GREAT

WHAT MAKES A GOOD SCRUM HALF A GREAT SCRUM HALF?

❝ **Work rate** is what stands out for me. The ability to change the game or do things others can't or won't try. They have time on the ball because they have practised it so many times they make it look easy. What makes good players become great is not being happy with good and wanting to be the best. Having that drive and then the tools to get you there can change you. ❞
Ben YOUNGS, England & Leicester Tigers

❝ **How you look at the game.** If you are a selfish No. 9 and look out for yourself a lot, you'll get nowhere. Talent will get you so far but to go to that next level you have to be selfless and a giving half back. ❞
Aaron SMITH, New Zealand & The Highlanders

❝ **Having a high skill level** along with the ability to make decisions under pressure will have a positive effect on the team. The 9 is the link between the forwards and backs, so you need to be able take control and make the split-second decisions. ❞
Ruan PIENAAR, Springbok & Ulster

❝ **The ability to make a difference** in the rhythm at which the game is played, and knowing how your forwards and backs will benefit from the options you take on the field. And, of course, a resilient mindset and never-say-die attitude that goes with all scrum halves against big forwards and fast backs. ❞
Rory KOCKOTT, France & Castres

❝ **I look at the best 9s** in the world and look at their games individually to find the best exponents of the different skills, i.e. Aaron Smith's pass, Will Genia's ability to bring others into the game, Fourie du Preez's kicking. ❞
Mike BLAIR, Scotland & Newcastle Falcons

❝ **The difference between** a good and great player is the number of mistakes he makes on the pitch at the highest level. It's someone who has time and space on the ball and then makes the right decisions for the team like Aaron Smith. ❞
Mike CATT, England Attacking Skills Coach

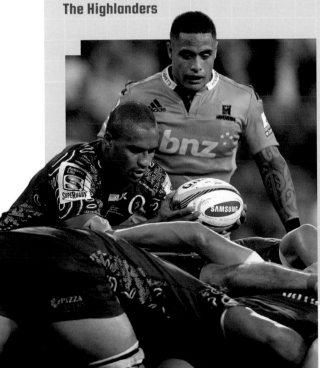

← Will Genia and Aaron Smith compete for their clubs in Super Rugby

FLY HALF

> ' One of the best *pieces of advice* I got growing up was from Alan Gaffney at Leinster. He said, 'You can think about all the things you want in the world but there are only four things you can do on a rugby pitch – pass, kick, run and tackle.' Get good at those four things and concentrate on them until you are excellent in the basics. '

Johnny SEXTON,
Ireland & Leinster

>> **The fly half** is the 'king' and key decision maker of the team. Given this pivotal role, it's no coincidence that the best teams have the best No. 10s.

Responsible for executing the coach's strategy on the pitch, whatever he wants he gets from the scrum half, who in turn gets it from the pack. The fly half needs to have vision, which means he is constantly scanning to help him decide whether to pass, to run himself or to kick for territory.

A highly competent communicator, he must be very proficient in his core skills and decision-making ability if his team is to compete effectively.

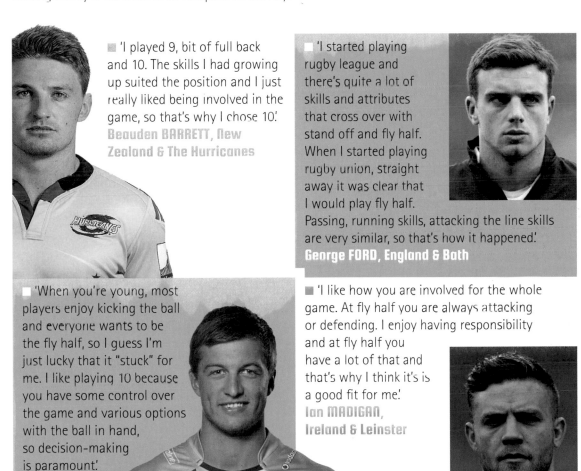

■ 'I played 9, bit of full back and 10. The skills I had growing up suited the position and I just really liked being involved in the game, so that's why I chose 10.'
Beauden BARRETT, New Zealand & The Hurricanes

□ 'I started playing rugby league and there's quite a lot of skills and attributes that cross over with stand off and fly half. When I started playing rugby union, straight away it was clear that I would play fly half. Passing, running skills, attacking the line skills are very similar, so that's how it happened.'
George FORD, England & Bath

■ 'When you're young, most players enjoy kicking the ball and everyone wants to be the fly half, so I guess I'm just lucky that it "stuck" for me. I like playing 10 because you have some control over the game and various options with the ball in hand, so decision-making is paramount.'
Handré POLLARD, South Africa & The Bulls

■ 'I like how you are involved for the whole game. At fly half you are always attacking or defending. I enjoy having responsibility and at fly half you have a lot of that and that's why I think it's is a good fit for me.'
Ian MADIGAN, Ireland & Leinster

⤏ Skills required to play fly half

The No. 10 has a pivotal role calling the shots on the field. They call on their skills and tactical knowledge of the game to shape the team's strategy. The fly half has to be a leader in the team because he is the major decision maker. South Africa's **Handré Pollard** is clear on what his core skills need to be, 'Kicking is obviously very important – for me kicking at goal as well as tactically. Decision-making skills are also very important, like when to attack the line, when to send the ball wide and so on. Solid defence is also a key ingredient, as your channel is often attacked from first phase. You need the necessary skill set and it is extremely important to be able to pass perfectly to your left and right.'

Game management

The ability to read the game and make decisions under pressure is at the heart of the No. 10's role on the field. There is a lot of responsibility on their shoulders. A young No. 10 must not be daunted by this and should be willing to make mistakes as part of the learning process. Having the ability to make the right calls at the right time is something that is learned through experience. Ideally, a fly half has to have the desire to learn and the drive to win.

Beauden Barrett believes the role of the No. 10 is about answering questions such as: 'What does the team need? How is the game going? Are the opposition doing what you think they are doing? Sometimes what you think is going to happen in a game doesn't happen, so it's about adapting. As a 10 it's a big job to manage that.'

To handle the pressure and be decisive takes a certain personality. Glasgow Warriors head coach **Gregor Townsend** outlines the type of strengths his ideal fly half should possess. 'A 10's ideal temperament is being confident to make a lot of decisions during a game, and keeping that confidence if mistakes happen. The best 10s are fierce competitors, driven to improve themselves, committed to high standards, and doing all they can to help the team win.'

Johnny Sexton suggests the key to being a good decision maker comes with experience over time, which can be frustrating for a young player, 'When guys would talk about experience when I was younger that used to drive me mad, but from a 10's point of view you have to play games. You've got to experience making a wrong decision, often to get better. A 10 probably makes more decisions than anyone else on the pitch. He might make 200 decisions in a game, of which one wrong one can mean defeat.'

Leadership

The fly half is a leader on the field and is charged with shaping the game. In collaboration with the No. 9, he delivers the coache's tactics based on what he sees play out in front of him. To achieve this he has to be a strong communicator, instilling confidence in his teammates through his decisions and actions.

'We put a lot of trust in our 9s and 10s as coaches that they know the game plan inside out and are in total sync with the coaching staff,' explains USA head coach **Mike Tolkin**, 'what we expect from each zone [areas of the field] and how we are trying to win the game. We have a lot of meetings at which we repeat it and repeat it to make sure we are in sync. They are real leaders of on-the-field tactics.'

Communication is a cornerstone of leadership, both 'on-field and off-field communication is very important; calling plays, guiding the forwards where to go on the field and explaining how this will lead to success,' believes Gregor Townsend.

For a young player, the role of the No. 10 can be especially challenging, as you have to instruct much more experienced and older players than you. **Ruaridh Jackson** uses his experience of joining the Scotland team to illustrate the point, 'It is hard as a young guy coming into a senior team where you are chucked in with a bunch of seasoned internationals and you have to boss them about. It can be intimidating but it's having the confidence that these guys will listen to you. They are knowledgeable guys and they will listen to you as the 10 because that is their role in the team structure.'

Distribution

The fly half's 'weapons' are his core skills. Due to his central role in the game he needs to be able to catch and pass in any scenario, and be equally skilled on both sides to ensure consistent accurate distribution of the ball. 'It's crucial the 10 has the ability to influence the game through his distribution skills,' says Northampton Saints coach **Alex King**.

Andy Goode sees the position as the fulcrum of distribution for the team, 'Fly halves need to have the whole range of passes available to them, short pop passes, long passes, flat passes and everything in between.' Stressing the importance of practising your passing technique, Ruaridh Jackson suggests that younger players, 'work off both hands, as a 10 needs to be able to get a long pass off both. Practise with your weaker hand and make sure you get your hands in the right position and push through to the target, that should help with the power.'

← In 2014 Beauden Barrett scored 239 points for club and country, including five tries and nine try assists.
Super Rugby and Opta Sports

Kicking

The fly half has to be a highly competent kicker of the ball, both out of hand and from the tee, if he has the added responsibility for goal kicking for the team. Andy Goode outlines the scope of the kicking role of the No. 10, 'You need to be able to execute long kicks for territory, high kicks for possible turnovers or ball retention, crossfield kicks for scoring opportunities, grubber kicks for

getting behind the opposition and a lot more. Add conversions and penalty kicks to this and you can see a lot of responsibilities on the 10.'

Johnny Sexton offers this advice to a young player, 'From a 10's point of view being able to kick with both feet as early in your career as possible makes your life a lot easier going forward.'

>> **Learn more about kicking** – *see pages 207-13*

>> A fly half's role

In attack

Playmakers who dictate the style, tactics and pace of the game, fly halves make decisions throughout a match aimed at creating scoring opportunities for their team. They look to expose opponents' weaknesses, and aim to continually get their team in the right places on the pitch to launch the next attack. **Ian Madigan** describes the role as 'making the most of your team's strengths and seeking out the weaknesses in the team you are playing against.'

They use what they see on the field but also analyse footage of their opponents ahead of the game to build an understanding of the other team. 'No. 10s are the players who "pull the strings" for the whole team, so understanding the game, looking for patterns in the opposition's game, and studying a lot of game film all goes hand-in-hand with being a good 10,' explains Andy Goode.

Handré Pollard agrees that analysing your opponent is one way to gain an advantage, 'It's

← Handré Pollard kicks for territory for the Springboks

vitally important to do your homework before a match – make sure you know where the possible weak spots could be on defence and try to attack that area.'

While the coach's game plan is based on analysing what the opposition defence will do, that can change during a game, so you have to think on your feet, believes Ian Madigan, 'Overall you play what is in front of you. You could make a play at the start of the game and ask the guys what they saw, then change your mind off the back of that. You are always thinking ahead and in rugby no play is the same.'

The fly half is constantly assessing options and processing information as Johnny Sexton explains, 'So much goes through your mind, like what's the next call, maybe a team call based on your video review, based on what you scouted during the week, what you expect the opposition to do, but often it changes.'

Fly halves are not controlling the game from afar, they are right in the thick of the action. Constantly looking for space, the fly half must focus on getting their team into attacking positions, 'You have to look to exploit possible mismatches as a back and always try to run towards their tight five,' suggests Handré Pollard.

George Ford says it's about looking up and playing what's in front of you, 'You are checking what the backfield is like in defence to see if there is a corner you can put the ball into or to see if they have three in the backfield and you have to run the ball to the edge to try and manipulate space elsewhere. You are constantly looking for space, so keep looking up and making as many decisions as you can based on what's on in front of you.'

There has to be a deep understanding between the Nos. 9 and 10 if a team is to operate effectively on the field. These two playmakers need to know the other's preferences in key

scenarios and be on the same page when it comes to delivering the coach's tactics. Ruaridh Jackson believes it's these two players that control the flow of the game, 'These guys dictate the speed of the game and what you are trying to achieve in attack.'

Jackson advises that as a No. 10, the time spent with his scrum half in practice makes the difference, 'You've got to make sure you know when your 9 wants to release the ball, whether he want to have a dart or take a few steps. You speak about things off the field but the more reps you can do in training the clearer your understanding of how they like to work the ball at the ruck will be.'

In defence

The No. 10 is usually one of the main organisers in defence. Their tactical skills are called on to optimise a team's defensive set-up after turnovers. 'A lot of the out half's role is managing the defensive system, so managing the forwards in the defensive line and off later phases of play,' explains Ian Madigan. 'For example, managing your props or second rows, making sure they don't get caught out by quicker, elusive guys. There's a lot of unseen work in managing the strategy in defence.'

At a turnover, the No. 10 and centres organise the defence, explains the Irish out half, 'You rarely see 10, 12 and 13 standing next to each other after a set piece: one centre stands on one side of the ruck and the out half and the other centre stand on the other side of the breakdown. This is to control the other players because the out half and centre would be deemed to be the strongest defenders on the team.'

When a turnover occurs the fly half has to be ready to get his team back into position. Handré Pollard sees his priorities as the Springboks 10 to be, 'ensuring the team immediately get width and ensure we are covered at the back in case of the opposition kicking deep.'

Turnovers are usually pretty chaotic and Ruaridh Jackson advises fly halves to focus on getting everyone organised because turnover ball is the best ball to attack with, 'You want to make sure you fill that field and get that space

right. You might want to concede yards on the first couple of phases just so everyone can get back in the line so you can attack their attacker from there.

'You want to consolidate, realign, and get the line set, then you can go after them again. Make sure the backfield is covered because quite often when you are attacking and you

GOOD V GREAT

WHAT MAKES A GOOD FLY HALF A GREAT FLY HALF?

A great 10 is either very good or world class at every part of the game. Kicking, passing, defence, and game management – that's what separates the top players. If you have every aspect of your game at a world-class level, you become a world-class player, and Dan Carter is one.

George FORD, England & Bath

One must never be predictable and always keep the defence guessing. A perfect example for me would be Dan Carter. He's someone who always varied his play well, and has a skill set second to none – kicking, passing, running, defending – call it and he could do it.

Handré POLLARD, South Africa & The Bulls

You rarely see Dan Carter have a bad game and his management of the team is first class. He might miss a couple of kicks every now and then but then he creates scoring opportunities all the time and has set the bar for how a 10 should play for almost a decade.

Andy GOODE, England & Wasps

lose the ball there is no one at the back, and a quick kick can cause a lot of damage. So your wingers and full back go back but quite often you'll see the 10 tracking back there as well to help in the backfield.'

The No. 10's channel is often targeted as a weak point, so fly halves need to focus on their defensive skills to ensure the defensive line stays intact. 'Solid defence is also a key ingredient as your channel is often attacked from first phase,' advises Handré Pollard. It's a tactic Ruaridh Jackson thinks is increasing in the game, 'teams seem to be sending big forward runners down the 10 channel more and more, so 10s need to enjoy tackling as well.'

↙ Fly half Dan Carter is the game's top international points scorer, with almost 1500 in his career for New Zealand

❝ **The difference between** a good 10 and a great 10 is the ability to control and manage the game when your team is on the back foot. The great 10s are the ones that keep the scoreboard ticking over, and drive their team when its forwards aren't dominating. Dan Carter is a fantastic player and when he's fit and playing at the top of his game he is certainly one of the top 10s ever to have played rugby. ❞
Alex KING, Northampton Saints Coach

❝ **Dan Carter** seems to make things look effortless. He's naturally gifted but he works hard at that. He always seems to have time on the ball, he can glide through a hole, and his kicking game is also up there. As a young player, he is a guy you'd love to emulate. I've been lucky enough to play against Jonny Wilkinson and they are both great in different ways. If you could combine those two guys – their mindset and natural ability would make the perfect 10. ❞
Ruaridh JACKSON, Scotland & Wasps

❝ **Dan Carter's all-round game** sets him aside from the rest. His ability to make the right decision under pressure, an exceptional kicking game, both out of hand and off the floor, coupled with his attacking running game makes him the complete 10. ❞
Paul BURKE, Backs Coach

❝ **Lots of good out halfs** will pass well, kick well, tackle well and be good on strategy, but really good 10s do one thing particularly well and that's what stands them above the rest. Johnny Sexton will score 10 out of 10 on strategy, which makes him one of the best out halves in the world. Whereas Jonny Wilkinson's passing was exceptional, Ronan O'Gara's kicking was exceptional. Those three are examples of out halfs who were very good in all aspects of their game but exceptional in one. ❞
Ian MADIGAN, Ireland & Leinster

❝ **I admired Jonny Wilkinson** and Dan Carter growing up, but I've taken bits of others' games too. Like the way Stephen Larkham would glide with the ball. His passing range was extraordinary; or Ronan O'Gara's spiral kick into the corner. You try to take the best bits of those guys' games and incorporate them into yours. ❞
Johnny SEXTON, Ireland & Leinster

CENTRE

" *I was a half back and 10 at school but I always preferred the midfield when I played half back because of the extra space and room to play ... I love the decision making defensively, and when you have the ball there is also decision making involved. Rugby is great as it changes, depending on the opposition or the weather. You never master the game but there's always a solution. Whatever you face, especially in the midfield, you are always trying to find that solution when you play.* "

Conrad SMITH, New Zealand & The Hurricanes

>> **The 'marshalls' of the midfield,** the centre partnership needs to display creativity and vision in possession and be the lynchpin of the team in defence. As likely to score a try as to stop one, a centre blends vital ball carrying and good offloading skills with an effective tackling technique.

Powerful, pacy and always alert, their speed of foot needs to be matched by a quick mind, as they have to analyse and react to take advantage of opportunities or shut down the opposition.

■ 'I thought one day that me and my brother Alesana would be wingers for Leicester Tigers, him on the right and me on the left. When I got my first-team chance, coach Matt O'Connor said, 'You're playing 13'. I'm always thankful to Matt as it's one of the best positions in rugby.

Playing centre lets you show what you can do in the game. In attack you get a lot more involved and get the ball more too'.
Manu TUILAGI, England and Leicester Tigers

■ 'I started my career as a full back and wing and did not play centre until my third cap for Wales. Shaun Edwards, the Wales defence coach, asked me, "How much rugby have you played at 12?" The last time was at U15s but I told him, "Yeah, I've played a bit of 12 in my time". It is great to have the ball but it is also satisfying knowing that you have run a good decoy line'.
Jamie ROBERTS, Wales & Racing Metro

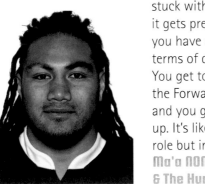

■ 'I was lucky enough to play with my older brother at an early age, he was second-five and I was centre, and I grew up in that position and stuck with it. I like it because it gets pretty physical and you have a lot of influence in terms of defence and attack. You get to be a link between the Forwards and the Backs and you get to really mix it up. It's like a loose forward role but in the Backs'.
Ma'a NONU, New Zealand & The Hurricanes

■ 'I've always been a natural centre but with the Crusaders game plan and set-up I'm suited on the wing. The good thing about centre is you get your hands on the ball more and you're more in the action. Your work rate is high and you have to be fitter'.
Nemani NADOLO, Fiji & The Crusaders

Fiji Vs France
8th November 2014
Marseille

►► Skills required to play centre

Explosive and skilful in attack, technical tacklers and leaders in defence, centres have to help their team control the midfield. Former South African centre, **Brendan Venter**, points out, 'The name says it all – you are in the centre of a backline, so that means you have to have distributing skills. You have to have a good voice, and you have to be a good decision maker in both attack and defence. You can play at a high level with just those skills. If you have speed and evasive ability, your effectiveness increases.'

Game awareness

Both in attack and defence, the centre has to be alert and make decisions. 'You need a better awareness of the opportunities on the field and to recognise the opportunities, make a good decision regarding skill selection required to maximise the opportunity and then execute the selected skill itself', explains Leicester Tigers coach **Aaron Mauger**.

'[A centre's] game sense must be top notch if he is to stay one step ahead of the opposition. It is about being proactive as opposed to reactive', explains **Jamie Roberts**. 'The more experience you get in the game, the easier it becomes to make decisions. You can kind of second guess where teams are trying to play, where the next breakdown is going to be and get a better understanding of what the opposition are doing, which buys you more time. This applies to both attack and defence.'

The Waratahs' assistant coach, **Daryl Gibson**, believes a centre's decision-making skills in defence should be more valued, 'The ability to make good decisions on defence and to make excellent reads is a very underrated and high-level skill.'

Distribution

A centre's distribution skills need to be strong to ensure he takes best advantage of every attacking opportunity. Jamie Roberts believes 'putting my teammates into space through good passing', is a major part of his role in attack as a centre. 'Make every touch on the ball count', says Aaron Mauger. To improve these skills he suggests young players 'focus on correct technique and then put those skills under pressure so you are constantly getting feedback on how your handling skill set is improving.'

►► **Learn more about catching & passing** – *see pages 100-3*

Running

Teams look to their centres to be explosive in attack, either carrying the ball or running support lines to help give the ball carrier options. They need to be able to manipulate defenders to get across the gain line. 'My strength has always been as a ball carrier, getting momentum for the team and getting us on the front foot. It is something I still take massive pride in being able to do', explains Jamie Roberts.

Fitness is critical for this hard working back, as 'you've got to be quick, skilful and have the pace to cover a lot of ground in attack and defence', maintains **Manu Tuilagi**. **Conrad Smith** agrees and highlights how their work rate differs from that of the equally busy back row, 'Centres are covering a lot of ground when you think of the kick and chase stuff we do with the wingers. We do long runs, whereas flankers also do the distance but in shorter runs.'

In attack it's a matter of knowing what lines you have to run as a centre for **Rene Ranger**. He suggests to young players, 'this comes from doing your homework by reviewing the opposition's attack and defence. You back your abilities to beat players and have a go, which comes from a good attitude and having confidence. Just as important is running good blocking lines and holding the opposition, which creates space for your teammates.'

»» Learn more about running – *see pages 104-7*

↓ Welsh centre Jamie Roberts' run is cut short by Sean O'Brien's tackle

Tackling

Heavily involved in open play, centres have the ability to snuff out an opposing team's attack before it has had a chance to take hold with a well-timed momentum changing tackle. It's not just about quality, it's about quantity, says Brendan Venter, 'If you look at the stats, the 12 and 13 make the most tackles in a game of rugby.' This ability brings with it responsibility, 'One of the centres is usually the leader of the defence,' as USA head coach **Mike Tolkin** points out.

Once again, the varied role of the centre is also part of its appeal. Jamie Roberts thinks it is great to have the ball, but 'it is also satisfying knowing that you have put in a big tackle or made a good defensive read or come up hard in the defensive line to stop the opposition from going wide.'

>> **Learn more about tackling** – *see pages 108-21*

↓ Crusaders' winger Nemani Nadolo was top try scorer in the 2014 Super 15 Championship with 12 tries. **Super Rugby and Opta Sports**

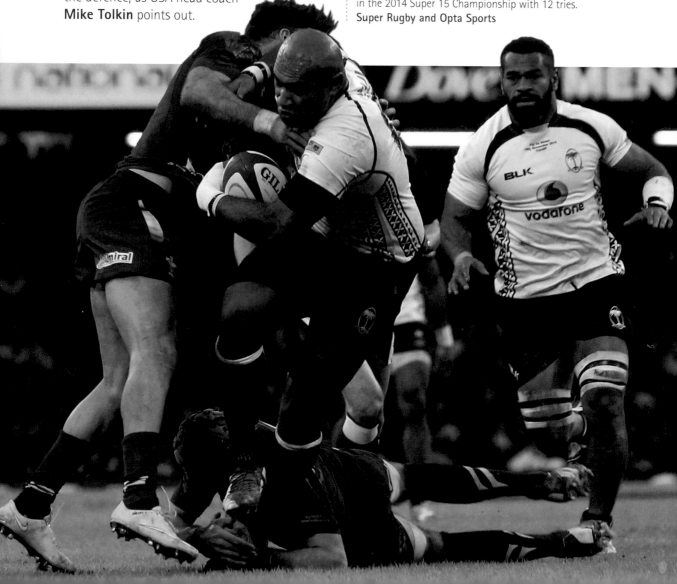

⇥ Differences between Nos. 12 and 13

The two centres can have the same roles and be played left and right, but more commonly in the modern game the responsibilities are split between the two. Different teams will place different responsibilities on their two centres. Usually the centres will be different types of players and tend to complement each other. There are no set rules for the type of players who wear 12 and 13 on their jersey, but having a deep understanding between the two of them is essential to the team's success.

Traditionally the inside centre (12) tends to be a barrelling, hard running centre whose primary focus is to get over the gain line and help his team get on the front foot. His role is to suck in multiple defenders and provide his team with a solid attacking platform in the next phase of play. He must also be able to act as another distributor of the ball, along with the fly half. He should be a vocal organiser within the team, in both attack and defence, helping his fly half to get the forwards into position following set piece play.

Rene Ranger suggests there are two types of 12, 'You have the hard-running, get-over-the-gain-line 12 and then you have the distributing 12 who looks to put players away. No. 12 should also have a good boot on him too, just in case he needs to help the 10 out and give him options'.

Conrad Smith's take is a little different. He points out how the 'No. 12 helps 10 a lot more with organisation, especially in attack and they distribute a lot more but they still need to ball carry.' While **Gordon D'Arcy** describes the position he has played throughout his career as 'the less glamorous facilitator role.' Compared to playing 13 he believes 'there is a lot more running

in traffic as 12. If you second-guess yourself, you get thumped by a 6 or 7 running down your channel. You are there to take pressure off the 10 who can get targeted in games'.

That relationship with the No. 10 is key for D'Arcy. 'You need to understand what the 10 wants around the field and help facilitate that by getting players in the right position to play the game he wants. You have a distributive role and you have to be able to organise when your 10 goes missing.'

The outside centre is afforded more space in attack by virtue of his position. He tends to be the slightly more skilful, elusive running centre with excellent distribution skills and an appreciation of the importance of preserving space for his wing outside him. Outside centre is the most difficult position on the pitch to defend, as there is so much space. It is imperative that the outside centre works tirelessly with his wing and full back as well as his inside centre to ensure he is not exposed by the opposition attack.

Conrad Smith highlights the defensive focus of his role in terms of organisation but also 'the higher work rate because of working with the wingers and full back.' Gordon D'Arcy believes it's a mixture of hard work and using your skills to get more time on the ball, 'No. 13 is an outlet and has to roll his sleeves up and get stuck into the hard yards when the work needs to be done. They do have to have those finesses, that outside break to make that connection between the inside backs and the outside backs. At 13 you might get an extra half-second on the ball and in rugby that is very important.'

⇥ A centre's role

In attack

There are many ways to approach playing centre and all can be effective if they suit the player's strengths. Using power and physicality is one style of play and Manu Tuilagi outlines his approach, 'I like to be a power centre, get over the gain line. I don't really care if I get smashed or not, so I just go hard.'

Other centres use their versatility to adapt their approach to attacking situations, which makes them difficult to read. Conrad Smith believes this is what makes a good centre because you never really know what they are going to do, 'Even the ones that look really good for a season or two, people catch on and realise they are doing the same thing over and over and that's when you can defend against them. The good ones realise you have to adapt and come up with something else. You are always trying to add different options.'

He uses his own experience to highlight how you have to adapt to stay ahead, 'When I started I was very different type of penetrating centre, I wasn't a bust centre but I was right on my running lines and guys put me through. I had to develop distribution and then defensive skills and even now a kicking game. You always have to keep them guessing so they don't work you out.'

Ultimately, centres look to create scoring opportunities and help give the team momentum. Jamie Roberts is a player who does just that for Wales and he outlines his options in attack, 'I help give the team momentum by carrying the ball and trying to cross the gain line or by running an effective decoy line, where I can hold a few players in the opposition defensive line and create space for my teammates.'

Roberts goes on to explain what you need to know if you are to exploit opportunities as they arise, 'Getting to know each other's traits and body language comes with experience. It is very important, but equally important is your relationship with your 10, your relationship with your wingers in attack and your relationship with your full back. So there are a lot of things that you have to get used to. Also, for me, the relationship with my 9 is very important because I like to run hard lines off scrum halves and they need to know that.'

In defence

Leaders in defence, centres have to be confident and physical in their tackling to shut down the opposition attacks. They need to be constantly communicating and instructing those around them to ensure the team is defensively sound. 'In defence you are the middleman. If the wingers or the full back says, "line speed" [the speed at which the defensive line moves forward] you've got to relay that to the forwards,' says **Nemani Nadolo**. Scanning is a vital skill for centres, as they must read the opposition's attacking threats. Jamie Roberts is captain of Wales' defence, and he lists analysing opposition traits and being vocal on the pitch as his key roles. He makes an important point, which all players should remember, as the leader of the defence you have to relay what you see to those around you. 'Communication is the first thing to go when you get tired and every rugby team, international or not, gets tired, but it is really important that you still scan and talk,' he says.

The type of system you play also has a bearing on the importance of these skills, as he explains. 'We defend with a blitz defence with Wales, which means we come off the line hard and try to beat our opposition to the gain line. It is a risk/reward defensive system with a high margin for error, so we need to make sure we are all on the same page. My role is to marshall that and to stay vocal.'

↑ Experienced No 12 Ma'a Nonu believes you have to make a lot of tackles 'tackling Backs as well as Forwards, you need to get your head around that'

Roberts relishes the responsibility that falls on the shoulders of the centre in defence, 'I enjoy that challenge and responsibility of shepherding the backs to try to stop the opposition from crossing the gain line.'

With space to attack comes space to defend, as Manu Tuilagi explains, 'Outside centre is one of the toughest positions to defend because you've got a lot of space around you. In the first phase you can hold back and let the play unfold. It is important to stay slightly behind your 12 so you're staggered and not in front of him. Then give yourself a bit of time to either jam in on the attacker or fall into the drift defence.

'If you move up in the defensive line, in front of your 12, you put yourself under pressure to make a decision, and you can end up having to guess what might happen. It's 50/50 so it's risky. If you guess it right then brilliant. If you get it wrong, it's a try for your opponents. You just can't let that happen.

'I've played with a lot of 12s, like Anthony Allen, and he is one of the best defenders. When you have that combination, you build that trust, and if you know he's going to be there if it makes your job a lot easier.'

Gordon D'Arcy highlights the challenges of tackling in the midfield, 'As a centre you'll be tackling big back rowers and ball-carrying forwards and trying to fight the battle on your own terms. Get up early so you can cut off his time and space. Work on your angles so you don't get hit straight on because it's the hardest tackle in the world to deal with. Control your angles, come in side-on and chop them at the ankles or grab them and keep them up.'

⏭ Centre partnerships

As one of the most influential relationships on the team, the centre partnership needs to have trust and a telepathic understanding between the two players. Playing together and building that relationship under game situations is key to gaining an understanding of your partner. Brendan Venter explains, 'The main thing is just playing together for a long time. It is like any relationship. When you spend time with people, half a word and the other person knows what you're going to say. It is the same thing with rugby. The more you play together the more you start to understand each other in defence and attack. It is very valuable and it is something we neglect nowadays because we like to chop and change teams too much.'

Jamie Roberts takes up the same theme, 'It is important to appreciate the relationships within the team and good coaches know to give players a run of games together to build that understanding. Myself and Jon [Jonathan Davies] have formed a good partnership in

→ Ma'a Nonu and Conrad Smith hold the record for the most international appearances as a centre partnership

the centre for Wales and by now we know each other's games inside out. We know what makes each other tick. You look at the likes of [Brian] O'Driscoll and [Gordon] D'Arcy who formed a formidable partnership but that only came from their experience of playing together for so long at club and country.'

Even the best partnerships can take time to build, as one half of the All Blacks most capped centre partnership, Conrad Smith, recounts, 'I've played with Ma'a Nonu the most and at the start we were just two individuals who wanted to do our own thing. We were almost forced by coaches to build a relationship and now it's a great relationship and we are good friends off the field.'

Again communication was the key, and Smith stresses the importance of honesty as pivotal in getting a better understanding of what makes the other person tick, 'You have to understand each other's game and you've got to have some pretty honest conversations to tell someone what you are worried about in a game, what scares you, what you feel like when you do this. It's possible to go through a career without having that conversation with someone. But if you do, you find out so much, often answers you wouldn't expect, like things Ma'a worries about in a game that I never would have thought he worried about. Now I know how I can help him and vice versa, so that's pretty important.' His partner on the field Ma'a Nonu agreed that communication had played a major part in their playing partnership. 'That's pretty much what a relationship takes. A lot of trust in terms of knowing you have each other's backs when you play together. Trusting he can make that tackle, he will pass the ball, or be behind when you make a break. Its having that trust that helps you make decisions.'

Ireland's Gordon D'Arcy concedes that the mistakes he made with teammate Brian O'Driscoll helped them to build one of the most successful, long-term partnerships in the game. The experiences they had as they grew into the game, both good and bad, helped shape their roles and build understanding between the two. 'There is no substitute for making mistakes and learning from it and we made more than our fair share of mistakes,' he says. 'You only make a partnership with a guy that you trust and trust doesn't come overnight. It comes from when you make a mistake he works hard to cover for you and you do the same for him. I had quite a steep learning curve when I moved into 12 with defensive reads that went wrong, but having one of the best guys in the world outside you made that transition really good.

'Know there is going to be a learning period and get frustrated with each other but instead figure out how mistakes happen. Then they happen less and less and the partnership happens seamlessly. Every now and then you'll look at each other and go, "Yeah we got away with that" but you only get away with it because you know how to read your partner's body language. It's that peripheral vision, you see what he is doing and know that he might take two steps and then shoot, and your body is tuned and ready for it. He might know you like to drift and then step back in on your inside shoulder. It's little things like that, there is no magic potion.'

As players, their learning experiences on the field were matched by their desire to learn and improve in training. D'Arcy describes how their efforts after practice helped build a bond, 'We were always the guys doing defence at the end of training, we were doing 1 v 1 tackles when the other lads were going in to get showered, we were still out there beating the crap out of each other. When you know the guy is working as hard as you are at the small bits that's when you go, "Yeah I'm happy to leave him to go 1 v 1 with whoever and I'll do my job."'

WHAT MAKES A GOOD CENTRE A GREAT CENTRE?

→ Conrad Smith made more passes than any other centre (42) in the 2014 Rugby Championship. @OptaJonny

The ability to kick, pass and run is very important. Look at someone like Brian O'Driscoll, perhaps not the greatest kicker of the ball, but later in his career he became more adept at putting little balls through in the wider channels, but certainly as a defender and attacker he was fantastic. He probably wasn't the greatest passer of the ball either, but later in his career he was certainly able to put players through gaps in the defence by drawing defenders and putting teammates away. **Jamie ROBERTS, Wales & Racing Metro**

It's all about timing. Brian O'Driscoll is one of those players who may not have been the best tackler or passer but he did it at the right moment. That is what set him above everyone else in his position for 10 or 15 years. The guys who make it count do it at the best moments, at those very high pressure moments they execute the basic skills really well. If you can make your pass with composure or make a tackle at the right time under the most pressure, that will make you a great player. **Gordon D'ARCY, Ireland & Leinster**

Making something happen. I love watching all the centres like Ma'a Nonu, but when you watch an Ireland game and Brian O'Driscoll's in it you just know he's going to make something happen. **Manu TUILAGI, England & Leicester Tigers**

→ Brian O'Driscoll is the most capped player for Ireland (133) and has scored the most tries (46)

The ability to learn and adapt in situations has a massive influence. There are hundreds of great players out there with great talent but those who learn faster than their opponents that makes all the difference. Brian O'Driscoll got better with age because his development as a player changed. Every three or five years he has focused on different areas as the game changed and he adapted with it. **Isa NACEWA, Blues Performance Coach**

❝ *Explosiveness and good decision making* set Brian O'Driscoll apart. He was probably one of the three best rugby players ever to play the game. I never played against him but I coached against him a lot. He had all the hard working characteristics, but it was that extra explosiveness that made him great. ❞
Brendan VENTER, Technical Director

❝ *Great centres,* like Brian O'Driscoll or Tana Umaga, have many strengths; there's not one thing. If you think you've got them figured out you'll defend that way and he'll throw a pass just when you think he'll carry. Or the other way around, he will have the vision to carry and split you open, and the same defensively. He gives you too much room on the outside but then he is always reading you and next thing you know he's got you covered. ❞
Conrad SMITH, New Zealand & The Hurricanes

❝ *Experience.* Two of the best centres in the current game are Adam Ashley Cooper and Conrad Smith. It's no accident these players are currently the best defensive players in the southern hemisphere. Both are over 30 years of age and have years of experience to shape their capabilities. I believe an outside centre gets better with age and experience from 28 years plus. ❞
Daryl GIBSON, Waratahs Assistant Coach

❝ *It's all about experience.* You look at the likes of Conrad Smith. He's been around for a while and he does his key roles right. His skill levels are always spot-on and he always works on the things he is not so good at, but also on the things that he is very good at. Another player that I look up to is Tana Umaga. He led by example and worked very hard. ❞
Rene RANGER, New Zealand & Montpelier

❝ *Being proactive in everything you do,* not just on the pitch but off it as well. Going to the Lions and just living with one of the best centres in the world, Jamie Roberts, and all those guys. It's the level of professionalism that they have, especially in training. He'd walk off the pitch and do his homework. He'd watch what he did on the pitch, knowing what he did wrong, did well, and what's needed to improve. Little things like that. ❞
Manu TUILAGI, England & Leicester Tigers

❝ *Just getting the clinical things right.* Your 1 percenters – your 1 v 1 tackles, your involvement in the game, making sure you track the ball the right way, making sure you are in the right place at the right time. Centre is one of the most important positions on the field so you are the middleman, directing play, so you have to be on guard for 80 minutes. ❞
Nemani NADOLO, Fiji & Crusaders

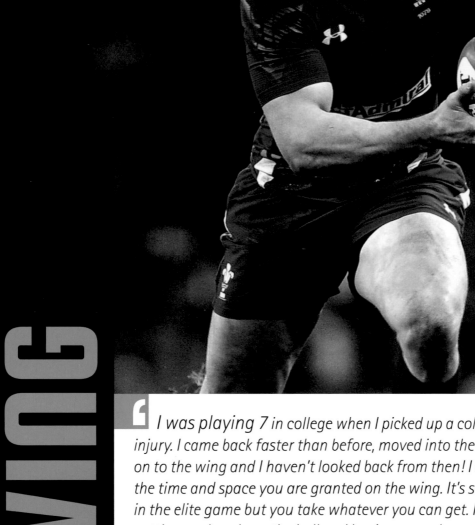

WING

'I was playing 7 in college when I picked up a collarbone injury. I came back faster than before, moved into the backs and on to the wing and I haven't looked back from then! I enjoy the time and space you are granted on the wing. It's so limited in the elite game but you take whatever you can get. I like getting my hands on the ball and having a good run.'

George NORTH, Wales & Northampton Saints

▸▸ **Speed merchants** and traditionally the top try scorers for the team, wings are increasingly involved in the physical elements of the game. Relentless in their search for space to give the team attacking options, they can have 50 or 60 sprints in a match, a lot of the time without getting the ball. When they do get possession they are experts at evasion, with good offloading skills.

Their speed is also put to good use on defensive duties, be that having to react to a situation, clearing out a ruck or getting back to defend a counter-attack or a kick.

■ 'I actually chose to play 7, but they realised I wasn't hitting any rucks so they thought I should be on the wing. Playing wing gives me the opportunity to score tries; it's one of the more exciting positions in rugby and I can exercise my skills in wide-open spaces.'
Marland YARDE, England & Harlequins

■ 'I played 15 until my second year of Ireland U21s. The coach said he wanted to try me on the wing and I have been there since.'
Tommy BOWE, Ireland & Ulster

☐ I started playing centre when I was young and I was quick so they started moving me around the back line and I also played a lot at full back for my club back home. When I first played for the Argentina team they put me on the wing because I was playing sevens as well.'
Horacio AGULLA, Argentina & Bath

■ 'From a skill set perspective, wing is the position I am most suited to. It allows me the opportunity to use pace, open field running and to catch high balls. I love to roam the field and look for work, make one-on-one tackles in the open field and, of course, score tries. Positionally it is challenging and tasks you to organise and communicate effectively with teammates inside you. While I have played other positions and enjoyed them, wing is the position I was meant to play.'
Blaine SCULLY, USA & Leicester Tigers

▶▶ Skills required to play wing

Pace is an essential part of a wing's toolbox, but they are more than just speed merchants. Positional awareness, ball handling and first-class evasion skills are all part of a wing's repertoire. They need to be able to anticipate and shut down opposition line breaks in defence and also be alert to any opportunity to attack. 'High ball catching, kicking and passing are important but as a back three player you need to work on all aspects of your game including running, outside breakdown rucking, and one-on-one tackling,' advises **Tommy Bowe**.

Running

A wing's time on the ball can be limited but impactful in terms of points on the scoreboard. Their challenge is to be in the right place at the right time to take advantage of the few opportunities they get. This takes tactical and positional awareness to find space while not becoming isolated or leaving your team exposed. USA winger **Brett Thompson** highlights the 'ability to beat a defender one-on-one with little amounts of space,' and also being able 'to insert in the line quickly and finish off attacking phases,' as being key skills for his position.

▶▶ **Learn more about running** – *see pages 104-7*

Distribution

Having the ability to pass the ball from both sides is a prerequisite for all players at the top level, but wings must be comfortable catching

→ Marland Yarde catches the ball during an Aviva Premiership match between Harlequins and Saracens

any type of pass that is thrown their way. As the last man in the attacking line, wings tend to be the recipients of long passes from teammates who are under pressure from opposing defenders. This means wings must fully understand the importance of depth and ensure they do not overrun the ball carrier. Catching kicks is also a vital part of the wing's game.

England's **Marland Yarde** lists the range of core skills required for a wing as 'your aerial ability so high ball catching and also being able to provide a range of short and long passes as well'. USA head coach **Mike Tolkin** is looking for a player that has finishing ability but also has 'strong kicking skills and is strong in the aerial game by contesting and re-gathering our high kicks'.

Welsh wing **George North** reminds players of the importance of working on both sides when practising, 'Players need to be able to pass off both hands, working the weaker hand a lot to try and get it up to the same level. Also the ability to kick off both feet is important. It's always important not to just train your good hand and foot but work on your weaker side as well'.

>> **Learn more about catching & passing** – see pages 100-3

>> **Learn more about kicking for territory** – see pages 207-13

Tackling

An effective wing can influence a game through more than their attacking skills. As the most mobile players on the field, the wings make an effective defensive contribution through their ability to track and tackle opponents at pace. **Brett Thompson** explains that, as a wing, 'you will be put under a lot of pressure to make one-on-one tackles with lots of space for the attacker to work with. Open field tackling is a very important skill for a wing'.

>> **Learn more about tackling** – see pages 108-21

>> A wing's role

In attack

A winger's pace, footwork and agility are essential components to allow them to evade defenders and gain territory. Blindside wings will often be found 'hunting' on the out half's inside shoulder, looking for any potential attacking opportunity, while the openside wing will usually be the player charged with finishing off the team's set plays. Wings should always be in support of the ball carrier and, more often than not, are the teams' leading try scorers.

'The back three always work as a unit and as a team', explains George North. 'In attack we are always working off the ball, whether it's running dummy lines and angles, supporting the play, or running inside lines off 9, 10 or 12'.

Marland Yarde enjoys the freedom his role has in attack, 'It's good to have freedom of movement and to get yourself around the field. As soon as there is turnover ball and the opponent has possession it's about getting back to the wing and communicating with your full back and the guys beside you and making sure you are in position'.

'Often as a wing you receive the ball in space. The ability to time your run off teammates and beat people in space (1 v 1) is a fundamental part of your game', highlights **Blaine Scully**. He stresses that 'it is important to "look for work" as a wing and not merely camp on your side of the field and wait for the game to come to you'.

In defence

The back three work as a 'pendulum' in defence – when one wing joins the defensive line, the full back will move across the pitch to cover the space behind them, while the opposite wing will move back to cover the space vacated by the full back. George North explains, 'In defence, it's about working as a team of three and working the pendulum. When one player goes up, two drop to different angles; it's about working together.'

Blaine Scully highlights the risks when this doesn't go to plan and how an exposed backfield leaves a team vulnerable to kicks leading to loss of territory and field position. 'In the game of rugby, if you cannot play in the right areas of the field and are put under pressure because of poor field position, more often than not you lose.'

This fluid movement is dependent on constant communication between the players to know where they are on the field at all times. 'If you stay in your head too much and do not analyse the opposing attack, next thing you know a try is scored that you could have prevented if you were in position,' warns Brett Thompson. 'Constantly scan and communicate with your back three in practice so it becomes natural in the game.'

A winger's speed is an asset in defence as well as attack to counterbalance the opposing team's running threats. 'You want the fastest guys out on the wing to cover their fast guys as well,' says Marland Yarde.

GOOD
V
GREAT

WHAT MAKES A GOOD WING A GREAT WING?

▪ *The individual skill sets* and physical attributes of the player often determines what type of wing he is. Jonah Lomu is an example of a large wing who had devastating power and the pace to finish. Bryan Habana is an example of the classic finisher, someone who has the ability to score tries from anywhere on the field. Ben Smith is an example of the wing/full back, a great all-round footballer who is solid in all facets, capable of playing multiple positions, while extremely effective as a wing. They may all have different styles but they are all very effective in what they do well. ▪

Blaine SCULLY, USA & Leicester Tigers

▪ *Confidence,* believing in your own ability to take on the opposition, getting the ball in your hands as often as you can makes a good winger a great one. Shane Williams used to get the ball into his hands 20-plus times. Wingers are a huge threat to the opposition so it is better to go get the ball in your hands than wait for it to come to you. ▪

Tommy BOWE, Ireland & Ulster

▪ *A great wing* needs an all-round good skill set, pace and the ability to read the game in attack and defence. Being a threat is an important part of it as well. ▪

George NORTH, Wales & Northampton Saints

← The Springboks' Bryan Habana has scored over 50 tries for his country and more than 70 in his club career

The ability to finish. *Everyone else on the inside does a lot of work to open up space and when you get the ball you need to make something happen. Bryan Habana not only has the speed but also the agility and power that makes him a super threat every time he touches the ball.*

Brett THOMPSON, USA & Edinburgh

Good vision and good decision-making skills. Sitiveni Sivivatu popped up in the right areas and made the right decisions when he got the ball as first or second receiver and was able to visualise the sequence in the field. That's a very rare talent.

Marland YARDE, England & Harlequins

FULL BACK

> 'I started my career and learned my trade on the wing. I always felt I could be a better full back than wing on the global stage because there are so many monster, powerful guys on the wing with an enormous amount of pace. My skill set was more suited to full back in terms of aerial ability, kicking ability and counter-attacking.'
>
> **Rob KEARNEY**, Ireland & Leinster

›› **The eyes of the team,** the full back observes the action from the back of the field and relays to his players where the main threats from the opposition are coming.

This versatile player is able to launch counter-attacks with the wings or shepherd opponents into touch as the last line of defence. Fearless under the high ball in pressurised situations and an aggressive tackler, this dynamic back has to be a good communicator and have the utmost confidence in his abilities, as he can be very isolated at times.

■ 'My first coach saw some qualities in me that suited full back and I'm really glad he did. When you have the ball you have more time and space than the centre and you can run more with the ball.'
Andrea MASI, Italy & Wasps

■ 'I played on the wing because I was fast and I could beat people one-on-one. Moving through the age groups I moved into centre and 10, and it was actually the start of things to come. Although I play full back with the US, I'm a utility back at my club Saracens. I really enjoy the challenge of the high balls. It's about attacking a high ball and when you come down with it, it's a great feeling.'
Chris WYLES, USA & Saracens

■ 'I played most of my rugby at 10 – I actually only moved to a more permanent role at full back aged 22. I enjoy the space, seeing the game from a different angle and having more time to do things with the ball and more space to do it in. I enjoy running with the ball, but there is also the tactical side to playing full back, which I like with my background at fly half.'
Willie LE ROUX, South Africa & The Cheetahs

⇥ Skills required to play full back

Effective full backs need to have vision, positional awareness at all times and a full array of core skills. They have an influential role in the backfield where they launch counter-attacks or maintain the team's defensive shape with the wings. It is essential for full backs to be effective organisers and communicators. For **Mike Tolkin**, 'Full backs have to be loud, vocal and organised and also be able to close down the outside. They need to be strong in anticipating the kicking game – reading the playmaker's hips, knowing what the attack are thinking of doing.'

Reading the game

The full back's position in the backfield gives them a comprehensive view of the action as it plays out. In attack they have to use that advantage to spot opportunities and position themselves to insert into the backline in the appropriate place. In defence they are constantly organising the back three to shut down opposition attacks and cover any kicking threats.

'Full backs should be "fast 10s"', suggests former Ireland and Leicester Tigers full back **Geordan Murphy**, '[you have a] bit more space at full back so you need vision and pace, be good under the high ball, a good communicator and organiser.' **Rob Kearney** explains how field coverage, the ability to position yourself to cover any running or kicking threats, comes from experience, 'You need to learn to read the play a couple of phases ahead. Learn the body language of the opposition 9 and 10 or some of the other key figures on their team.'

Catching a high ball

The full back has to have a sure pair of hands under the high ball. Constantly under pressure from the opposition who are looking to 'find grass' and gain ground with their long kicks, the No. 15 has to relish the challenge of contesting the ball in the air. 'It's about having the bravery and commitment to take those high balls. Though

you've also got to have good co-ordination', explains **Chris Wyles**. Rob Kearney suggests that 'aerial skills and your timing of the ball are about practice in games and training. When jumping you have to make sure your peak velocity is well timed with the flight of the ball.'

›› **Learn more about catching the high ball**
– *see pages 183-4*

Counter-attacking

The full back will often be the player to lead a team's counter-attack after catching an opponent's kick. They must quickly analyse what is in front of them, as well as be aware of their support, and decide if there is an opportunity to launch a successful counter-attack. If they are isolated or face an intact defensive wall, the full back will usually look to kick the ball downfield. This means they must be comfortable and confident in their ability to kick into space. Initiating a well-thought-out counter-attacking move can heavily influence the game, so there is a responsibility on the No. 15 to stay calm under pressure.

Rob Kearney believes 'you need pace to counter-attack. You need to be able to assess the situation and decide whether you should run, pass or kick.' While **Willie le Roux** recommends young players 'work on [their] kicking game because [they] have to be able to kick good touch-finders, up and unders to the corners and sometimes even dropped goals'

›› **Learn more about counter attacking**
– *see page 185*

← Springboks full back Willie Le Roux goes up for the high ball against Argentina

Tackling

A strong and effective tackler, the full back is often the last line of defence and is under pressure to make every tackle count. 'If you are going to make the tackle, it has to be aggressive, has to be through the thighs so the attacking player doesn't have the ability to offload the ball,' explains Geordan Murphy. 'As the last man, shutting down the ball is key. If you can't make that aggressive low body tackle then it has to be a higher tackle in order to shut the offload down.' **Andrea Masi** prefers going to meet the ball carrier rather than waiting. 'Some full backs like to stay at the back, but I like coming forward and making tackles.'

›› **Learn more about tackling** – *see pages 108-21*

›› A full back's role

In attack

The full back's role is to give the team momentum. They will insert into the backline in various positions, based on a team's rehearsed moves or where they see an opportunity in open play. Full backs also act as a team's second out half if the 10 is caught out of position, or if there is an attacking opportunity down the blindside.

Chris Wyles suggests, 'In terms of attack you are communicating where you are going to come into the attacking line because you have options and can enter at different places.'

The back three can be a pivotal unit for the team through their ability to change a game with a significant counter-attack. A good understanding between these three players ensures attacking opportunities can be maximised. Rob Kearney believes the back three unit working together is vital and is an aspect of the game that is hugely important but massively underrated by those watching rugby, 'Coaches put a huge amount of emphasis on it and guys in the team do as well. It has the potential to be a 60 or 70 metre shift and a turning point in the game at any given time.'

A full back should always be on the lookout for space or a weakness in the defence to exploit. Andrea Masi explains, 'Look for a mismatch in the opposition defence, someone slower than you, maybe a front row. If you don't have time to spot the mismatch get someone to tell you where you have to attack. When attacking, it's important to have very good timing on the ball because usually we get the ball from a long pass, maybe 10 to 15 metres away, and you can't be too early in the ball.'

In defence

Full backs have to read the opposition, anticipate if they are going to run or kick the ball and react accordingly. This means they must constantly keep an eye on the opposition out half and anticipate his next move. The full back must constantly organise his wings and ensure everyone is in position to deal with any attacking threat. The back three work as a unit and the full back has to be vocal to lead this group to ensure integrity in defence.

Rob Kearney believes that 'as a full back you are the marshall of the back three so you need to understand your wingers. You need to work together as a pendulum a huge amount and your scrum half has quite a bit of a role in terms of that pendulum working with regards to the chip line.' The Ireland 15 sets high standards for his teammates, 'I consider the back three to have a good game if we win all our aerials for the ball, and if the ball ever doesn't find grass when the opposition is attack kicking against us.' 'Defensively you have to be alert,' agrees Chris Wyles. 'Not only are you coming into the line as a defensive tackler, but you've also got to be aware of all kicks, so the more you communicate with your wings the better a position you'll be in.'

Springboks full back Willie le Roux has his own take on the importance of communication between the back three, 'Good communication is the most important thing – as a full back, life can get pretty lonely and tough at the back if you don't have your wing partners around to assist with those long kicks or to talk you through what could be coming your way.'

Often the last line of defence, full backs must be very effective and confident tacklers if they are to prevent scoring opportunities for the opposition. Anticipating whether to aggressively tackle the ball carrier or to hold off and buy his team time to react is another vital component of the full back's skill set. USA Coach **Mike Tolkin** explains what he values in his full backs, 'I really feel confident in my wide defence when I know I have a player who has great anticipation. Knowing when they need to shepherd the attack towards the sideline and when to jam down hard and cut down an attack in the backfield is important.'

Geordan Murphy played full back for 16 seasons with Leicester Tigers before starting his coaching career with the club so he speaks from experience when he says the 15 is 'trying to shut down anything that comes through the line. It's a difficult position when you find yourself isolated and there's maybe two or three guys coming through the line. It's bite on the attacker and leave the two-man overlap. It's very much a judgement call for back three players, but if in doubt, tackle the guy with the ball.'

WHAT MAKES A GOOD FULL BACK A GREAT FULL BACK?

GOOD V GREAT

❝ *You need to have* a strong kicking game and aerial ability like Israel Dagg and Israel Folau. You need to be able to read those couple of phases a few steps ahead. That's what separates the goods from the greats. ❞
Rob KEARNEY, Ireland & Leinster

❝ *Great full backs* are players who don't make mistakes, are very safe in the high balls and in attack are really threatening with a long kick. They have to be confident. One of the best full backs is Israel Folau, he is so threatening with the ball in the air and on the high ball he is the best full back ever probably. I never saw him drop a high ball. ❞
Andrea MASI, Italy & Wasps

❝ *Israel Folau pops* to mind because of his athletic ability and his evasion skills and one-on-one ability to beat players. Similarly Israel Dagg, who has that ability as well, as does Mike Brown. ❞
Chris WYLES, USA & Saracens

❝ *A great full back* is someone whose all-round game is brilliant, meaning he can kick, catch, defend, attack and is always in the right position on the field. There are two full backs I've always rated for the way in which they livened up the game: Percy Montgomery and Christian Cullen. ❞
Willie LE ROUX, South Africa & The Cheetahs

→ The Wallabies' Israel Folau has enjoyed success in rugby union, rugby league and Australian Rules football

2.THE

SKILLS

CORE SKILLS

Catching, passing, running and tackling are the core skills of rugby. Every player needs to practise and develop these skills if they are to contribute to the team's success. The players and coaches in this book stress how having a good foundation in these skills is critical to a player's development and ultimately their success.

During a game, in the heat of the battle, players do not have the luxury of time to think through the process of each skill before executing it. The higher the level of rugby, the less time and space players have to execute skills. A player must practise the correct technique for each individual skill over and over until it becomes the default action in any given situation. Players must train their muscle memory to execute the correct skill during a game, through hours of practice and repetition. Fly half **Ruaridh Jackson** explains, 'When you are in a pressure situation you want to follow your instincts so you can do something in a split second.'

Any rugby player who makes it to international level has spent many hours practising and honing their core skill set. These skills are the basic foundation for your success and are a prerequisite if you harbour ambitions of playing professional or international rugby.

The difference between the elite and novice is the ability to perform your core skills consistently under pressure with diminishing time and space.

Daryl GIBSON, Assistant Coach, Waratahs

Along with these core skills, this section includes communication as another core skill. It takes time to develop your confidence to become an effective communicator, but it is an integral part of your skills toolbox. You must communicate with your teammates on the rugby pitch. There is no alternative. A quiet player will struggle to develop trust with his teammates. Communication is key to your success on the field.

The core skills are a fundamental requirement to play the game and are universal to all positions. All players have to develop these skills as England head coach **Stuart Lancaster** explains, 'It's not good enough now for a forward to say, "well, I'm a great tight-head but I can't handle the ball". You've got to be able to do everything.'

▸▸ Core skills win games

Every action in rugby stems from core skills. Without them, a team cannot function. The higher the individual and collective skills within a team, the more successful that team will be. Accurate passes, well-timed runs and momentum shifting tackles are the raw ingredients of a skilful team. Stuart Lancaster believes it's what makes the world champions the best, 'You look at the best in the world at the moment, New Zealand, they have a great core skill set which is pretty much ingrained through touch and pass games and the amount of rugby that they played in their early years. Under pressure, particularly at international level, you have very little time to think or breathe never mind execute subconsciously.'

There is no substitute for hard work

Any player's proficiency in core skills comes from practice and repetition but the benefits are worth the effort. Improvement in an individual's core skill set is an ongoing process and should start with a good understanding of proper technique, which is reinforced in games. In my own experience I played touch rugby at lunchtime every day for 10 years. I believe that's why my school, St Mary's College in Dublin, has produced so many international players. We got our reps, our 10,000 hours, without even realising it. Leicester Tigers coach **Aaron Mauger** would expect all elite players to be focusing on their core skills every day, 'Planning your week and making every touch on the ball count is the difference between the great players and the average/good ones.'

Mike Tolkin explains the advantages of developing the core skills of individual players. 'We coach them in isolation to make the players technically sound and we work them also in small sided games and warm-ups when the players are being tested under pressure but also in a fun environment,' he says. 'The key is to get the guys working on their skills without them really thinking about it, making sure they are learning good habits and repeating good technique.

'Players have to learn the proper fundamental techniques and the best way to practise them and then put in the extra time before and after practice. Looking at video of themselves, be critical of themselves, get feedback and continuously put in the hours so the muscle memory is done right.'

England attacking skills coach **Mike Catt** believes the core skills message is clear, 'Focus entirely on core skills. There is nothing better than to see individuals develop their core skills so they are more accurate and make the right decisions on the pitch.'

CATCH AND PASS

↗ Fly half Beauden Barrett practices the core skill of catch and pass

To build pressure and create scoring opportunities you have to have possession of the ball. A fundamental part of that is your ability to catch and pass. International teams average nearly 700 passes in a game so it's vital to build and maintain a high level of proficiency in these areas if you want to progress.

Players should be comfortable on the ball. Work with a ball in your hands away from training to get a feel for how it behaves and how you can influence the speed and direction through subtle movements and effective technique. Throwing and catching to yourself will not only improve your catching but also your hand-to-eye coordination.

⚡ How to catch a rugby ball

⚡ CATCHING

- Big eyes
- Soft hands
- First job first
- Your right hand (power hand) should be towards the back of the ball and your left hand (guide hand) towards middle/front of the ball

If you take your eyes off the ball, you won't catch it. Focus on the ball until it is safely in your hands.

Keep your hands up with fingers towards the ball. It gives the passer a target and helps them place the ball in front of you, which is of paramount importance if you want to maintain momentum in attack. If your hands are down it takes time to lift them, speed and timing are critical. USA Rugby development coach **Alex Magleby** talks through the process, 'It's "make a window" with your fingers (thumbs together), especially if the ball is above your waist, and "show ten" (ten fingers). So "soft fingers, big eyes, looking through the window".

'If the pass is below your waist, then it should be pinkies together and "make a basket" (as opposed to a window) – that's the difference between the two. Now you have a quality catch and it makes the next pass much easier.'

If the ball hits the palms of your hands, it's likely to bounce out of your grip, so you want your fingers to do the catching. 'We don't want to hear the thud of ball hitting palms; stresses

Alex Magleby. All Blacks skills coach, **Mick Byrne**, explains the concept of soft hands and the importance of pointing your fingers towards the ball, 'The effect of "soft hands" is the ability of the wrists to react to the pressure of the pass. If you have your fingers forward towards the ball, you are using your fingers to catch and the wrists have the ability to slightly bend back, which creates a suspension of the catch. Young kids are often taught to put their hands up, so they put their fingers to the sky, which creates hard hands. You need to have your fingers pointing towards the passer.'

Often a player misses a catch because they have already mentally moved on to the next job. You can't score a try or make the pass if you don't have the ball so make sure you get the first job done, catch the ball, and only then move on.

⚡ How to pass a rugby ball

Always look before you pass and know where your options are. At the top level passing the ball has to be completed accurately and consistently at high speed.

Alex Magleby highlights foot position as another factor in the passing process, 'On the pass, we teach foot forward in the direction the ball came from, with the other leg open to the direction you are passing, hips upfield so you are square and moving towards your tryline to hold the defence. The ball stays away from your body, bent elbow, push through your core/wrists and punch, then follow through in the direction you want the ball to go.'

Magleby explains two ways players can generate power in the pass and uses an unusual way to explain passing to young players, 'For lack of a better term, "Kiwi" style is getting that punch and shoulder rotation, "English" seems to be more about using the core pushing through the ball. They coalesce around the same point, push in the direction you want the ball to go – the space in front of the receiver – and follow through to that point. Pretend there's a gremlin popping out of the receiver's chest and you have to knock it off. Take the head off the gremlin. Fingertips follow through and you are just a magician.

'Show 10' at the beginning, cast a spell to receive, then, finish casting a spell where you want to go.'

Mick Byrne believes one of the key parts of the pass is to continue your running line and not slow down. To do this you have to focus on your upper body, 'You have to be less reliant on your feet position and more reliant on your arms for the pass. It's really important that you pass above or across your hips so that your legs are free to continue running at your current pace and you generate power using your elbows and wrists.'

Coach **Paul Burke** advises the catch-pass process must be a single motion, 'The most important thing when running is to get your hands up, catch the ball early over your inside hip and transfer the ball across your body in one action.'

▸▸ The different types of pass

When you are developing your skills, lots of consistent short, accurate flat passes are better than a poorly thrown long one that could be dropped, knocked-on or intercepted.

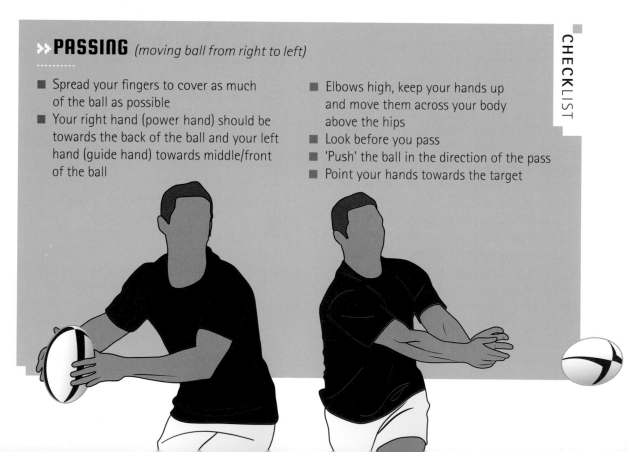

▸▸PASSING *(moving ball from right to left)*

- Spread your fingers to cover as much of the ball as possible
- Your right hand (power hand) should be towards the back of the ball and your left hand (guide hand) towards middle/front of the ball
- Elbows high, keep your hands up and move them across your body above the hips
- Look before you pass
- 'Push' the ball in the direction of the pass
- Point your hands towards the target

Be really balanced *and use good technique to the pass, punching and flicking your hands straight to the target. Practise until it becomes second nature.*

'I don't just practise standing still; I practise under pressure and under fatigue because that's how you are for 80 per cent of the time in a game. Sprint from one side of the field to the other side and make a good pass, then sprint back across the field again and make a good pass. Practising when you are dead calm and fit means you should be able to make every pass.'

Aaron SMITH, New Zealand & The Highlanders

Alex Magleby explains the thinking behind your pass selection, 'It depends on how far you want to move the ball. The motion is the same throughout, at any point you can make a short or a long pass so you are making a read as a distributor. If you are a prop or a fly half, I [as the No. 9] may be giving the ball 2 metres away but we have another option 3 metres away and another 5 metres away. The mechanics are the same – I still have my elbow bent, that window, and I can bring that pass through my core.

'I have a choice between three types of pass [each team will have different names for these passes]. The Yo-Yo – that's just a fingertips pass, I can leave the ball right there, in front of the short runner. There's the Pistol – a 3-metre pop pass where I push the ball a little more. Big window, follow through with my wrists. And the Rifle – mechanics are the same but I'll follow through with my arms all the way to the target. There's a slight variation in what I'm doing with the ball and with my fingertips.

'If I keep ball in my fingers the whole time between the catch and the release I can manipulate the pass. With the Rifle pass I'm going against the grain with my fingers. If it's a pop pass my fingers are with the grain. The only difference between the two is moving your fingers slightly in relation to the grain going from pop to spin pass.'

How to improve your passing

Glasgow Warriors head coach **Gregor Townsend** believes, 'that getting as many catches and passes as possible will improve ball handling very quickly', while Paul Burke suggests, 'static passing is good to master the technique. Make sure you're passing off the right leg and that your weight is going through the ball.'

↑ Rene Ranger has used his speed to good effect in both Sevens and XVs for New Zealand

RUN

Rugby is about forward momentum. The teams that are going forward are the ones that will have the better chance of winning the next contact situation and continue to build momentum.

It's important that you always try to run straight or at least, forward. Young ball carriers have a tendency to run sideways across the field to avoid a defender but this cuts down the space for their teammates outside of them. Remember 'hips to try': keep your hips square to the try line and then use a sidestep or a dummy to beat your man 1 v 1.

Saracens coach **Mark McCall** outlines how players should think about their running, 'Think about your footwork and being able to manipulate the defender. Thing about what you should do with your 'weapons' i.e. your hands, your hand-offs, and finally try to inject a change of pace at the right moment.'

▶▶RUNNING *A good running checklist reads 'ABCD':*

Angle change – as you get the ball step off one foot, change your angle, then step back up again.
Ball transfer – keep the ball away from your opponent
(C) Separation – keep as much distance as possible between you and the defender
Drive your legs – through the tackle

Angle change [A]

You want to keep as much distance between you and the would-be tackler because the closer he gets to the ball carrier, the more his chances increase of making a good tackle.

It's important that you get the tackler off balance or caught in two minds so he doesn't get himself set to make a good tackle. A sidestep or swerve brings attention to your legs and will hopefully get the defender to plant his feet, which means he slows down for a split second and you gain the upper hand. Coach **Alex Magleby** breaks down the process, 'For 1 v 1 there is space on either side of the tackler. The ball carrier has to make the defender aware of that. It is important to change the hip angle of the defender so he doesn't sweep us into the way he wants us to go. We try to square up the defender by letting him know that we may be going to his left or his right shoulder.

'Make sure you change angle before the ball arrives. Once the ball arrives, I've already started the manipulation of the defender, changing the angle of attack to offset the tackle. If I want to

go to his left shoulder, I pretend I'm going right for a split second and square him up so he doesn't know where I'm going ... then I can choose my direction.'

A change of pace is something England's centre **Manu Tuilagi** recommends for beating your man, 'If it's 1 on 1 or even 2 on 1 and I get the ball early with lots of space, I'll try and beat the guy on the outside and get the hand-off. Run your line and trust your tempo running; not just running fast the whole time, you slow down then accelerate at the right time. Makes it a lot harder for the defender.'

Rugby is a fast-paced game and there is very little time to assess the situation. Deciding on how best to beat an opponent has to become almost instinctive, as Ireland's **Gordon D'Arcy** explains, 'When you are at your best you haven't even thought about it. If there is a thought process necessary, the moment has gone. There are times when things just happen, "click", and it's about perception, lateral vision, timing, footwork and reflexes but if you have to think – it's too late.'

D'Arcy's Irish teammate **Cian Healy** is known for his mobility as a loose-head in open play and he describes how he can use opponents' perceptions of a player in his position to his advantage, 'There are lots of different things you can do. You can stop and start, change pace and completely shift. The best kind is a simple shift of direction, which is not usually expected from the heavier lads. When one of the front five players takes the ball up and can change direction, you will more than likely break the gain line because the defender is probably going to plant his feet in an attempt to tackle a big guy. By applying the sidestep, changing direction and aiming for an inside shoulder, it can be pretty easy to beat a weak arm tackle.'

Fijian centre **Nemani Nadolo** uses two of the great wings in the game to explain why size doesn't matter, it's about believing you can beat your man, 'Guys like Jonah Lomu, who could beat a man easily in his sleep, then you look at Shane Williams who can beat his opponent just as easily. It's about having that faith in your skills and ability to beat the person in front of you. Once you know you can do that the thing in front of you becomes just an object.'

Ball transfer [B]

You need two hands on the ball to be able to pass. If you hold the ball in one hand, that is a cue for the defence that you aren't going to pass, so multiple defenders can focus on you. This means you can end up getting hit pretty hard. Holding the ball in two hands plants a seed of doubt in the defender's mind that you might pass the ball rather than carry. This may cause the defender to hesitate momentarily, buying you a vital second or two.

If you are going to take contact, that is when you make the ball transfer and you put the ball in one hand, the one furthest from the opposition. If you lead into the tackle with the ball, the chances of that tackler disrupting the ball increase. You want to get that ball as far away as possible from the tackler. Alex Magleby emphasises the point, 'It very important to hold the ball in two hands so at any time I can hit my support, left or right, so the defender doesn't know. I use my "wand" (the ball) to get the defender to move and to commit to space. Ball transfer happens at angle change, so I now have to transfer the ball away from the defender.'

Separation [C]

When you transfer the ball to one hand, you want to use your other hand for a fend (hand-off) because it maintains separation between the tackler and you. You want to power it out because you are not just trying to maintain distance you are trying to push off him and use his momentum to drive you forward. You want to time that hand-off so you push yourself forward. That, coupled with your leg drive, will help power you away from the contact area. 'Put the defender in two minds, try to get them off balance and then use your fend,' advises All Black **Rene Ranger**.

Alex Magleby describes the space around the ball carrier as a hula hoop to help players visualise the area they are trying to protect, 'I don't want the tackler to get into my space or near my centre of gravity. I want to keep him as far away as possible, as if I have a hula hoop and I don't want to let him inside the hoop. It's a violent separation. I want to get that separation with a fend or power step.'

Back row **Sean O'Brien** describes the separation process, 'When you see someone in front of you, try and get that separation and that distance. The defender is trying to get close to you; you're trying to get away from him. Using your feet, get your hips square and get a fend out if you can. Get as much distance between you and them as possible, then get your hips and legs square and go forward from there.'

Drive your legs [D]

Once the defender has come towards you and you are using your weapons, you want to make sure you really increase your leg drive. Power through with high knees, fighting, fighting, fighting, which makes you more difficult to tackle and, as a ball carrier, that's what you want to be. You can also lower your centre of gravity at the hips when running to make yourself as small a target as possible.

If you have the mindset that you can bust

through that tackle, as coach **Ben Herring** says, the chances are you'll get over the gain line and maintain momentum. 'Sometimes young players think of a line of defence as a brick wall that cannot be crossed and flop into contact accordingly. Run at weak shoulders and arms, accelerate into contact, transfer your momentum *through* the tackle or the opponent. Twist, turn and force the tackler(s) to tackle you', is his clear advice.

Alex Magleby believes the leg drive is key to getting you back in the game quickly, 'You've got to drive – drive through the process, try to get your hips square, get back up field, get continuity, get the ball back to two hands and make the pass or go yourself'.

How to improve your running

When running lines, the timing of the run is crucial. Welsh wing **George North** highlights 'quick footwork and hand-offs at the right time' as being an important aspect of the skill. While Argentina's **Horacio Agulla** focuses on how to judge your speed, 'You have to control your pace and catch the ball at the perfect time when you are at speed. You have to practise that in training and find the right timing'.

Prop Cian Healy uses the warm-ups to figure out what he can do as a ball carrier in a game, 'In warm-ups, I love getting out there and throwing the ball around with a few sidesteps and that helps you figure out your abilities. We work on footwork, evasion and agility at training as it is an important part of your game'.

↓ Run like Manu Tuilagi

TACKLE

Defending is as much a part of rugby as attacking is. You can increase your value and impact for your team by being a very good tackler.

Technique is king when it comes to tackling safely. A deep understanding and application of the tackle technique will minimise chance of injury, and maximise the effectiveness of the tackle. Knowing how to optimise your feet, legs, shoulders, arms and head in the tackle will help you develop into a very good tackler while keeping you safe. Coach **Les Kiss** is clear that players should learn good habits from the start, 'Begin with the basics of tackle technique. It may sound simple but it is at the core of a good, sound and confident defender.'

Learning to tackle

For young rugby players and those new to the game, tackling practice should be an area of focus, starting with the tackler hitting a pad and progressing up to contact. Ideally, the tackler should be on his knees with an attacker slowly walking towards him. The tackler executes the technical tackle, going through each point on the checklist and off both shoulders. Progression should only be considered after the tackler has demonstrated proficient technique and understanding of the safety issues. Flanker **Kelly Brown** suggests it comes down to practice, 'I started in my back garden when I was about six and I tried to tackle my older brother who at the time was significantly bigger than I was. Get the basics of the tackle technique right, start off at very low pace or start off tackling on your knees,

and just gradually build up your confidence.'

Coach **Ben Herring** has an unusual but effective way to describe why a player should commit fully to a tackle, 'Know this: every percent less intense you go the chance of getting hurt goes up by one percent. The quicker you can get to someone the less speed they get to build up. The more you decide where the tackle takes place the less ability they have to hurt you.

'The closer you get the safer it is! (In hockey if you hesitate when someone is swinging the stick, you will get it in the face – if you rush in, you get it in the shin!) I personally loved this advice from when I was a young boy and I applied it to my whole career.'

↓ Geoff Parling tackles charging Steffon Armitage

›› TACKLE

CHECKLIST

Tackle technique can be broken down into individual elements to allow a player to understand how to tackle safely and effectively:

- Body language
- Eyes up
- Head placement
- Foot placement
- Shoulder contact
- Arm wrap
- Leg drive
- Bring to ground
- Back on feet

Tackle technique

DEFENCE COACH ROB HOADLEY explains how to help a player develop individual tackle technique: 'All players must work on consistently getting the tackle technique right in order to build up their confidence. Practices should start on tackle shields and focus on consistently working through the process of correct tackle technique. After building up confidence working against tackle shields, defenders should start to tackle ball carriers in full contact drills. Repetition of this process to master the technique in practice is crucial, so that it becomes instinctive during a game. When a player enters the game, there is no time to consciously go through the entire process of each tackle. Rather, the tackler must be able to trust his training and muscle memory, leaving him free to focus his energy on committing aggressively to the tackle.

'By doing this, we eliminate clutter from the mind and simplify the process of making a tackle. When clutter, or distractions enter the mind, so does fear of failure.

'By training consistently to commit to contact, the player will build up their technique and belief as they continue to see improvement in training. Defenders must understand that intensity and commitment brings out the best in us. Some may feel that they are protecting themselves physically by shying away from contact or going in half-hearted. But ask them, "has taking on a challenge half-hearted ever helped you, or been successful?" I can't think of an occasion where it has helped anyone on the rugby field. In fact, it makes it more likely that the player will be injured by an opponent who is fully committed to contact. Instead, get them excited about the opportunity to actually inspire intensity in others. I find that the best motivation can be in seeing the reaction of teammates to a player that previously struggled with physicality, who commits to a regular training regime, and now produces positive grade tackles on match day. Offer opportunities, praise and rewards to produce positively contagious behaviour.

All players must comprehend the impact on the team if just one defender avoids their defensive responsibilities. If a player's intensity is slightly off their best, their performance drops dramatically. As previously stated, intensity and effort does not take skill, experience or understanding of the game; it is actually a choice of which each player is in control. It can be a tough choice when we feel low or lack confidence. Yet the only thing that will get us back to our performance goals is to bring total commitment to the process and the moment. While it is vital for coaches to foster an environment that encourages and rewards effort, once this culture is established it then becomes essential to be harder on effort lapses than skill errors – intensity is a choice, skill involves ability. No matter what your ability is, effort is what ignites that ability and turns it into accomplishment

'Such discipline to bring sustained intensity must be driven from within the team. Being a good teammate is calling out those that take their foot off the gas physically. Players must be honest to help each other get over such lapses in order to benefit the team performance.'

↑ Sam Warburton ready to tackle ball carrier
Johnny Sexton

Body language

The tackler should always look like he is willing
and ready to make an effective tackle. This starts
with his body language. Ideally, the tackler is in
a boxer's stance with one foot forward, knees
slightly bent, hips low, hands up and elbows in.
The tackler is on his toes, resembling a boxer,
ready to fight. Head should be 'on a swivel',
surveying the threat in front of him.

Eyes up

The tackler must be aware of who he is tackling
and ensure that his eyes are on the ball carrier.

Head placement

It is imperative that the tackler places his head
to the side of the ball carrier to ensure safety.
Welsh back row **Sam Warburton** stresses the
importance of getting head placement right to
avoid injury, 'The most important thing is to make
sure you don't get your head on the wrong side.
A lot of concussion injuries occur because of this.
I am a fan of tackling low, so to hit around the
knees with your shoulder and using your arms
to clamp the player's legs together. That is my
preferred choice of tackling. It allows me to get
on my feet more easily to compete for the ball
or allow teammates to compete for a turnover.'

Always remember – cheek to cheek: this
means that the cheek of the face of the tackler
should be against the bum cheek of the ball
carrier. Never put your head across the ball
carrier, as the chance of getting a knee to the
head will increase. Always place your head to
the side, and tight against the ball carrier's bum
cheek. 'Use his backside as a cushion,' suggests
English flanker **Tom Wood**. 'It helps you make
a tight contact so you don't swing your arm.'

Foot placement

The tackler should aim to get his lead foot as close to the ball carrier as possible and, ideally, between the tackler's legs. The power of the tackle is generated from the legs, so ensuring that the lead foot is as close as possible to the ball carrier will help to maximise the power of the tackle. If you imagine that the ball carrier has a hula hoop or circle on the ground around his legs, the tackler wants to invade the ball carrier's hula hoop, by getting his lead foot inside it.

It's not just placement that contributes to the effectiveness of the tackle, it's also about timing. If you get your lead foot in the right position but you plant it too early, you will have problems, as Wales centre **Jamie Roberts** outlines, 'Technically, you want your feet in the right position and to get as close to your opponent as possible. Try not to plant your feet early and tackle with your arms.' All Black skills coach **Mike Byrne** explains the importance of getting your tackle right, 'It's about getting your feet in close and keeping them alive, shoulder on and wrapping at the same time. That's one of the keys – you see players plant their feet and lunge, leading with the shoulder, but they don't get their arms wrapped and bounce off. Players will plant their feet and at the last second the player steps around them and gets away. Keep the feet alive, get your feet in close, getting your shoulder on and wrapped, with your feet working hard after the contact as well.'

Scotland's No. 8 **David Denton** believes it's important to learn early how to get yourself aligned before the tackle, both head and feet, 'Get into a position where you are effective but also in a safe position. Slightly inside the defender, a good foot placement, followed by a good head placement, making sure your head is on the right side of the body, driving your legs and squeezing your arms together.'

Shoulder contact – same foot, same shoulder

This means that whichever foot is planted between the ball carrier's legs, the same shoulder makes contact with the ball carrier in the tackle. If the tackler has his left foot planted between the ball carrier's legs, the tackler will use his left shoulder to make contact. The tackler's head should always be on the opposite side of the shoulder he uses to make contact with the ball carrier.

Arm wrap – punch/pull

The tackler's arms should be in the boxer stance with his hands up and elbows in tight to his body. As contact is made with the shoulder, the tackler punches his arms forward and wraps them around the ball carrier's legs. With the ball carrier's legs in the tackler's arms, the tackler then pulls his arms back towards himself.

Leg drive

Once the ball carrier's legs have been wrapped in the tackler's arms, a strong leg drive from the tackler will knock the ball carrier off balance and knock him backwards and down on to the ground. But, as Mick Byrne emphasises again, 'The one thing that's common in all the successful tackles and turnovers is keeping your feet alive. When you speak to NFL coaches, the players whose job it is to sack the quarterback don't focus on the tackle, they focus on keeping their feet alive. At all times when he's changing direction and tracking back, he keeps his feet alive. He can't plant his feet.

← Horacio Agulla fights to stay on his feet against the New Zealand defence

'This is one of the key things for a young player to learn. Once both feet plant on the ground there isn't much else you can do. If you get your shoulder on while keeping your feet alive you'll be able to get back up on your feet and secure the ball if that is possible.'

Bring to ground

The tackler should have driven the ball carrier backwards and the momentum of the tackle will knock the player down on to the ground. Ideally, the tackler should aim to land on the ball carrier, chest down.

Back on feet

Following your tackle it is essential to get back on your feet quickly, because if you are on the ground you are effectively out of the game. It is a lot easier and quicker to get up if you are chest down, either on the ground or on the ball carrier. Push yourself up off the ball carrier or ground and get to your feet as quickly as possible so you can either contest for the ball, or clear out the ball carrier's support.

'Get to your feet quickly' is back row **Shane Jennings'** message. 'Flankers should always believe that the tackle is not complete until you are back on your feet. If you are on the ground, you are out of the game and therefore not much good to your team.'

How to improve your tackling

As with any skill practice makes perfect and tackling is no different. You want to test yourself against different opponents and in different situations in training, so come game day you are ready to react.

England back row **Steffon Armitage** explains the secrets of his success, 'Developing and improving your technique comes from doing 100 tackles in training during the week. Going over and over again. Getting big guys and small guys, so you learn how to take different people down. Most of the time you go high and you bring him down and you get over the ball. With the big guys you can't do that, they are too strong. If you go high they are just going to bump you off. So try to find the best tackle technique for different types of opponents.

'Start on your knees, making sure you get that good tackle in the hips. From there get backs in who can do a bit of footwork. '

Familiarising yourself with your opponent's running style and how others have counter acted that can make your job a bit easier. Here's how Ireland's **Gordon D'Arcy** did his homework on Australia's Israel Folau ahead of their match-up, 'Video is a very important tool. Before we played Australia, I watched how Conrad Smith tackled Israel Folau, how he went in, how he didn't get stepped, and how he kept his feet alive. I tried to emulate that in training by getting someone who was big and rangey like Folau and just practised. Practising good technique is crucial.'

As an opponent comes toward you, you want to shorten your stride length so you don't lose the power and lunge at the player. It's difficult to change your feet and if he steps you and adjusts at the last minute and if you are too long in your stride length you can't react to that. If you get your feet underneath you, shorten your stride length; let him make his move. When he does, try to have a good sink in the hips, keep your head up and drive your front leg in between his legs as close as possible. That means you have a good foundation at the middle of his centre of gravity or below and rock him with your tackle.

'As you make impact, you chase your feet through, wrap your arms tight and try and drive him backwards

'I've always been taught that the point of contact is about a yard beyond his body. So you don't hit him where he stands and lunge, you imagine you are driving and hitting him a yard behind and your momentum is carrying you through the tackle. Of course, it's easier said than done, especially on a moving target and one that is trying to fend you off or bump you into the floor.

Tom WOOD, England & Northampton Saints

►► Different types of tackle

The various situations the defender is faced with will determine the type of tackle they chose to execute. The decision should be based on which tackle will be the most effective, and that depends on the situation. As a player's skill level improves and the time spent playing rugby increases, so too will the player's decision-making process in all facets of the game, including defence and tackle selection.

Size of the opponent

Naturally, players take into account the size and strengths of the opposition ball carrier when choosing which type of tackle to make. Picking the correct option to bring down a fast agile back or a strong direct forward is important if you want to stop their progress.

↑ Flanker Shane Jennings tackles the ball carrier

When the opponent is equal to or smaller than the tackler, coach **Scott Lawrence** recommends a 'front-on high tackle to prevent the offload and send them backwards'.

Back row **Sean O'Brien** describes his process for deciding how best to tackle an opponent, 'If it's a player I can manhandle a bit, I'll hit him a little bit higher, get my feet nice and close and get him going backwards. If he's a bigger man, I'll try and eat the space away and get my feet as close as possible to his feet, get as low as possible and take his legs'.

Man and ball

Where you hit an opponent on their body (always below the shoulders) can have a big impact on the success of the tackle. Tackling the ball carrier high is usually done with the aim of tackling 'man and ball', thereby preventing the ball carrier passing to a teammate. The decision of how high to tackle an opponent is not always obvious, but it's something a player develops with experience, as flanker **Kelly Brown** explains, 'Some guys you can get high and you can tie up the ball and then there are others where you'd try to hit them high and you'd bounce off. So it's about working hard, learning the different techniques but also your decision making so you know exactly which type of tackle to deploy and when'.

You would only decide to hit high if someone else is going low so it's an option when there are multiple tacklers. You want to be tackling 'cheek to cheek' for safety, which is a tackle around or below hip height. For teaching purposes when you are starting off with a new tackler you should always look to get them to hit the ball carrier low and bring them to ground.

>> Angle, distance and speed

Front on, side on, from behind, up close, at a distance, at speed – these are all factors in tackle selection. Defence coach **Rob Hoadley** outlines some of the options which players should consider in just a few of the different situations.

Choke tackle

An attacker runs into a congested area of defenders.

'Defenders in the area all close in on the carrier and squeeze him upwards so that he cannot get to the floor and recycle the ball. Tacklers should attempt to get a bicep under the armpit of the carrier to hold him up.'

Leg tackle

Generally on a drift formation, or any open field situation (i.e. kick return or turnover possession). At these times there will be a big enough space between defenders for attackers to get to the defenders outside, forcing a more passive leg tackle.

'Aim for the hips, clamp the ball carrier's legs together and drive through the initial contact point to take him to ground.'

>> Turnover tackles

First and foremost a tackle should stop the opposing team from crossing the gain line. The aim should then be to regain possession, so there are a number of options that allow players to tackle for turnovers. Coach Scott Lawrence outlines the front-on chop tackle; 'Generally a fast-line speed tackle, used to chop down the point runner and expose for a poach.'

Even when the attacker is protecting the ball it is possible for the defender to choose an option that helps them to make the most of contact with the aim of winning the ball. Here defence coach Rob Hoadley explains one such technique, which he calls the 'knock fend'.

Knock fend

On a drift defence, the attacker is on the outside of the defender using their fend in an attempt knock the tackler away.

'If the tackler can get close enough, he has the option of knocking the ball carrier's fend down with his inside arm, while wrapping the tackler with the outside arm. He should continue to leg drive through the tackle. Alternatively, if he cannot get close enough to knock the fend down with his inside arm, the tackler can duck under the fend and use the leg tackle technique.'

>> Multiple tacklers

In an ideal scenario, the defence will remain intact, keeping its shape and discipline. The defence is patiently waiting for an opportunity for multiple defenders to tackle an isolated ball carrier with the aim of turning over possession.

Lock **Joe Launchbury** advises players to recognise these situations so one defender can tackle the ball carrier low, taking them to ground, while the supporting defender can attempt to jackal [steal] the ball, 'If I go low, I can take their legs away straight away and let one of my teammates come in and jackal on the ball'. Back row **Jerome Kaino** is in full agreement when he says, 'It's really effective when you have good jacklers around you who can jump on the ball. If you have a big guy coming towards, you can chop them, another guy can jump on them and you get the turnover'.

Coach Rob Hoadley explains two tackles where the defenders work together to bring down their opponent and regain possession.

Double tackle

Often used when the ball carrier attempts to run hard between two defenders.

'The two defenders must get their hips close together in order take away the gap the ball carrier is attacking. After the initial hit, both tacklers can leg drive to knock the ball carrier back. Ideally one of the tacklers would also work on stripping the ball from the ball carrier's grip'.

Hit and strip tackle

Used when a ball carrier is fending another tackler and the ball is exposed in their non-fending arm.

'The player arriving as the second tackler must first hit the carrier hard with his shoulder to stun him. Then get a close grip on the ball with bicep tight on it. The defender must then explosively rip his arm away from the ball carrier to dislodge the ball.'

▶▶ 'Red Zone' tackles

Teams divide the field up into zones to allow them to identify the best tactics to implement in certain areas. Different teams will use different names for these zones and the number of zones can vary too. For example, the rugby pitch can be notionally divided into three zones – the red zone (from your defending tryline up to your 22-metre line), the white zone (from your 22-metre to the attacking 22-metre line), and the green zone (from the attacking 22-metre line to the tryline you are trying to attack). In your red zone defences tend to be a lot more aggressive because you can't afford to give up ground. The types of tackle used here reflect that.

These three tackles suggested by coach Scott Lawrence all aim to stop or drive back the opponent before they can cross the try-line and ground the ball:

Front-on low to high tackle

'Frequently used in red zone or in hips up slow line speed defence when driving the attacker backwards.'

Drive tackle

'Used in and around the ruck, like an American football drive block.'

The turtle

'Covering tackle sliding under the ball carrier and rolling them up like an upside-down turtle to prevent them grounding the ball.'

← Shane Jennings wraps around the ball carrier's legs to take him to ground

⊁⊁ Attitude in contact

If you want to stop the opposing team's attack and bring down the ball carrier, you have to commit to a tackle. Flanker **Kelly Brown** explains, 'A lot of tackling is about bravery and having the right mindset. It's about wanting to tackle the person and not being worried about it.'

Wales centre **Jamie Roberts** puts it clearly, 'Tackling is about getting your shoulder in the right position and getting your whole weight behind the tackle to smash the opposition player. If you are not mentally willing to do that, then you are already one step behind. You do need the right mindset of being brave and wanting to stop the opposition ... This attitude comes from confidence, which builds up as you develop your tackling technique.'

Some players get that attitude early but it's not something that everyone has in their game from day one, as Roberts remembers from his younger days, 'I remember, turning up to youth training sessions when I was about 14 and I was a bit sheepish in contact. I used to grab the opposition player by the jersey and swing him around!

'At a training session, when I was 16, the coach literally lined up two sets of players and told us that we had to run as hard as we could into the player opposite. You were not allowed to sidestep; you had to run as hard you could and the other player had to tackle you. That session changed my whole approach to tackling. It is a bit of a man test but tackling for me is very much about mindset. There is technique to it but the mindset is important.'

Scott Lawrence makes no bones about it when he says, 'The mindset for the tackler is purely confrontational. The athlete is looking to put themselves or the team in a position to get the ball back at the tackle.'

USA back row **Scott LaValla** explains how young players need to think about what they have to do and not what they think could happen. They should trust their training, 'Don't look at a player and think "he's big and fast", look where you want to make contact and focus on your cues. That might be "hit low and drive", or just "dominate".'

Tackle selection

DEFENCE COACH ROB HOADLEY offers his advice on how coaches can help players learn the tackle and develop their decision-making skills: 'The key is to teach the isolated skill component of each tackle in controlled training drills. When players feel comfortable with the isolated technique, then teach the decision-making process of what tackle to use in any given scenario by practising them in game situations. The idea is first to add tools to the toolbox, then to teach players to decide what is the right tool for each job.

'There are many different styles of tackle used in different game situations. For example, a small player tackling a bigger player will use a different technique from a bigger, slower player who has to tackle a quicker player. There are numerous varieties and names for different tackles. Ensure that your team has a language for each tackle that they are comfortable with. While players must practise all styles of tackle, they should also (often by position) focus on the type of tackles they are most likely to make in the match.'

Commitment to contact

COACH ROB HOADLEY shares his opinion on why a player must have an aggressive mentality in contact if they are to make successful tackles: 'A defender can a) be in good position through the team's defensive shape/organisation, and b) have great technique BUT applying this without c) the aggressive mentality in contact, will lead to failure. On the other hand, it is possible for a player with a great mentality to make great tackles without an experienced understanding of positioning or technique. He will need guidance and coaching on a) and b) to be consistently successful – this is the sort of player that coaches can work with.

'The key question then becomes, can you train c) an aggressive mentality in contact? We don't want to ignore young players who may have a good understanding of positioning and technique but lack a natural commitment to contact. We are essentially asking then whether physical intensity is a fixed trait or something that can be taught and learned. I firmly believe that with the right guidance and training, players can drastically improve their commitment to contact and therefore the overall defensive quality of their team

'Ultimately, commitment to contact is a choice that each player is in control of. It can be a tough choice, but it is a choice nonetheless.'

accenture   ❯❯ RBS ⬤ NATIONS

No 2. Welsh Defence v Ireland

Wales

| 88 | 60 | 41 | 35 | 21 | 5 |

Own 22   22 – 10m   10m > < 10m   22 – 10m   Opponents 22

#seebeyond   Direction Of Play   ⬤ Successful Tackles

31
Vs Ireland

23
Sam Warburton
Vs Ireland

23
Toby Faletau
Vs Ireland

Accenture's defining moment number 2 – The Wales v Ireland game will be remembered for an outstanding defensive display from the men in red. Between 45-55 minutes they made 77 tackles, the majority of which were inside their 22. If Ireland had managed to break through they may well have been celebrating a Grand Slam.

❯ High performance. Delivered.

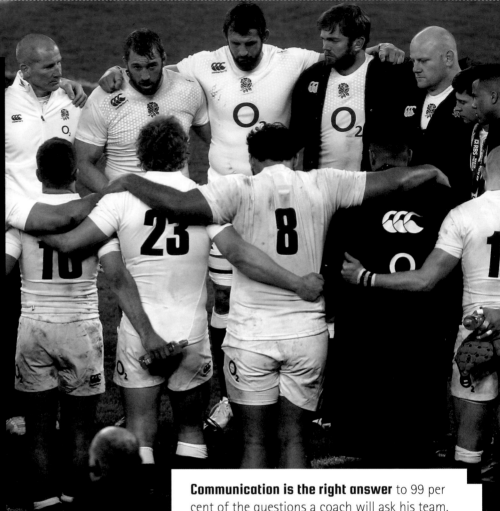

Communication

↑ The England team form a huddle after the game

Communication is the right answer to 99 per cent of the questions a coach will ask his team. It's the most understated yet valuable and vital component for a team's success in attack and defence. It's the difference between informed collective decisions by teammates and educated guesses.

Lack of communication comes when players are uncertain in their roles, uncertain of the team's goals and have a lack of confidence in certain situations. Leicester Tigers coach **Geordan Murphy** recommends patience and positive feedback, 'You need to tell players what they are doing is correct, help them understand by slowing things down and help them understand what they are trying to achieve and then just encourage them to talk.'

USA full back **Chris Wyles** believes a player shouldn't be quiet on a pitch but rather talk to people about what they are doing and communicate through game, 'By doing that you are telling your teammate what your intentions are and you're also feeding them information. It's also about the quality of the information and not just saying things for the sake of it.'

Geordan Murphy suggests starting small to get players talking, 'Encourage the guys to give the small talk, not calling plays just saying "do this" or "do that", encourage teammates to have that interaction with each other. It's not always about the big talk; it's about the little talk.'

There are two parts of communication – talking and listening. It's important to acknowledge that we have heard and understood but these don't have to verbal, there can be physical cues and non-verbal. If you are in the defensive line and you hear a teammate behind or outside you instructing you to do something, raise your hand to acknowledge you've heard it. You are unlikely to have time to reply and anyway you might be out of breath, but they'll know you heard if you've raised a hand or given a thumbs-up. As Argentinian wing **Horacio Agulla** reminds players, 'Communication is important, both spoken and visual, as sometimes it's so loud you can't hear on the pitch.'

Communication can be the difference between pre-empting a situation and reacting to it, it's a key to success. A team that is quiet cannot be successful. As coach **Ben Herring** says 'Constant loud direct communication is gold!'

Murphy sums up his thoughts from 20 years in rugby, 'The best attacking players I've ever worked with have all been incredible communicators. They've also had great vision and understanding of the game. They understand where the defenders will go and what they will do. They are also able to communicate that and put other players into holes by talking and organising the guys around them. For me world-class players are creative but also tremendous organisers as well as tremendous communicators.'

How to improve communication

As with any skill it is about practice. While the aim is to improve effective communication on the field, the work really starts away from the rugby pitch.

England's attacking skills coach **Mike Catt** has a suggestion for coaches to help both a player's communication and their understanding of the game, 'Get players to do little presentations so that they have to study specific parts of the game like catching a high ball, passing, tackling, etc. Get them to watch one player in their position, someone like Dan Carter, and get them to present to you what he does and they don't.'

Fly half **Ruaridh Jackson**'s former coach at Glasgow Warriors, **Gregor Townsend**, was keen on getting him to speak off the field to help improve his skills on it, 'I was confident in front of the team at meetings so when I was on the field my communication was clear, confident and concise. I was comfortable bossing the big guns around from an early age and it stood me in good stead.'

SET PIECE

The purpose of these technically, physically and mentally challenging set pieces is to restart the game after a minor infringement on the pitch. Scrums are a pushing contest, lineouts a jumping contest, and kick-offs are a catching contest. All are races to act before your opponent can react.

They offer attacking opportunities, as the grouping of 16 players (unless a shortened lineout is elected) in a relatively small area of the pitch creates space for the backs to exploit, if the forwards can provide a solid attacking platform for the backs to launch an attack. First phase tries are a thing of beauty, as it means that everybody from 1–15 has done their job.

Fundamentally what you are looking for from the forwards is to provide a solid platform. What that means is to be able to get a quality of possession that allows the backs to play or strike. They need to be able to launch an attack that puts the team on the front foot and gives them the very best chance of being successful from an attacking point of view.

Gary GOLD, Director of Rugby at The Sharks

THE SCRUM

↑ Shane Jennings in the scrum for Leinster

A scrum is a way of restarting play, usually after a knock-on, accidental offside, or an unplayable ball from a ruck or maul.

The scrum is a pushing contest that requires excellent technique, the ability to handle physical and mental pressure along with a unified drive from all eight forwards. Props, in particular, bear the brunt of the force of the scrum and must aim to be dominant at scrum time. Successful scrums can have a significant impact on a game and allow a forward pack to exert their will over the opposing pack, while providing their own backline with a stable platform to launch attacks.

The psychological impact of scrum dominance should not be underestimated. Argentina prop **Marcos Ayerza** describes the scrum as, 'a hugely important weapon and a unique part of rugby'. Italy's **Martin Castrogiovanni** accurately describes this scrummaging contest against the other prop as 'a sport within a sport, another game within the game'.

›› The formation of a scrum

There are three rows to a scrum. The front row consists of the loose-head prop, hooker and tight-head prop. The second row consists of the two locks and they are flanked by the back row, which consists of the openside and blindside flanker along with the No. 8.

Both sets of forwards' front rows bind against each other and, on entry of the ball into the scrum, the pushing contest commences in an attempt to win possession. The team who throws the ball into the scrum has the advantage of knowing when the ball will enter the scrum.

Scrums can provide excellent attacking opportunities for the team in possession, as 18 players, [16 forwards and 2 scrum halves] are concentrated in a small area of the pitch. All remaining players must be 5 metres behind the scrum. This means there is a lot of space for the attacking team to launch a strike move through their backs.

›› SCRUMMAGING

If a scrum is to be safe and successful, all players must understand their roles:

- Role in the scrum
- Feet position
- Bind
- Profile
- Pushing technique

CHECKLIST

Role in the scrum

Each player should understand their role in the scrum in both attack and defence. Attacking teams will have set plays that they will launch from the scrum, so it is important that every player in the pack understands the desired outcome from each individual scrum.

Blues coach **Nick White** sums it up as follows, 'The front row creates a platform for the locks and the loosies [back row players, also known as loose forwards] to generate power through the scrum into the opposition. Their role is to generate constant pressure on the opposition or create a stable platform on their own ball.'

Feet position

It all starts with the feet. The aim in scrummaging is to drive your opponent back, or at least maintain your field position, so having a stable footing is critical to this. Feet position also contributes to how much power the individual and collective eight players can generate.

Bind

The bind is the term given to how you connect with your fellow players to form the scrum. How and where you bind on your teammates depends on which position you play. Each bind type is outlined in the next section, but the principle for all is to ensure a strong and tight bind. Nick White highlights the important point that the best bind is not just the hand but the whole arm, 'You use your hand to bind but if you use your whole surface area of your arm, it fixes everyone tight and locked and loaded.'

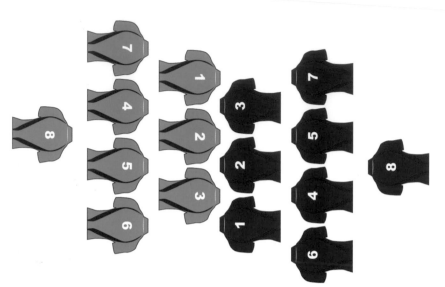

SCRUM POSITIONS

I Loose-head prop
2 Hooker
3 Tight-head prop
4 Lock
5 Lock
6 Blind-side flanker
7 Open-side flanker
8 No.8

→ Players generate their power from a strong pushing profile

Profile

Optimal technique in the scrum comes from understanding how each part of your body needs to be positioned to generate maximum power while ensuring you are protected. The position may not be comfortable initially but it will be powerful if you keep this checklist in mind. Forwards coach **Mike Cron** sums it up best, 'Basically all we are is squatters in the squat rack doing it horizontally rather than vertically.'

Keep your chest proud, shoulders back and spine straight to maximise your power. Poor form (head below hips/legs too far back) reduces your power and provides the opposition with an opportunity to attack. The two areas of the body that young forwards need to work on are the chest and the hips, explains Mike Cron, 'Having a proud chest and hips tilted backwards allows the player to transfer power through into his opponent. Tilting the hips back like a duck's arse maintains strength through a player's core and legs.'

Poor hip positions leads a lot of teams to scrum too low, believes set piece coach Nick White, which causes them to lose vital power, 'To get low they drop their shoulders below their hips which is dangerous and depowers them. The ground is your friend to an extent but you need to scrum at a level where you can generate power in a strong pushing position between 90 and 120 degrees with your knees and hips.'

Bending from your hips and having good knee flection, but not too much, is England forward coach **Graham Rowntree**'s advice, 'You keep good "scaps" shape, so I say imagine you have a 50p between your scapulas and try and hold that position on your back.' He also stresses the importance of keeping your head in a neutral position but your eyes looking up. You want your eyes looking forward not down, like you are looking over the top of your (imaginary) sunglasses, 'If you look down, you'll go down. Keep your bind up and don't have your feet too far back then you can't collapse.'

Pushing technique

Technique is the combination of all these elements coming together to drive your team forward and your opponent's team backwards. Graham Rowntree recommends players think about the alignment of their spine, their eyes looking forward and their feet firmly on the ground, 'Then all you have to do on engagement is hold that position – looking forward, keep that bind, keep that 50p between your shoulders, keep that hip flection – and squeeze and bear down. That's scrummaging.'

↓ A successful scrum requires eight players to act in unison

CHECKLIST

▸▸ *The All Blacks' Mike Cron lists what players need to understand to develop an effective body position in the scrum:*

■ Players need to understand the strongest pushing position bio-mechanically
■ Players then need to be able to stay strong with movement
■ Players need to understand how their body operates
■ They need to understand the forces of a scrum and how you want the scrum to operate as ONE unit working together at the same time and in the same direction

✙✙ Scrummaging by position: loose-head prop

The role of the loose-head prop is to attack the opposition tight-head prop with the aim of destabilising him by trying to push him backwards. The loose-head does this by working to get under the tight-head prop's chest and driving forward. He must do this legally and maintain his bind on his hooker and on the opposition tight-head prop throughout the scrum.

In attacking scrums, Mike Cron says the loose-head prop's aim 'is to stay absolutely connected to his hooker and not to kill [attack] the opponent at the expense of putting added pressure on his tight-head prop. You have to control the power and stay connected with the hooker.'

While in a defensive scrum, Cron explains, 'Props will say they like to "get the angle" and kill their opponent and that's up to the team and individual. Our ball is the main aim and I'd be keeping him focused on maintaining a strong connection because the closer to the hooker you are the better.'

Pre-engagement

FEET POSITION

The loose-head prop must provide the channel for the hooker to strike the ball between his legs, so feet should be shoulder-width apart with their outside leg slightly advanced before engagement in the scrum. Different teams have different set-ups but all stress the need to have as little movement as possible, so a player needs to find their strongest position and try to stick to it.

It starts with your feet, as Graham Rowntree explains the ideal set-up, 'If you are a loose-head, you want your left foot advanced in front of your right foot with a bit of a split.'

Mike Cron takes us through the set up for his All Blacks props, 'For us our props set up with their outside leg up ahead of their inside leg for balance. On the "bind" call they bring their inside leg up roughly square with their other leg. Teams that set up with their feet square right from the word go, they need to have balance and their locks have to take a lot of weight backwards to allow their props to do that. Props having their leg up a wee bit takes off a bit of pressure, then on the bind call they can bring their leg up square or wherever they feel strong.'

BIND

For positive straight line pushing it's important to have a very strong connection between the loose-head and the hooker at the shoulder and hips. If they are only bound at the shoulders but their hips are miles apart, they lose the lock's power, advises Mike Cron. He outlines the order of the bind between the pair and describes where you bind on the hooker's body can impact the scrum. 'Traditionally it was the loose-head who bound first to the hooker to get the best bind. Different teams do different things so generally speaking you have your loose-head bind first and bind higher', he explains. 'I don't like them near the shorts because I don't like the hooker's hips being pulled one way or the other.'

Post-engagement

FEET POSITION

It is important to find the feet position that allows you to feel at your strongest pushing position. If your feet are too far back, then you cannot exert any forward momentum. The same can be said about having your feet too close under you. Ensure your feet are in position to allow you to exert forward pressure, while maintaining the channel for the ball to go through your legs. Imagine exploding up from a squat position and try to position your feet and legs in that optimal position. Work to get into that position as early as possible explains Graham Rowntree, 'Our lads have got their feet organised and back early. For a loose-head the best guys in the world, like Alex Corbisiero, get their feet back and in a pushing position before they're even engaged. Then it's about maintaining that position for as long as possible.'

Loose-head **Jack McGrath** echoes the words of many when he says, 'Feet positioning has become more important, the less movement the better, tension from the whole pack at all times in the scrum no letting up, all eight together, especially the back rows as they are more important than ever now.'

BIND ON OPPOSITION TIGHT-HEAD

The loose-head's bind on the opposition tight-head is critical. Legally, the loose-head must bind with his left arm inside the right arm bind of the tight-head. The loose-head can only bind on the back or side of his opponent's jersey. Individual loose-head props will have their own preference about binding long with a straight arm or binding short on their opponent. Ideally, the loose-head will ensure that his bind is strong with his elbow high to maximise his control over the opposition tight-head prop.

Crusaders coach **Dave Hewett** is ideally looking for a long bind on impact, 'This provides more strength in the bind and also allows the loose-head more control over the tight-head.' Mike Cron highlights the downside of choosing to bind short, 'The bind round the belly with elbows pointing down is a very loose, limp bind. Loose-head props are able to get a really tight bind right from the "bind" call.'

Irish loose-head **Cian Healy** describes a change he made to his bind that helped him improve his scrummaging, 'When I reached out to bind with the opposition tight-head, I was getting my arm knocked by his shoulder and I was going down a lot in the scrums. So now, I have a shorter bind which keeps me coiled up like a spring and when I have the opportunity to push, everything is in the right place rather than being long and stretched out. That is something that has really worked for me.'

>> Scrummaging by position: tight-head prop

The role of the tight-head is to keep the scrum steady. He must do everything he can to ensure he does not take a backward step. If he does, the entire scrum will be disrupted. He does not have to move forward but he cannot move backwards. Due to the formation of the scrum, the majority of the pressure and force goes through the tight-head prop. He is the key man in the scrum and has one of the toughest roles within the team.

Mike Cron explains, 'The tight-head is the anchor of the scrum who sits in and holds down, while the loose-head sits in and holds up. As the axis of the scrum is on the opposition hooker's right shoulder, the tight-head has much more pressure on him than the loose-head'. He sees the tight-head as the most critical position at scrum time, 'You need your tight-head to hit, sink and load as he is your anchor – if you don't have a good tight-head prop you don't have a scrum'.

Graham Rowntree agrees, 'You've got to have incredible core strength to be a good scrummager as you have all the pressure going through you'.

Pre-engagement

FEET POSITION

The power that the tight-head has to transfer from those behind him means that he needs a strong base from which to drive into his opponent. Ireland's **Mike Ross** describes a split stance in his set-up, 'I try to have the same set-up before every scrum, feet shoulder-width apart, split stance, with my left foot back where I want it to be on the engagement.'

BIND WITH HOOKER

Usually the loose-head will bind with the hooker first and the tight-head will bind over the arm of the loose-head and on to the hooker. The exact whereabouts of the bind with the hooker is a personal preference, with some props looking to bind on the shorts to remain tight at the hips, while some props prefer to bind on the hooker's jersey. It is important that the hooker feels comfortable and unrestricted by his props' binds, as he needs to be able to have the freedom to strike for the ball.

The tight-head needs a strong connection with his hooker if he is to take on the opposition, 'If you get isolated away from your hooker, it's basically you against two guys on your own,' explains England's **Dan Cole**. 'I make sure I bind on his shorts and he binds underneath my armpit.'

Ireland's Mike Ross describes his bind and relationship to his fellow front row players, 'I make sure my left arm is bound on the hooker's shorts or shirt (depending on the width of the hooker!), my left shoulder is pulled out from under his armpit and my head is ahead of my loose-head's.'

Mike Cron prefers his tight-head binds to the hooker 'around the kidney area rather than down low, which is stronger because the prop's forearm and bicep has more connection with the hooker's body.'

BODY POSITION

Height plays a big part in scrummaging and hips are key when it comes to the most powerful body position for a prop. They adopt the same 'squat' position as the hooker and locks with a flat back but they aim to get as low as possible, so they sink down in the hips to gain the advantage over their opponent in an attempt to stop the opposition loose-head getting under them. Ireland's Mike Ross explains his process, 'On the "crouch" command I sink my hips down, and on the "bind" I move my right foot back parallel to my left and sink down further.'

'It's easier to win a pushing contest if you are low rather than high,' believes England's Dan Cole. He explains that as a prop you have to be good at pushing but you have to be able to transfer the weight, 'Behind you are a lock, a flanker and the No. 8 and you have to transfer that weight through yourself to the opposition.'

Post-engagement

TIGHT-HEAD BIND ON THE OPPOSITE LOOSE-HEAD

The tight-head's bind is important not just for transferring power and stabilising the scrum, it is also about controlling the opposition loose-head who is looking to attack. The laws of the game state that the tight-head must bind outside the arm of the opposing loose-head's bind. The challenge for the tight-head is to ensure he does not bind too long on the opposite prop, exposing his ribs and allowing the loose-head to get under him.

England's Dan Cole explains, 'On "set" your bind stays on his back and you have to keep that bind high and legal. Then it's a question of gritting your teeth and pushing. You co-ordinate with your hooker and the second row behind you so the power is transferred through to the opposition.'

Coaches Mike Cron and Dave Hewett, who works with many players that feature in Cron's All Black pack while they are on club duty for Crusaders, describe their preferences for the position of the bind between tight-head and loose-head. 'I would suggest if you bind too high you are in trouble. If you bind too long, you are in trouble. The right place for most tight-heads is just under the armpit – not on the arm or chest because you are not allowed to do that by law,' says Mike Cron. Hewett agrees, 'I am looking for the tight-head to bind on the back of the armpit of the loose-head. Looking to grab some underarm hair, not cranking down on the loose-head's arm.'

On the "set" call, Ireland's Mike Ross describes how he binds on the back of the opposition loose-head prop and launches forward, drops his chest down and tries not to move his feet except to go forward. He advises young players to 'keep your hips low, back flat and a strong bind. Having your legs back at 120 degrees from your body is the optimum pushing position, so always work to have your feet back sufficiently at the engagement.'

How props improve

Young players who come from wrestling backgrounds tend to excel at playing prop. Understanding the biomechanics of the body and how to manipulate your opponent are very important components for this position. For the majority of players looking to develop their pushing technique, it is simply a case of understanding your strongest pushing position [scrum profile] and continuously developing it. This can be done as an individual against a scrum machine, ensuring your back is flat, your bind is up [replicating the bind on the opposition prop] and your feet are not too far behind you. Your profile should mimic a squat in a vertical position.

It is widely accepted that props get better with age and experience. Ireland's Jack McGrath is a young player who is making his mark in the top flight and cites learning from 'older guys who have been playing for a while. You pick up tricks [scrum technique] from experienced players.' Italy's Martin Castrogiovanni echoes McGrath's point by recommending that 'young props should watch a lot of videos of scrums. You can learn a lot by watching videos of other rugby players, such as good technique and timing.'

When it comes to practice, Dave Hewett stresses the importance of learning good technique early and explains how best to avoid picking up bad habits, 'It's important they get the right coaching because what you don't want to do is reinforce bad habits. My philosophy is the more you do the worse you get. You get fatigued and then you tend to develop bad habits, which you reinforce again and again. Do it right, do it enough to get it right, but don't overdo it so you don't reinforce bad habits.'

Super 15 Blues coach Nick White offers advice to coaches looking to make improvements across the whole forward pack. He believes players can develop their scrum technique individually on the scrum machine, then work in their units before putting it all together with the entire pack to develop their collective timing and synchronisation, 'You can break it down into the front row working together to get their timing. Then add the locks and then the back row. Putting it all together with the binding and their sync linked, which means their collective pushing profiles. Get it right individually before bringing it together and work against a scrum machine or another pack to get in sync with each other.'

How props prepare for scrums

A checklist is an option used by some players, as it helps them with the consistency in their routine. Tight-head Dan Cole explains how the process works for him, 'I prepare by having a picture in my mind of what a good scrum looks like and feels like. You know that because you do the training to get the body position and develop a checklist – feet in position, bind with my hooker, get nice and square, then get the second row to come in and then crouch and after that the freeze command is there.'

Mike Ross has a similar routine, 'I follow my set-up routine, making sure I'm happy with my feet placement and distance of engagement. I take a deep breath, hold it, and wait to get out of the blocks as quickly as possible at the "set" call, keeping good form all the way through and trying to impact as hard as I can.'

Loose-head Cian Healy, however, finds that a checklist is not necessary for him any more, as the experience he has gained over the years means he is more relaxed going into a scrum. It was not always the case, 'I used to be a ball of stress before a scrum. Now I have one area I pick to work on for each training session or for a game, such as making sure my head is in the right place. If you stick to that, then everything usually comes together.'

So much of scrummaging is about the mental pressure players are under. Dan Cole explains it is something players have to embrace to play at the highest level, 'The mental side of scrummaging is knowing that it will be a physical challenge. It will be tough. It's like a staring contest with your opposite number – they are working really hard and you are working really hard and at some point one of you will give up. You just need to make sure it's not you.'

When you come to a scrum you don't want to overthink, you want your head to be clear so go through a process. Your body takes over from all the repetition in training of good technique and there's a checklist you go over in your head. Feet position, nice and tight through the core, bind with your hooker and you want to feel nice and connected to your lock. After that it's muscle memory and what you have trained.

'I like to be a little bit in front of my hooker in the set-up and I like to have my right foot up to give me some balance. As I come down my

focus is to get a good brace on the shoulder of the opposition loose-head then get my right foot back into the perfect position for me to scrum on 90 degrees.

'My bind on the opposition prop tends to be longer, then when they say "set" it comes back to a 90-degree angle and quite short. My main focus at this point is to rock the loose-head back a bit so I am in control. I'm not going forward too much, just trying to knock him back enough so I can stay in control and keep him there. I want to be able to move him where I want to move him and not be dictated by what he wants to do, this is the ultimate goal for a tight-head.

'No matter what the situation or what happened before, I want to feel calm and ready. I go through my checklist and when I'm down there [in the scrum] it's about aggression and staying in control. ❜

Owen FRANKS, New Zealand & Crusaders

↑ New Zealand had the most successful scrummaging unit in the 2014 Rugby Championship, winning 90% of scrums on their own put in. Dependable @OptaJonny

►► Scrummaging by position: hooker

The role of the hooker differs in attacking and defending scrums. In attacking scrums, the aim is to hook the ball back to the No. 8 once the 9 throws the ball into the scrum. In defending scrums, they work with the loose-head prop to destabilise the opposition tight-head prop. The hooker is the leader of the scrum and sets the height for his team. Springboks **Schalk Brits** reminds players, 'If you scrum on their terms they'll always win, so try to make them scrum on your terms.'

France's **Benjamin Kayser**, explains a hooker's concerns, 'The main connection is with your props and you need to understand each other's bodies, balance, what they like or don't like. A little chit-chat before a hit is probably the best tactic you can use because you need to be connected. When you tell your tight-head you are going to go on the opposition tight-head you need your tight-head to come with you or there will be too much gap. You are the extra key man who is going to direct the pressure.'

Pre-engagement

FEET POSITION

Hookers have the task of having to raise one foot momentarily to hook for the ball while still maintaining a strong pushing position. This requires flexibility and timing to ensure they can quickly strike the ball and get back into their most powerful pushing position.

Prior to engagement, the hooker will usually have one foot forward, holding the weight of the pack back. The scrum revolves around the attacking team's hooker, so when he feels his team is ready and on the referee's command, he releases his foot and the two forward packs engage.

Benjamin Kayser sees hookers as 'leaders of impact' and describes their role in releasing their foot to initiate the "set" call, 'think of the right foot of the hooker being a wedge and one of the only brakes that there is on the scrum. There is the No. 8 holding the two locks at the back, and the hooker holding the props at the front. As soon as I let that go I'm going to send everybody into a hit. So the timing needs to be perfect so you are the general of the scrum!'

BINDS WITH PROPS

The front row engages directly with the opposition so it is important for the hooker and props to form a solid connection to push against the opposing front row. It is vital that the hooker feels confident and comfortable with the binds of his props. Personal preference will dictate the exact whereabouts of the hooker's binds on his props.

In All Blacks **Keven Mealamu**'s experience, some props like a really tight bind but he thinks this can put you off as a hooker, 'If you are too tight, it means you can't get low enough. Being

← Bismarck Du Plessis has worked hard to develop his scrum technique over the years

able to spend some time understanding what is comfortable for the three of us is key. That is probably somewhere in the middle for everyone so we can all do our job!'

In terms of where to bind, Mealamu describes his preference, 'I like to bind with my props under their armpits because it helps me feel very connected to them at the scrum and helps us get nice and low when we are ready for the set. Being a shorter hooker helps!'

The relationship between the hooker and prop in terms of their position relative to each other is something **Graham Rowntree** highlights, 'Not enough hookers advance their tight-head forward, I want my hookers to be just behind his tight-head, or rather I want my tight-head's left shoulder to be advanced of my hooker. That ultimately protects the hooker's hooking foot!'

Post-engagement

The front row must stay connected and concentrate on the task at hand, which is to push against their opposition front row, while ensuring the hooker has the freedom to strike for the ball. Flexibility is an understated requirement for hookers, who must strike for the ball while dealing with incredible force and pressure in the middle of a scrum.

It is important that the props stay connected to the hooker and continue to drive straight and not get involved in any personal battles with their opposite prop. All Black **Corey Flynn** highlights where one player's actions can impact on another's ability to do their job, 'You want your props nice and tight and you want your loose-head to keep his arse in, you don't want him swinging out because it pushes the tight-head into your ribs, which isn't comfortable. I like my tight-head to be about an inch or two ahead of me and tight in as well!'

▶▶ Scrummaging by position: locks

The lock provides power and support to the prop in front of them. They 'lock' the scrum through their bind with the prop and by ensuring they maintain contact with their prop at all times, throughout the scrum, as Ireland's **Devin Toner** emphasises, 'You always have constant pressure from your shoulder to the prop's backside, if the pressure is let off they're going to get into trouble.'

Pre-engagment

FEET POSITION

If you ask a player to lean into a scrum machine in their strongest driving position, their body profile will resemble a vertical squatting position. This is the optimal position for a prop or lock to drive in the scrum. Then the player must work hard to ensure that his feet stay connected with the ground.

Feet position is all about giving the pack stability and traction when the push begins. Every player should have their feet in a strong position when they engage and locks have to ensure they are not caught out during their set-up by the referee's calls. With a short engagement, it is very important that second rows have both feet on the ground during the "set" call, and that there's a solid bind between them and the front and back rows. Canada's **Jamie Cudmore** explains, 'Having both feet on the ground enables a much more solid hit and you make sure that hit follows through with a step forward. You can't have hit and then step back because then you are playing catch up.'

Mike Cron stresses the aim is to have all 16 feet on the ground, roughly square when you make contact with the opposition. The gap between the front row's hips, which the locks have to work with, is a factor in achieving this goal and he describes how he teaches his pack, 'If you have a reasonable gap in the front row, your locks can have staggered feet and they can release that leg like a trigger on the "set" call. If there is little or no gap and the locks try to do that, it means when the front row hit they will have a leg in the air. I coach them both ways – big gap so staggered leg, release the trigger, next scrum no gap so locks have to go square.'

LOCKS BIND ON EACH OTHER

Locks will bind with each other, with one lock's arm around the back of the other lock, gripping his jersey in the armpit region. The other lock will bind over the arm of the first lock and also grip his teammate in the armpit area. Locks want to be nice and tight to each other, but not too tight that it undermines the common goal of the scrum, as Mike Cron explains: 'You want your two locks tight, but when they go into their "hole" [the head between the hooker and prop] you want them spine in line and not angling outwards. If they are too tightly bound at the shoulders, their hips are angling out towards the flankers rather than facing straight ahead. You are better off having the power going straight, so you want a strong connection, nice firm bind, but you want them spine in line.'

'How' locks bind is one factor but 'when' they bind also impacts on the scrum and how their teammates bind to them. If the locks prepare for the scrum with their knee(s) on the ground, it prevents the back row from binding on to them early. Mike Cron suggests, 'if the locks want to bind on their knee I would look to get them up reasonably early; some teams do it on the "bind"

call. My guys don't bind on the knee and cut out the middle-man, they just come in and bind on the props. This also avoids having to readjust your feet when you come up because the gap is too big.'

LOCKS BIND ON PROPS

The locks' bind is between the props' legs with their heads in the gaps between the three front row players' hips and their shoulders in contact with the backsides of the players in front of them. There are slight variations of this to allow for players' preferences or team's styles, but ultimately the goal is the same – creating a strong, tight connection.

Blues Coach **Nick White** stresses the importance of this connection in having an

↑ Once the props and hooker form their binds the locks can come in and bind to the Front Row

effective drive, 'The shoulder connection on the back of the prop's backside is key. They are connected with their shoulder and their crutch grip with their bind is crucial for the scrum working.'

Which side of the scrum a player is on has implications for the lock and where they get the best bind, as Devin Toner explains, 'I mainly lock down on the loose-head side these days and my bind is on the waistband of the shorts, this gives me some flexibility to get right under the props arse and also shift the pressure to the hooker if needs be. If I'm on the tight-head side, I would bind around the upper part of the prop's leg to get a more secure bind.'

England's **George Robson** walks us through his process for getting his bind, 'I put my head forward for the bind and make sure my right shoulder is pushed forward a bit and is in contact with the hooker's left butt cheek, and if I do that my left is automatically in contact with the loose-head's right butt cheek.

'I then put my elbow through the prop's legs and bind with my hand facing me, this gives me a better contact with the front row and means when engagement comes I am already in a good position to get my body weight through them.'

Italy's **Marco Bortolami** outlines the benefits of binding on the outside rather than between the prop's legs, 'An outside bind around the external hip of the prop keeps the hips of the prop straight but it's very important to control the level of the shoulders to avoid shifting up. I keep both knees on the ground at the same level, very close to the prop's heels.

'When the bind of the prop is complete, I lift my knees off the ground and apply a little pressure to engage on the "bind" call. Ideally you shouldn't move your feet and finish the engage with maximum pressure on the "set" call. Balance your upper body to apply pressure from your legs through the hips and into the prop through the shoulders.'

Post-engagement

PUSHING TECHNIQUE

As the centre of the scrum, the locks have to have optimal body position and pushing technique to ensure their force is transferred forward. Ireland's Devin Toner advises locks to 'keep your back straight, shoulders in contact with your prop, and your knees as close to the ground as possible. The angle of your legs to your back should be about 120 degrees, to get the most force.'

▶▶ Scrummaging by position: flankers

The flankers' role at the scrum is to push. While the ball is in the scrum their one and only focus should be on their contribution to the pack in driving the scrum forward. Their role after the ball comes out is to make a tackle or get to the breakdown.

Steffon Armitage explains his thinking, 'If I don't push in the scrum, [after watching] the video on the Monday that prop is going to be having a go at me. I don't want to let anyone down and my job as a flanker is to scrummage first and then get off, so you have to be fit. Without a good platform from scrums and lineouts you can't win games.'

Pre-engagement

BIND

A flanker's bind to a lock is similar to a prop's to a hooker in that they only bind to their teammate on one side. The shoulder of the flanker should be just under the outside bum cheek of the prop in front of them. This means that the prop is being driven forward by both the lock and the flanker. A scrum is eight people working in unison and the flankers have to add their power to the scrum if a team is to maximise its forward drive. The bind is a big part of ensuring their power transfers into the scrum and in helping keep the unit together.

In coach **Nick White**'s opinion, flankers should, 'Bind the same as props, using the whole surface area of their arm to connect with each other. Although the loosies bind on to the lock they still have to keep tension through their binds to stay connected.'

Steffon Armitage looks further ahead, 'I bind on to the second row because by law, I have to and that's where I get more of a connection.

Sticking everyone together, shoulder on the bum of the prop because that's where you get pressure. My foot closest to the scrum is forward, and my other one back, so not only am I pushing as hard as I can but I'm ready to go off the scrum to hit the breakdown or to make the tackle.'

↓ Wales Captain Sam Warburton ready to launch from the scrum

▸▸ Scrummaging by position: No. 8

The No. 8 controls the scrum from behind to ensure the agreed first phase play can be delivered. While the ball is in the scrum he is part of the eight-man push, guiding the ball with his feet until the 9 wants it or until he picks it up and goes himself.

Pre-engagement

BIND

Last to join the scrum at the back, the No. 8 slots his head between the two locks' hips. The No. 8 applies force through his shoulders, which are just underneath the locks' buttocks. By binding on either lock in front of him, the No. 8 should ensure that the locks remain tight at the hips. Mike Cron explains how he ensures a strong connection and bind between his players to help generate power for the drive, 'I get them to do an isometric squeeze so when he binds on to his locks he opens up, comes down, and then squeezes them into his shoulders. It's another connection and that takes a wee bit of weight off the front boys too. By law he must stay where he is; he can't hit between the two locks then move.'

↓ The No 8 has a pivotal role in the scrum and has to be vigilant for opportunities

❯❯ Sequence of forming the scrum

We refer to pre-engagement as the time before the two sets of forwards engage with each other at the scrum. Post-engagement is after the referee's call of 'set' and both packs have come together.

Pre-engagement includes

- Loose-head bind to hooker
- Tight-head bind to hooker
- Locks bind to each other, then to the props
- Flankers bind to locks
- No. 8 prepares to bind with locks

Referee calls 'crouch'
- Forwards crouch into pushing position

Referee calls 'bind'
- Props bind against their opposition props, using their outside arms

Referee calls 'set'
- Packs come together and pull binds tight.
The scrum is now said to be in post-engagement

Post-engagement

When the scrum is formed, play can restart:
- **Throw:** when scrum is steady and stable the referee signals to the No. 9 to throw the ball into the scrum
- **Push:** when ball enters the scrum, the packs push to contest for the ball
- **Hook:** the hooker 'hooks' the ball back to the No. 8's feet
- **Options from the scrum:** the pack can drive forward to gain ground, the No. 8 can pick and go himself or the 9 can pass the ball to the backs from the base of the scrum

Throwing the ball into the scrum

The attacking team's No. 9 throws the ball into the scrum. The ball must be thrown in straight or else it's a free kick to the defending team. Mike Cron explains the challenges facing the hooker at the top level, 'It's physically impossible to get your foot out in front of your shoulder at the top level of the game because of the pressure generated, so referees need to be a bit more lenient. I agree the ball has to go in straight but it has to be a wee bit to your side if the hooker is going to be able to hook it.'

Push

A unified drive is required in a scrum with all eight players pushing together with the correct technique. Mike Cron outlines how he gets packs to work together by isolating their senses so they can focus on the drive, 'I have the players close their eyes in certain drills so long as they can do this safely. We get most of our information from our eyes, so by taking the eyes out of the equation players learn to FEEL what is happening around them.

'Put your pack into a scrum machine with a lot of weight on the machine. After they engage have all members close their eyes and no one is allowed to talk. They then have to push the machine forward. If they do not work together the machine will not move. If they cannot move the machine on the first try then do it again. After two or three attempts they will learn to work together and the machine will move.'

Hook the ball

It is the hooker's job to 'hook' the ball in the scrum. Supported by their props, the hooker raises his right leg briefly to hook the ball and direct it back to the No. 8. The skill requires strength, flexibility and balance. 'It's all about your front foot and hip movement and making sure you can extend far enough to hook the ball without losing any power', explains Saracens No. 2 **Schalk Brits**. Mike Cron recommends young players do Pilates or other forms of flexible training to help increase the flexibility required.

Graham Rowntree describes the hooker's set-up to hook, 'Hookers have to put their right foot and right shoulder forward to hook but it's hard to do. It's the set-up that's key, so the hooker's job starts earlier than anyone else's. They have to have their foot on the mark, in advance of the tight-head so they can get their right shoulder forward'.

Former All Black **Corey Flynn** feels that the challenge of hooking is that of not losing power while your foot is raised, 'If you take your foot off to hook the ball then they have eight men pushing against seven'. While his leg is off the ground, the hooker is not fully contributing to driving the scrum forward, so it is important to hook the ball as quickly and efficiently as possible. 'Hookers shouldn't have their foot up for ages, so the sooner you can get your foot down and give yourself a strong platform to scrum off the better', advises Brits.

Timing and delivery of the ball into the scrum is critical. Hookers and scrum halves must devise their own system so both players understand what is expected of them. 'You try to tell the 9 when to throw the ball into the scrum because they don't understand how hard it can be sometimes to hook the ball when the pressure is on', explains hooker **Benjamin Kayser**.

All Black **Keven Mealamu** outlines why it is important for the hooker and scrum half to develop a good understanding when it comes to the timing and speed of the ball into the scrum, 'It is important to give your 9 feedback on the speed of the feed. Is he putting the ball in quick enough or does he need to slow it down? Little things like that make a big difference, so practising with your 9 for 10 minutes after training really helps'.

If hooking isn't an option because of the pressure in the scrum, there are other ways for the hooker to get control of the ball or contribute to winning the scrum. France's Benjamin Kayser describes some of the ways in which he uses the momentum of the scrum to walk over the ball, 'My right leg is always in front so sometimes I stop it with my knee and walk over it and then strike it nice and easy. Some guys now throw their right foot and hook it between the loose-head's legs, the number one channel, but I mainly try to hook it while we are pushing. The ball comes in, you call for a shove, everyone's feet start moving and that's when I just quickly hook it. Or if the scrum is very, very stationery because there is a lot of pressure I block it with my right knee, leave it there and then walk over it and hook it'.

There are traditionally three 'channels' for the ball to travel through during the scrum. Channel one is through the loose-head prop's legs and will end up at the No. 8's left foot. Channel two is straight through the middle of the scrum, the ball travelling back to the centre of the No. 8's feet. Channel three is the most difficult for the hooker to strike and should end up at the right foot of the No. 8.

Lifting your foot to hook the ball in the scrum is a challenge. As a hooker you can only do your job if the five players behind you and the two guys either side of you are working as hard as

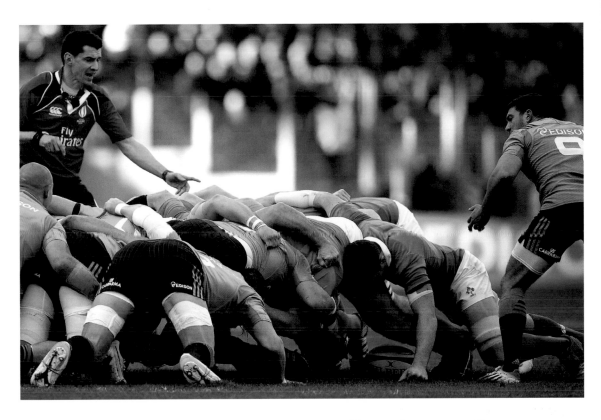

↑ RBS 6 Nations Champions Ireland had 85% set piece retention and 90% kicking accuracy in the 2015 championship. @AccentureRugby

» Options from the scrum

they can to support you. Flexibility is essential to hook the ball properly and players should practise by lying against the scrum machine and striking for the ball. Springbok **Bismarck Du Plessis** works on his hooking skills every time he hits the scrum machine, 'When I started playing rugby, my dad used to help me by clamping my head between his legs and making me hook the ball from both sides. Hooking the ball is important because the scrum half can't put it [the ball] under his hooker's feet any more, and I like that.'

Communication and understanding between the No. 8 and scrum half at scrum time is important if a team wants to exploit all first-phase options. USA back row **Todd Clever** explains that as a No. 8 it's about knowing exactly where [the scrum half is], knowing where the opposition No. 9 is and having great communication together, 'You need to know if your scrum half wants a flat ball to attack the line or if he wants it deeper so he has more time on it. It is also important to have that relationship, so if the scrum goes down, he gets the ball in your hand as fast as possible so you can take the free kick.'

THE LINEOUT

A lineout is a contest between the two forward packs to restart play after the ball goes into touch. It's critical that all players understand their roles based on pre-rehearsed calls if a team is to retain possession and launch an attack. The team throwing the ball into the lineout has the advantage as they know where the ball will be thrown, as opposed to the opposition who have to react to the throw.

Lineouts produce the most tries from any set piece, as both sets of backlines must be 10 metres back from the lineout. This means there is plenty of space to launch a first-phase strike move. As such, All Blacks forwards coach, **Mike Cron**, sees them as an opportunity, 'Lineouts are a perfect place to allow your mind to think laterally. Just because it has never been done, it doesn't mean you can't do it!'

'It's not just about winning a lineout, although that's critical', explains Sharks director of rugby **Gary Gold**, 'it's about trying to win the lineout in the most optimal area (middle or back) and then being able to deliver the path of delivery that best suits the type of play you are looking to make.'

›› Action v Reaction

The team that is throwing the ball into the lineout has the advantage because they call where they want ball to go. Action v Reaction means that if all the technical elements of the lineout are in sync, the throwing team should win possession. 'Lineouts have to be done with all players knowing the timing of movement, lift and throw and then each player's role once the ball is won', explains Mike Cron. Hooker **Schalk Brits** agrees that lineouts are about every player doing their job, 'Like the scrum, it's not just an individual that makes a lineout, it's a team effort.'

CHECKLIST

›› **LINEOUT** *There are multiple components to a successful lineout:*

- The call
- The race
- The jump
- The lift
- Timing
- The throw
- The catch
- Ball transfer

The call

Ideally the lock jumping in the middle calls the lineout. This is because he has the best view of the space around him. You shouldn't call a lineout for the sake of it; the opposition can't defend everywhere. It's important to understand that and call to the space. If the back is open, throw there until the opposition defend that space. Then throw to where the new space is. Remember, the first priority of the lineout is to secure possession.

The call will be determined by the location of the lineout on the pitch and whether or not the backs want the ball. Teams usually have three areas to throw the ball – front, middle or back. Each team will have its own unique lineout calling system. Second row **George Robson** explains that those three options can be reduced based on the abilities of the pack, 'You have to work with what you've got and recognise there could be plays you can't do, if you have a hooker who can't throw to the back, for example. You work to the strengths of the people in the lineout, get them performing consistently and play to them.'

Fellow lock **Jim Hamilton** reinforces the message about keeping it simple, 'so everyone can understand the call and react accordingly.' Not least for the thrower. Hooker Schalk Brits explains a successful lineout is 'definitely down to making the right calls and everyone understanding the calls too.'

HOW TO IMPROVE YOUR LINEOUT CALLING

South Africa's second row **Eben Etzebeth** warns young players that they have to do their homework when it comes to lineout calling, 'In the Springboks, we've really got a lot of variations and calls, so it entails a fair bit of studying. But like anything in the world, practice makes perfect

– the only way to improve your lineout calling is to keep working on it every day and making sure you do the basics well.'

The race

Think of the lineout as a race into position and into the air. This is referred to as 'speed on the ground'. Speed on the ground is hugely important as it gives the advantage to whichever jumping pod can get into position the quickest, before jumping and contesting for the ball. Beat your opponent on the ground and it will make the rest of the lineout much easier.

Not every lineout involves the jumping pod moving into space, but all lineouts have an element of a race within them. Once the call has been made and the lineout initiated, speed into the desired space, whether that is on the ground or in the air, is critically important for a successful outcome. As a jumper, you must get to that space before your opponent does. Therein lies the race.

Mike Cron describes how the team in possession have a head start, 'We are saying "GO", so we have an advantage. So long as you have an explosive jump, explosive lift and timing of the throw you should win most of your balls'. Or, as lock George Robson puts it, 'action beats reaction. If you get everything right, the opponent should always be playing catch up'.

Teams with the throw-in may look to improve their chances of success further by employing movement and deception before the ball is thrown into the lineout. As Robson states, the purpose is to confuse the opposition and manipulate space, 'In the lineout technically everything has to be good but you also need to be able to manipulate space. Being able to deceive someone that you are going somewhere then go somewhere else very quickly enables you to win the ball'.

The jump

A lineout jumper cannot expect his lifters to simply lift him; he must jump as high as he can, while maintaining control of his body. Movement before the jump will vary, depending on the lineout call, but the fundamental technique of the jump itself remains consistent. Power off the ground, drive your hands up towards where the ball will be and maintain a strong core by squeezing your glutes and quads. It is important to maintain this posture and ensure you keep your legs straight and together while in the air. This enables your lifters to focus on their job of keeping you safe during the move.

Flanker **Tom Wood** describes the jumping process, 'You want to be as dynamic as you can, throw your arms up as if you were jumping on to a wall. Stay strong through your core. You have tape on your legs for the lifters so keep your legs tight together, squeeze your bum cheeks so your core strength is all fired up and there is no movement, that also provides a good shelf for the back lifter to push from'.

Lock **Joe Launchbury**, who aims to replicate the same routine every time he jumps so his lifters know when he is going to jump, highlights consistency as the key to success, 'If you jump around every time, the more likely they are to miss you, so I do the same footwork pattern every time and jump on the same spot, which helps a lot'.

Italy's **Marco Bortolami** also states the importance of jumping and landing in the same spot regardless of the flight of the ball, but emphasises the coordination of the jumping pod, 'A good jumper is able to coordinate the lifters to enable them to lift him properly. A lineout jump is more a coordination between three players than a basic athletic skill'.

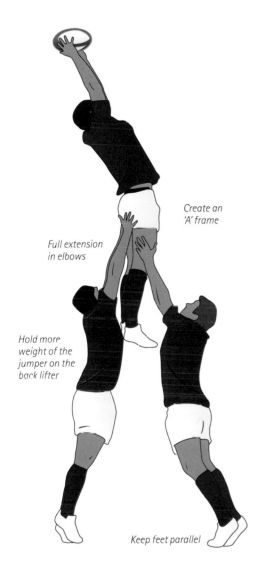

Full extension
in elbows

Create an
'A' frame

Hold more
weight of the
jumper on the
back lifter

Keep feet parallel

⋙LIFTER'S CHECKLIST

England's Dan Cole *shares his lifter's checklist: 'Your main job is to lift and there are some big lads so you have to use your big muscles to get them off the floor:*

■ Squat position and fire up from the floor to the air
■ Good grip of the lock's legs
■ Hand-eye co-ordination, knowing where the target is. The bloke often runs towards you so you have to have your hands in the right place
■ Then power through the straight spine and through the arms and lift
■ Your big muscles basically work with their momentum and you can throw the guy up and catch him at the top and have the strength to be at full extension and hold the guy in the air. Sometimes if there is a lineout next to you the opponent might be very good in the air but you have to have the physical strength to hold him at full extension'

The lift

The lifters' job is to help the jumper get as high in the air as they can, and then ensure they bring him back to ground safely.

For the lineout to function effectively, it is important that the lifters grip the jumper in the right areas. The front lifter aims to lift the jumper just above his knees, while the back lifter should lift the jumper at the top of his hamstrings, or just under his glutes. The lifters explode through the lift from a squat position, aiming to lock out their arms and get as close as possible between the jumper's legs. Ideally, the lifters should be chest-to-chest under the jumper with arms locked out and at maximum extension.

Cian Healy adds his sage advice, 'Lift technique is just about putting your full power into it. At professional level, we work on explosive Olympic lifts in training. Throwing a bar up over your head isn't too dissimilar to throwing a lad up in the air like a lineout lift. The lineout lift itself is fairly basic. I rely more on speed across the ground to get to the jumper. That is an important area. If you are powerful in your lift and get your hands in the right area, it is going to be a good one, but it is the speed into position that is going to make the big difference. If I can get from the front to the tail of the lineout in two seconds, then hopefully I have been faster than the time it takes for the opposition to react, and by that time, hopefully, we have won the ball.'

The hooker throws to space and not to a person, so if the jumper is early or the hooker is late the lifters have to provide a stable base and be strong enough to keep the jumper in the air to adjust, as second row George Robson highlights, 'Lifters should be able to hold you there for a length of time, which allows for a margin of error with the hooker's throw if it's late.'

Safety is paramount and prop **Mike Ross** makes it clear that it's the role of the lifters to look after their man in the air and bring him back to ground safely, 'At lineout time, always look after the man you're lifting. You put him up there, put him back down. I've seen a few long-term injuries from not doing this.'

Tom Wood explains what a jumper is looking for from a lifter, 'They've got to try and keep a firm hold of you. They have to go from that upright locked out position to a half squat position themselves, very tight to the jumper and get their heads almost together behind the jumper so you have a strong foundation to maul on or to set a play off.'

Timing

As a forward pack you will have to work out the optimal time to throw. This depends on the lineout call and takes practice. The best way to start is by going through the lineout call without the ball for a few reps.

With the jumping pod going through their roles without the ball, the hooker can observe when the jumper is at maximum height. That's why it's a good idea to do a few reps, as it lets the jumping pod concentrate on doing their individual and collectives job(s) without the pressure of the having to catch the ball.

When the jumping pod and hooker are ready, it is time to get the timing of the throw right. Depending on the lineout call, the ball should leave the hooker's hands as the jumper is about to jump.

The only exception to this is when the call is for a flat throw at the front, on the 5-metre line. This is because there is such a short distance to throw the ball it doesn't matter if the jumper is in the air; they just need to get in front of their opposition jumper to win the ball.

It is important to repeat that the hooker throws to a space in the air above the lineout based on the lineout call. They do not throw to, or at, a jumper, unless the call is a flat ball at the front. For all other lineouts, the hooker throws the ball as or before the jumper jumps. If they wait until the jumper is in the air to release the ball, the jumper will be on their way down by the time the ball gets to them.

There are various triggers within the lineout that determine when the hooker should commence his throw. This can be a nod from the jumper, the movement of a lifter or, on a timed throw, the hooker's throw itself is the trigger. Eben Etzebeth outlines the technical aspects of the play, 'Decision-making and communication are very important when it comes to winning lineouts – between the caller, the jumper and the supporters. Lineouts are actually very technical and, as a jumper, I have to ensure I get off the ground on the right spot, at the right time and the right speed, so timing is also very important.'

HOW TO IMPROVE YOUR TIMING

England coach **Simon Hardy** reminds us to 'make sure the hooker understands the lineout movement e.g. speed of jump.' Mike Cron believes it's about understanding and communication among the entire pack while practising the calls, 'Allow time to discuss and walk through each throw so the thrower/jumper/lifters are all on the same page. It sounds simple but quite often teams move on to the next throw without really nailing the last option and getting a full understanding of each other's role.'

The throw

I played hooker professionally for ten years and loved the technical challenge of throwing consistently under pressure. I can confirm that composure, mental fortitude and technical skill, along with endless hours of practice are all required to perform the task of throwing.

Throwing is not a case of one-size fits all, each thrower has their own routine and technique but there are guidelines that, if you adhere to them, will improve your throwing. More importantly, your confidence will improve. Remember that there is no substitute for practice and to improve a skill takes time.

HOW TO FOCUS BEFORE A THROW

The mental aspect of lineout throwing is very important and similar to that of a golfer or a goal kicker. For me, having a checklist was crucial as it helped me be in the moment to focus on each individual throw. It also provided me with a way of analysing each throw. Confidence in anything comes from repetition and practice. Practising your throwing by using a checklist may seem cumbersome at first, but stick with it and before long, you will automatically go through your checklist without even thinking. This is the key to becoming a competent and confident lineout thrower.

Schalk Brits gives his perspective on this, 'When someone kicks the ball out your heart is racing. You're tired most of the time, you have to compose yourself to get the call, remember the call, understand the call and then throw the ball with pinpoint accuracy.'

Simon Hardy describes how he uses three boxes to help hookers focus:

Box 1

SAYING (from field to touchline)
You can talk to yourself about anything, chances are you are breathing heavily, have just been hit, made a big tackle, scrum etc.

Box 2

SEEING (just behind the point of touch)
You visualise the throw(s), control breathing and prepare the ball/yourself (e.g. towel)

Box 3

SHOOTING (on the point of touch)
Step up and use trigger word/phrase/physical action, clear head, let the training take over, throw

>>THROWING CHECKLIST

My own lineout throwing style evolved over the years until I became confident in my own technique. My checklist developed through working with throwing coach Simon Hardy. The aim was to create a consistent process like a kicker, which also helps with focus. His advice was very detailed, 'Technique is relative to the issues a player brings re: height, size, flexibility and coordination. The basics are – get square re: hips, chest, feet, relaxed knees, promote hips or squeeze backside in, stretch your neck, good breathing, snap hands and elbows, turn hands slightly out, stay tall, use big muscles groups (abs, back triceps) keep same release point, hands to follow ball, step after the throw.'

■ **Focus**
Take your time before each throw to compose yourself. Take a deep breath and focus ... Schalk Brits explains the process he goes through before each throw, 'I get the call and I normally don't rush to the line to throw in. I use that time after the call to compose myself, get my breathing slower and then just throw. From a mental point of view it's just focusing on the process not anything else. I never think about whether I'm going to lose a ball. Control the controllables: I'm trying to get my heart rate down. Adrenaline plays a big part in throwing.'

Working from the ground up:

■ **Feet** Make sure they are square, or toes pointed slightly inwards, feet shoulder-width apart. Though **Benjamin Kayser** has his own preference, 'Unlike the southern hemisphere throwers I throw with one foot in front of the other, left foot first.'
■ **Knees** Relaxed, not locked or caving in.
■ **Hips** Square to the lineout.

■ **Hands** If right-handed, right is the power hand and is back towards the end of the ball, left hand is the guide hand and towards the front. Fingers are spread to cover as much of the ball as you can with your fingertips on the seam. **Corey Flynn** explains his own technique, 'I find the valve with my ring finger on my right hand and then I place my hands in relation to the valve.'
■ **Position of ball** Line the ball up in front of you then move it into the starting position behind your head. You want to start the throw with the ball behind your head, with only the forward throwing motion to be executed, otherwise you give the opponent more time to react to your backswing. Corey Flynn describes the ideal moment to throw, 'As I take the breath I pull my arms up into my throwing position. Then I am ready to go.'
■ **Nose of ball** Should be square – straight down the line. If the ball isn't square you'll probably make a crooked throw. 'When I hold the ball I prefer to line it up straight down the middle of the lineout, because I feel it leaves less room for error,' notes **Bismarck du Plessis**.

■ **Elbows** Should be tight, which gives the ball power and spin. Do not let the elbows splay on any backwards motion.

■ **Head up** Exaggerate your head up (look down, going down) or you could underthrow the ball.

■ **Throw** Starts from the core, small backswing from your core then a snapping motion, arms forward, hands forward, ball forward. It is vital to make sure your fingers point towards the target. Exaggerate this – like the follow-through on a golf swing. Different hookers have different concerns for the throw, for example, for Benjamin Kayser smoothness is paramount, 'I've worked a lot on using power of the abs and having a smooth, fast throw because that's what my jumpers ask for'. For Bismarck du Plessis, however, consistency is key, 'I grip the ball the same every time, I like keeping my elbows close to my body when I throw, finishing with my hands held high and my palms to the outside'.

■ **Quick self-analysis – good throw or bad throw? Then move on** If it was a good throw, try to remember how the set-up and execution of the throw felt. Then aim to replicate that for every throw. Schalk Brits also uses the golf analogy, 'To me it's like a golf swing, you need to figure out what works for you and then, when it goes wrong, why it went wrong. It's only practice that lets you understand your throw'.

→ Lineout throwing requires the hooker to master physical, technical and mental skills if they are to throw with accuracy and consistency

Position of ball

Nose of ball

Hands

Hips

Knees

Feet

Types of throw

There are two basic types of throw:

- **Flat throw** – hard and direct
- **Lob throw** – softer throw with an arc to get over opposition jumper

Both throws have the same mechanics to them. The main difference is the power of the throw and the timing of the release of the ball, as hooker Corey Flynn explains, 'You try and keep it as similar as possible across all throws. It is just the position of release of the ball from your hands. When you throw a flat ball you throw hard and fast, and release the ball later. When you throw a lob you release slightly earlier with less power in the throw.'

HOW TO IMPROVE YOUR THROWING TECHNIQUE

Coach Simon Hardy takes us through his coaching process with hookers to build confidence in their ability while also improving their technique, 'I get players to watch what is good so they can create a picture in their head plus feel-good technique. There is no point in them watching poor throws, as the key is not to correct from mistakes but to keep going back to what is good. They only need to recognise they have made a mistake and then attempt to do the next throw correctly.

'I use video analysis myself to see what faults they have; particular recurring issues and look at how to eliminate them, i.e. use of drills, see physio, etc.

'In practice I use consequence drills. It is very important to understand the player's maturity, feedback ratios, reaction to stress, etc., so some of the below I do not use on everyone:

- Negative consequence drills, e.g. as soon as you miss two throws (or similar) we finish = means session finishes on a negative note
- Positive consequence drills, e.g. must hit five (or similar) in a row to finish = means the session finishes on success
- Passive consequence drills e.g. have ten throws to finish (or similar) which may finish well or poorly Also play games which create significant throws.'

For those looking to add spin to the ball, skills coach **Mick Byrne** suggests players have to work hard at the wrist and fingers, creating spin but still heading towards the target, 'On a throw or pass, the hands head towards the target and the spin comes after the throw. The arms head towards the target and the spin comes out through the wrist and fingers. The fingers still need to come to the target. There is a subtlety there to work on.'

When things go wrong, and they inevitably will, hooker Schalk Brits recommends looking at all the variables, not just the throw, 'There are a lot of different ways of throwing but the other variables for me are definitely the opposition, your pod's lifting, the lock's jumping in the right space, then, getting that timing. Finally if the call is correct or not correct.

When I look at the lineouts I've lost I look at all the variables and if it's the throw – ball too high, throw too hard – then it's my fault and it's something I have to work on.'

How to deal with throwing under pressure

'When I was younger it would crack me that I would lose a throw' says Schalk Brits. Handling the pressure of throwing is something I believe improves with age and experience. I know I certainly learned how to deal with a poor throw late in my career.

This is one of the first things I tell any hooker I work with now. If you throw a poor lineout throw, forget about it immediately. Move on. There will be time to reflect, but in the middle of the game, the most important thing is what happens next – not what just happened. While it is very important to forget about the poor throw in the middle of a game, it is important that hookers take the time to analyse and understand why the throw was not accurate.

Corey Flynn, Schalk Brits, Keven Mealamu – all hookers miss throws and all say 'bin it' and move on. 'You have to put it behind you. When you are in a tight situation on the rugby field, you need to be in the moment and think about the job at hand', says Keven Mealamu. 'Save all the analysing until after the game when you get a chance to review the film and break down your throws to see where you went wrong. Just be in the moment and think about what you need to do to nail your throw now.'

Lineout throwing coaches, like Simon Hardy, can help players understand the issues they are having, and he outlines common reasons for problems, 'A run of bad form suggests either a lack of preparation, possibly a young inexperienced thrower developing a base knowledge or simply the player's base skill level is not good enough. Anyway, in both cases, go back to doing repetitions and start the whole coaching process again.'

> **Throwing requires** *a lot of time to develop a good technique and a routine that works for you. The more time you put into your throwing, the better you will become. People will show you different techniques but once you find your own and really nail it down by putting in the repetition you will feel comfortable when you have to go out and perform under pressure.*
>
> *'It is important to ensure that your throw is as efficient as possible. When there is too much movement in your body, there is a lot of room for error. Ensuring minimal movement throughout your body helps for a good technique. You have to have strong shoulders and triceps but it's important to make sure you have a strong core.*
>
> **Keven MEALAMU, New Zealand & Blues**

The catch

Catching the ball at the lineout requires the same mechanics as catching the ball from a kick-off. It is an overhead catch, using both hands. In an ideal scenario, the timing and throw are perfect, the lifters are chest to chest, the jumper is at full stretch, and they catch the ball with their fingers spread wide, thumbs together to create a window like we did in Catch and Pass (page 101).

The catching mechanics change depending on where the jumper is in the lineout, as lock George Robson explains, 'If I'm at the front, I try to go up quickly and win a pre-grip ball. The catching mechanism is part of the jump for me. I start quite low with my hands either side of me. When I jump I use my arms to get momentum and then, when I'm in the air, my arms are forward and up, not straight above my head. This way I can reach forward and grab the ball before anyone else – it's closer to me and others have less time

to react and get the ball. In the same movement I snatch the ball into my body as quickly as possible. It's the same thing with drive ball – you want to draw the ball into your body as quickly as you can before anyone else can get an arm in.

'If you are going backwards for a lob and trying to beat someone behind, I would use the same jump mechanism but I would lean back with my arms and reach back to get the ball behind me.

'Straight up the middle, like at the front, you want to gather it a bit in front of you. If the throw is top dollar, you want to be reaching at the top of your jump to get it, as that gives a crisp ball to play off. When you catch off the top, use your arms, reach and catch, move your head to where you want the ball to go, bring your arms down, and put the ball where the scrum half is going to go so he can run on to it and do that quickly.'

'Don't twist your upper body too much because you will compromise your jump stability,' advises lock Marco Bortolami. While skills coach **Mick Byrne**'s key message is to remind young players that their hand is a continuation of their arm and should be kept straight so their fingers are pointed up and not backwards, 'Their hand continues on from their arm so there are no cocked wrists. For a lineout jumper if he cocks his wrists and then reaches above his head his fingers are actually pointing backwards. We really work hard on keeping their hands as an extension of their arms with no cock in the wrists so that when they reach for the ball their fingers are available for the catch.'

← Like scrums, successful lineouts depend on the Forwards knowing their roles and doing their jobs in unison

Ball transfer

The primary objective of the team throwing into the lineout is to win possession of the ball. The secondary objective is to win the ball in the optimal position to launch the next attack. For example, if the next play from the lineout is to launch a backline attack, the best place to win possession of the ball is towards the tail of the lineout. This puts less pressure on the scrum half's pass to his backline. What the team wants to do with the lineout ball will dictate what happens next. The options are usually:

- A pass off the top to the 9 and out to the backs
- A down and pop – the jumper comes down with the ball and pops the ball to the 9 with the intention of holding the opposition back row in the lineout
- A peel to another forward
- A maul

Flanker Tom Wood has his own recipe for the perfect take, 'Catch the ball cleanly, then rotate yourself so you can deliver the ball cleanly. The more you can rotate and the quicker that ball is, the quicker you can play it into midfield.'

Locks should always try their best to catch with both hands to ensure full control over the ball, but on occasions where this is not possible, Italy's Marco Bortolami provides some tips to get the ball to the scrum half, 'If the throw is catchable only with one hand, because is not straight or a little bit too high or you are under pressure from a defender, only use the inside hand to flip the ball to 9. Practise the delivery with one or two hands standing on one foot.

'Develop a one hand gesture to make sure you are able to control the ball above your head with your fingers; don't deflect the ball with your palm because you will have very little control of it.'

KICK-OFFS AND RESTARTS

The game of rugby commences with a kick-off. Which team kicks off will be decided before the game. The kicking team's kicker gets the game underway by drop kicking the ball from the centre of the halfway line. Depending on the strategy of the kicking team, they will either aim to contest the ball by kicking it just beyond the required 10-metre line or else kick the ball deep within the opposition territory, forcing the attacking team to play out of their 'red zone'.

Following the scoring of any points by a team, the team that was scored against restarts the game by the same method – drop kicking the ball from the centre of the halfway line.

The kicker can kick the ball anywhere in the opposition half of the pitch as long as the ball travels over the 10-metre line. The strategy of where to kick the ball will depend on a number of factors that will be discussed by the coach and practised by the players during the week leading up to the game.

Your team's strengths play a big part in strategy, so look to kick to your players' talents. Fly half **Ian Madigan** outlines his advice, 'If your wingers and second rows are good in the air, try to kick the ball so it's contestable for them in the air. If you have a good lineout, you'll look to kick the ball deep so the opposition kick it into touch so you'll have a lineout.'

The kicking team should identify and kick to the opponent that provides the least threat. Ideally, find an isolated player or deep into opposition territory, in the hope that the ensuing play results in a lineout to the team that kicked off. (Usually, when the ball is kicked deep, into the opposition 22, the team who catches the ball will set up a ruck and kick the ball out of bounds to relieve pressure. This results in a lineout for the team that originally kicked to restart play.)

Blues coach **Nick White** is clear in his preferred tactic at this set piece, 'Kick to a centre who is by himself in the middle of the field or kick long to a half back who is either going to kick it out or pass to a winger or 8. However you want to do it, kick to the opposition where they are not expecting it.'

The scoreboard is another factor in the equation. The options you choose will be different if you are looking for points or looking to run down the clock. 'Chasing a game you are going to try kick it to win the ball back straight away,' explains Ireland's Ian Madigan. 'If you are ahead, you'll kick it long and force the other team to kick it out.'

›› How to catch a restart

As with any catch, keeping your eyes on the ball until it's safely in your hands is crucial. Argentina's No. 8, **Juan Leguizamon** explains why, 'You should never take your eyes off the ball, because that will make you lose focus.' All Black No. 8 **Jerome Kaino** warns of distractions, 'No matter what is in your peripherals, just keep your eyes on the ball and time your jump.'

You can't catch the ball if you are in the wrong position so learning to judge the trajectory of the ball and anticipating where it will land is something to focus on in practice. Alternatively, you may find it easier to go to the most commonly targeted areas of the pitch. There may be some cues from the kicking team that indicate where the ball will be kicked. The receiving team should assess if the kicker is right- or left-footed, and what the formation of the kicker's teammates look like.

George Robson explains his approach, 'At kick-off you don't know where the ball is going, so you need to take a second to look at the flight of the ball and work that out. If it's going to you and you get the position right and are there first, others coming in to compete will struggle to win the ball.'

Catching the restart is very similar to catching the ball at the lineout. Usually, a second row will move into position and jump for the ball, aided by two lifters. 'In the restart you get lifted, similar to the lineout, so you try to jump in the same pattern every time,' advises **Joe Launchbury**. Different but no less valid advice comes from Argentina's **Juan Leguizamon**, 'A good jump involves turning your body in the direction of your posts in order to protect the ball and yourselves in the air.'

Although the technique of catching the restart is similar to catching the ball at the lineout, it is important to practise the movement, jump, lift and catch at training to improve this set piece skill. The amount of pressure the kick receiver is under will determine what type of catch technique is utilised. If the kicking team are contesting for the ball, the receiver will move into position as quickly as possible and jump for the ball, aided by his lifters. In this case the catch will be an overhead catch. For Joe Launchbury practice is the key to this, 'The more confident you are catching the ball above your head the easier the skill becomes. It's something I practise as much as I can, even if it's just on my own, throwing the ball up and catching it overhead. The more times you repeat it, the happier you will be in a game.'

If the kicking team kicks the ball deep into opposition territory, however, the receiver will have more time to catch the ball as he will be under less pressure. In this case, he will most likely not jump for the ball but catch it by creating a basket with his arms and chest.

Alex Magleby sets the scene, 'If the ball is fairly long and I'm not under as much pressure I'm going to basket catch it for stability, as there's so much noise around that contact area. The support players then build a nest around the receiver.'

HOW TO IMPROVE YOUR CATCHING FROM A RESTART

In terms of practice, England's **Geoff Parling** builds his confidence by practising his technique of catching ten high balls after sessions when he is fatigued, while Italy's **Marco Bortolami** suggests practising in progession, 'the receiver should first catch the ball on the ground from another player who throws with his hand, then

kicks. Repeat with the receiver lifted.'

Catching the ball from a 22-metre kick is no different from catching any other type of kick. The only real difference is that the receiving team must be aware that they will potentially be under more pressure as the ball just has to cross the 22-metre line to be live, so it is adviseable to practise catching under pressure in training.

Where I position myself on kick-off receipts varies on the opposition and where they are most likely to kick it. The two locks would generally go to most kicked-to areas between the 22-metre line and the 40-metre line, one on the touchline and one on the 15.

'When you are catching overhead, try and get into the air as early as possible, arms straight up, fingers spread and keep your eyes on the ball. Try not to catch it in your palms as it can be tricky, relax the fingers and after a while it should come naturally. If you're catching it on the chest, keep your elbows together to stop the ball falling through.

'To catch the ball you should already be in place when the ball has reached its highest point in the air. I practise this regularly with the other second rows. You can just kick the ball high to each other but you're only allowed to move when the ball is on the way up, by the time the ball is on the way down you have to stay where you are and try to catch it overhead. It sounds simple but it is quite hard to get the hang of.

'I would usually have two lifters to get me high in the air to catch it. If the ball is caught comfortably, it is a good opportunity to set up a maul as soon as you touch the ground and get some momentum driving them back.'

Devin TONER, Ireland & Leinster

OPEN PLAY

DEFENCE

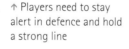

↑ Players need to stay alert in defence and hold a strong line

Rugby is 80 minutes of relentless effort with one objective – to win the ball and score.

Teams can find themselves under sustained pressure on defence for long periods of time but ultimately the final result often comes down not to how good they are on attack but how disciplined and focused the team is while they fight to regain the ball.

Defence is something to get excited about. A momentum shifting tackle can have a very positive impact on a team. It's a really big boost for a team when they keep their defensive shape for a long time until the point that they can turn over the ball.

Todd Clever speaks of the ability of a turnover to 'rally a tired team and give them confidence', while **Steffon Armitage** highlights the potential impact on the scoreboard, 'Do what it takes to get your team back on the attack. Defending for five minutes and then getting one turnover could be the change of the whole game. Most tries are scored from turnovers, now that's when you get it, from loads of pressure-turnover-finish.'

Any team that has aspirations about winning silverware needs to have a solid defence, 'Your role in defence is just as important as your role in attack. Identify what defensive situation you are in when your team concedes a turnover and make sure you connect and communicate with your teammates so your system can be as strong as it can be from a turnover situation', says Leicester Tigers coach **Aaron Mauger**.

►► Defensive philosophy

Teams must apply pressure in defence. The aim of the defending team is to win the ball back through aggressive and disciplined defence. There are numerous defensive structures that teams' use, but they are all designed to put as much pressure on the opposing attack as possible. Ireland's defence coach **Les Kiss** looks to build a mentally tough defensive mindset in a system that is extremely hard to break down. For him the defence focus is on 'attacking without the ball' and he looks for his teams to generate scores through defence. 'It is not about just stopping the opposition, it is more about "how will we win the ball back?"'

Factors for a successful defence

The success of a team's defence depends on a number of factors. As with all situations in rugby, any given moment is dynamic and constantly

Contest possession and go forward, applying pressure to prevent territory being gained. Supported by or in support of teammates to regain possession and counter-attack.

WORLD RUGBY (formerly known as the IRB) outlines the principles of defence

changing. Ensuring players fully understand the defensive structure of the team, as well as having confidence in their individual tackle techniques is the basis for a successful defence, but there are other elements that players and coaches should focus on.

Types of defence

There are various factors to consider when creating a defensive structure for your team, but the two main types of defence used in rugby union are a drift (up and out) defence or a blitz (man on/up and in) defence. The line speed of these two forms of defence is the main difference.

With a drift defence, the defending team is attempting to push the attack towards the sideline, with a relatively slow defensive line speed. Defenders align themselves inside their opposite man, looking to tackle their opponent with their outside shoulder. If the attacking team passes the ball before the tackle, the defending team will 'push' across, with each man in the defensive line responsible for covering the inside shoulder of the defender next to them.

With a blitz defence, the defending team will launch quickly off the line and try to force the attacking team to the inside. Defenders align themselves outside their opposite man, looking to tackle their opponent with their inside shoulder. This high risk/high reward defence is seen as more aggressive, aiming to stop the opposition attacking in the wide channels of the pitch by congesting the midfield.

At the top level of the sport, teams will aim to integrate a number of different styles of defence during each game. This is based on their analysis of the opposition before the game, and on what the attack is doing during the game.

Les Kiss outlines some of the defensive styles he aims to employ during a game, 'I coach to ensure my teams can apply varying styles of defence to suit the situation in front of them. Analysis of the opposition will be the driver in terms of which style of pressure to apply at any given time. These different styles include such things as blitz strategies, safety/recovery methods, individual shooter defence tactics (shooting out and attacking the 9 relentlessly, key defenders shooting out of line into the blind spot of the first receiver, fake blitz defence strategies etc.).'

Understanding your role

In any situation you should know your own personal role and aims. There may be slight variations based on the defensive system your team uses but you should understand the key principles. **Rob Hoadley** explains, 'No matter what style of defence a team adopts, as soon as the ball is out of the ruck, defending players must move forward to deny the attacking team the time and space they attempt to create through setting deep and wide.'

A team reacts to an opposition attack by forming a wall, known as the defensive line, and your role as a defender depends on where you are in that wall. Your position in the line will usually be determined by your skills and where

they best serve your team, as coach Hoadley outlines, 'Ideally, the defensive team would position their slower players in the middle of the field and faster players on the outside so that forwards can make the heavy tackles on the inside and backs are in position to mark the faster opposition backs where there is more space out wide.'

Trust and communication

Trust and communication, along with execution, are the cornerstones of a solid defence. It takes time to trust yourself and your individual tackle technique. It takes even more time to build trust between multiple players in defence. Trust is a vital part of defence as it means that you can trust your teammates to perform their tackles, which leaves each individual to worry only about doing their job. Alex Magleby is very clear on this, 'If I am hesitant in my job because I don't think they can defend me on the inside, I'm not going to be as effective as I possibly could on your outside. If everybody does *their* job I can do *my* job effectively.'

Trust is built on communication and execution. This means that the players communicate by commentating on their actions, for example, 'I have the ball carrier', and then executing, by performing the tackle and doing what they said they would do.

Letting your teammates know what you intend to do and then following through with actions builds trust. There is no shortcut in this area of paramount importance to the defence.

Maintaining 'defensive line integrity'

The vast majority of defending relies on maintaining the defensive line integrity or defensive shape. This means that players must stay connected with each other, forming one solid wall, all moving forward together. If one player falls behind or shoots out in front of his teammates, a hole is created for the attack to exploit (unless the defensive structure does this on purpose).

'Chain of three' – is a way of breaking the defensive wall into smaller units to help the players. If each player works very closely with the player to his left and right, they form a chain of three. Together the various chains of three form the defensive wall. Communication between defenders in their chain of three is a vital part of a successful defence. Coach **Scott Lawrence** describes the system, 'Each player should be able to cover the space between themselves and the next defender and make an effective tackle. Thereby the integrity of the imaginary line connecting all defenders is intact.'

Rob Hoadley explains why a team needs to work at the pace of their slowest player if they are to maintain the solid wall of defenders, 'Generally spaces between defenders get bigger the further away they are from the ruck. The launch should always go at the speed of the slowest man so that the defence keeps a consistent line. Therefore, the attack will not have any holes to attack between isolated defenders.'

Tackling mindset

There is limited space on the rugby pitch to defend, so if everyone performs his own job and maintains the team's defensive shape, it should be possible for the defending team to put pressure on the attack and hopefully force a turnover. This philosophy is based on the assumption that each player understands the team's defensive structure and has the ability to tackle.

Ireland defence coach Les Kiss suggests the complete defensive profile of a player is not only about being technically and physically proficient but also about attitude and having 'the mental

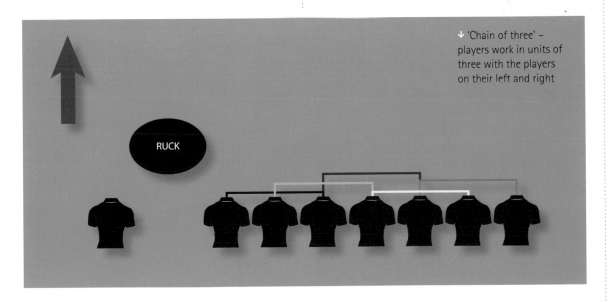

↓ 'Chain of three' – players work in units of three with the players on their left and right

RUCK

strength and fortitude skills required. Every player must have the mindset, skills and technique to apply pressure at the tackle contest.'

Rob Hoadley believes a player's confidence in contact comes from understanding the team structure, 'An aspect that can help eliminate a fear of failure in the tackle is improving the player's understanding of the team's defensive structure. They can then feel a connection with defenders around them so that players are not asked to make unrealistic difficult one-on-one tackles, for example, a prop tackling a wing in space.'

In training, Hoadley recommends players focus on 'the best process of making a tackle, rather than the outcome. Regardless of success

↓ Two Welsh back rows tackle Scotland's ball carrier in an RBS 6 Nations clash

or failure, success comes from full commitment to the process and the moment.'

Coach Hoadley gives the outline of a routine for players on the field, which he believes sets them up for success in the tackle. This six-step process aims to help players build a basic mind-set for conventional defensive situations from set piece or phase play:

1 SET EARLY
vision to connect with our defence (correct spacing with the two defenders either side, in relation to the match scenario), in order to cover attacking threats across the field.

2 KNOW YOUR ROLE
and which defensive channel you have responsibility to cover within the team system.

3 POSITIVE BODY LANGUAGE

a player who has positive body language is always engaged in the task at hand. You are much less likely to see a mistake from this type of player than one who is switched off in terms of body language. Each team must understand precisely what defines positive body language so that it can be assessed constructively. Even if you are the worst tackler in the world, there is no reason why you shouldn't look like the best tackler in the world before you make the tackle.

4 COMMUNICATE

with the two defenders either side of you, and call the launch when the ball is out of the ruck. There are two great benefits to consistent communication. Firstly, like positive body language, it focuses the mind of the defender on going through their process. Essentially, we are asking the player to commentate on what he is doing while he is doing it. It is very rare that a player will communicate the right process to himself and others but then follow it with a completely different action. Very rarely will the corresponding action not follow the commentary. Secondly, a good aggressive launch call for the defensive team has the effect of distracting the attacking team from going through their own process, as they become aware that they are facing a well-organised and engaged defence.

5 LAUNCH

again the speed of launch depends on the team system (drift or blitz)/area on field/numbers of attackers v. defenders. Most simply put, the defensive team can be more aggressive and have greater launch line speed the more numbers they have. With fewer defenders than attackers, the defensive team is more likely to use a drift defence.

6 TACKLE COMPLETION

the most positive aim being to create a turnover in the tackle. As we have seen, there are many types of tackle but the aim of any defensive system is ultimately to get the ball back. Attacking from turnover ball can produce the best opportunities to score tries as the opposition are immediately disorganised in defence, having all started in attacking formation. Practising attacking from turnover ball against a disorganised defence should be a regular part of training.

Dealing with mistakes

As the pressure mounts and fatigue sets in, players and teams can and do make mistakes and present opportunities to the attacking team. Coach Les Kiss reminds players that it's how the team reacts to a situation that is important, 'Shit happens. Things can and will go wrong and we will make errors. How we respond as a team under pressure and in adversity will determine how great we will be. Fighting through tough moments will ultimately define us.'

Coach Rob Hoadley uses the words of a great player from another sport to highlight the importance of having the mentality that failure is part of success:

> *I've missed more than 9,000 shots in my career. I've lost almost 300 games. Twenty-six times I've been trusted to take the game winning shot and missed. I've failed over and over and over again in my life. And that is why I succeed.*
>
> **Michael JORDAN, Chicago Bulls & Washington Wizards**

➤➤ Reading the attack (scanning in defence)

'Scanning' is a term that is used to describe the process of looking up and analysing the immediate threat in front of you, as well as any potential threats that may come into play. As a defender, it is very important to assess what the attack are trying to do and where they are trying to attack.

As coach Scott Lawrence describes below, an attacker can sometimes unintentionally inform the defence of his intentions by giving cues. Defenders must look for these cues and then make decisions based on them:

■ Who is carrying the ball? If it's a lower passing skill player, like a prop, there is a higher likelihood of a hard carry and we'll condense the defence accordingly.
■ When a player tucks the ball in one hand, usually this is a sign of a carry. The opposite is true when it's in two hands, they can run or pass.
■ Small things like the angle of the 9's feet can cue the first defender of their intent.

Here is an outline of some of the scans players should do during a game, which gives them key information on what the opposition is intending:

■ The shape of the attack. For example, a deep kicker with a flat backline around the 22-metre line means a kick is coming.
■ Forwards scanning other forwards coming out of a set piece to see where they are going.
■ Finding the 10 in most attacking systems and rotating accordingly.
■ The number of players inside the 10 is another scan and may dictate line speed.

England back row **Tom Wood** offers the simple advice of focusing on an opponent's hips if you want to know which way they intend to go, 'Watch the shorts because his hips don't tell lies; his hands and his feet will. He is trying to show the ball with dummies and move it around and sidestep and shuffle quickly, but it's more difficult to do that with your hips so that's where you focus.'

Decision making in defence

All facets of rugby involve decision making and defence is no different. The decisions of who to tackle, what type of tackle to perform and the aim of the tackle change based on the situation the defender is faced with, i.e. area of the pitch and support in defence.

Better decision making comes from confidence in yourself, confidence in understanding the team's defensive structure and through experience. Looking out for the cues of the attacking ball carrier and attacking team, as discussed above, can aid with the defensive decision making.

A player not only has to understand what the opposition is aiming to do but also what outcome they want. The aims of a tackler are dependent on the match situation and players need to factor in other aspects like support and field position. Rob Hoadley explains, 'If the defender is in a strong position to make a double tackle with a teammate, the aim will be to make an aggressive tackle and drive the opponent backwards while stripping the ball. On the other hand, if faced with a counter-attacking full back in a lot of space, the aim will simply be to complete a leg tackle.'

HOW TO IMPROVE YOUR DECISION MAKING IN DEFENCE

Playing and analysing the game are key to improving the skill. The Super 15s winning Waratahs assistant coach **Daryl Gibson** believes, 'defensive decision making is developed through experience and learning from your missed tackles and game situations'. For the former All Black it's also about 'having a thorough understanding of the team's defensive system and your role within it'. He strongly recommends 'watching and learning from the best in the game'. The Sharks' **Brendan Venter** also believes it's about learning from experience and where the 10,000-hour rule is relevant, 'The more often players can be put in those situations, the better their decision making will become'.

Read and shut down

Knowing who to tackle when the attack is going to run an intricate attacking play can be tricky. This is part of the decision making process in defence and requires all the components of the defence to work together. That means working in your chain of three, scanning what is unfolding in front of you, looking for any incoming attacking threats and communicating to your teammates who you intend to tackle. You should also listen to your teammates and what they see or intend to do.

Knowing your opposition's attacking strengths will aid your defensive decision-making process. For example, some teams will have elusive individuals, while others may run an attacking pattern that defences can pick up on. All Blacks centre **Conrad Smith** looks for trends in the opposition attack and observes what they like to do as a team, 'You'll look at individuals, [and know that] he's really quick so you've got to worry about that. Some guys you can read so you know when he's going to pass or when he's going to carry'.

Experienced Irish centre **Gordon D'Arcy** speaks about the importance of patience when you are in defence. Go too early and you gift the opponent the advantage, 'One of the key things is not getting ahead of the ball, when the defender inside you has the ball carrier. If you shoot out of the line, you have made his decision for him and he'll make a fool out of you. When you are marking three or four guys outside you, all running different angles, you can't pick someone until the ball carrier passes the ball'.

A player has to focus on his skills and make sure his technique is right. 'Learn how to control your feet as you are decelerating and then accelerating again on the pass. You have to learn how to get your feet underneath you, the contact and the bite, getting him to ground and speed to feet', continues D'Arcy.

Defence at set piece

The best way to defend a set piece is to win possession. It may sound obvious but exerting maximum pressure on the attacking set piece is the first step in winning the ball. At worst, it will mean that the attacking team will have to be very accurate in their execution. At best, the defending team will win possession.

Defending scrums

The same mindset is needed for a defensive scrum as an attacking scrum. All eight forwards should aim to put their opposition under as much pressure as possible in the hope of forcing a turnover. Canadian lock **Jamie Cudmore** thinks it's pretty simple, 'For me, scrums are always attack – there is no attack or defence – there is only attack'.

If the opposition win their own scrum, the defending back row must get away from the scrum quickly to tackle the opposition. No. 8

Jerome Kaino speaks about the relationship with the flankers in this scenario, 'Defensively, a No. 8 is the inside link with the blindside and openside flankers. They will have the first defender off the scrum so you will clean up anything that comes inside them. You are a crucial link in defence.'

Defending the lineout

Defences should compete aggressively for the ball – hookers do not like having to make pinpoint throws every time, especially if it's windy or wet. Put a couple of pods up in the air every time and force the thrower to throw the ball over them. Consistently putting the hooker under pressure in the lineout can damage his confidence and potentially starve the opposition of prime lineout ball.

How to steal the ball at the lineout

Pre-game analysis of a team's preferred calls can also help you anticipate their most likely options. During the game the jumpers hunt the ball in the air by reading and reacting to the opposing jumper's movements. Watching the hooker and assessing his style of throw can also help a defending lineout predict where he intends to throw the ball.

Tom Wood stresses the importance of being able to read the opposition, 'You have to watch a lot of clips and get to know how the opposition operates, how their key lineout calls work and what makes them tick. Then, on the day, it's important to be able to read their body language, pick up triggers of movement and get in the air quickly.'

Not only does analysis help with how quickly you can get to the ball, **Jim Hamilton** suggests you can also use it to manipulate the hooker's throw, 'If you have studied an opposition hooker and know he struggles to throw to the back, then your team should contest the front and middle of the lineout.'

Perhaps the most direct approach is suggested by **George Robson**, 'you just want to get to the ball and steal it.'

How to decide when to stay down and contest on the ground

Defending teams can decide to stay down and not compete for the ball in the air. There are benefits but this is not without its risks, as Tom Wood outlines, 'There is merit in that but most teams prefer to stop it at source by winning it in the air. If they are allowed to win free ball, it makes it a lot easier for them to set a maul.

'If you can get up alongside your opposite guy, even if he wins the ball, you land in among them and can be disruptive from there. The problem arises if you misread it, make the wrong call and jump in the wrong place. Not only do you lose the ball and let them construct a maul, you are in the air and slow to get into the maul.'

Field position plays a part in whether to try this strategy or not. **Joe Launchbury** explains how the options differ depending on where your team are on the field, 'If we are close to our defensive tryline, we may say we'll stay down for this one and make sure they can't set up a drive against us. If we're inside their half or even close to it we are more likely to compete harder and try to nick the ball.'

→ Rather than contest in the air, Joe Launchbury waits for opponent Kelly Brown to return to ground with the ball

⟩⟩ First-phase defence

Defences must be 5 metres behind the scrum and 10 metres behind the lineout. This provides the attacking team with space to execute first-phase plays [moves], as all the forwards are in a condensed area of the pitch (unless a short-man lineout has been called, in which case, a number of forwards may be in the back line).

Attacking teams will have a number of first-phase moves that they will attempt to execute, given the extra space on the pitch. Defences must scan, organise and react to these first-phase attacking moves as Rob Hoadley explains. 'Scrums and lineouts will have pre-determined roles from a static and organised start. The key in these scenarios is the inside connection between back row and backs.'

Gordon D'Arcy outlines the difficulties defences face during first phase and highlights the importance of scanning and reacting to the unfolding attacking play, 'Someone runs short and someone else runs short with them and then the 10 throws the ball out the back and you're left thinking, "Oh, but I had the guy short?" You have to be able to be in that fulcrum of the midfield at 12 and 13 and you have to be able to defend two or three players at any one time and be ready to tackle every one of them as the ball leaves the 10's hands.'

⟩⟩ Multi-phase defence

The more phases an attacking team can hold on to the ball and continuously attempt to penetrate the defence, the more pressure will mount on the defending team. The aim of the defending team is to remain patient while maintaining its defensive shape in the hope that an opportunity to turn the ball over will present itself.

The aims of the defending team are summarised by Ireland defence coach, Les Kiss. He believes that at the core of a great defence team is their ability to handle massive and sustained attack pressure and that the key to being excellent in this area is discipline:

- **Discipline in knowing** the laws of the game (especially the ruck/breakdown law);
- **Discipline in being excellent** in your technique despite pressure and fatigue (mental toughness);
- **Discipline to commit** to the system (individuals staying focused on their role and not breaking defensive shape – mental toughness);
- **Discipline in rallying** and scrambling your defence line when broken (which will inevitably happen);
- **Discipline and focus** on great set piece defence – good defences begin with good set-piece pressure;
- **Discipline in off- and pre-season training** to be as fit, strong and powerful as possible to ensure you can be depended on.

Defending the ruck

Discipline and patience are the cornerstones of a solid defence. Defending the ruck is all about decision making and that is why it's hard for a young player to appreciate the decision-making process, as it comes with experience and time.

Decision making at the ruck

As you approach the ruck a player should ask himself a number of questions: Is the ball won or lost? If I join the ruck, what will that do? Can I see the ball? England's second row Joe Launchbury lists the decision making process for a player considering joining a ruck, 'You try to assess as quickly as possible, how many of your teammates are making their way to the ruck? Are you going to be needed? Is there a chance of you turning the ball over? Can you see the ball? Is there a chance you can get the ball back for your team?'

If there is nothing to be gained by going into the ruck, do not go into the ruck. Get into the defensive wall. That's discipline and patience. Discipline is knowing that you are not going to vacate your position in the line to join the ruck, or you are not going to join the ruck if you are not needed. Patience is staying in the defensive line and launching again until there is an opportunity to turnover the ball.

Les Kiss is clear in his thinking on this matter. 'Post-tackle skills involve effective decision making and technique around legally contesting for the ball, putting pressure on the opposition ruck clearance or bailing out of the contest to reload in the defence line.' If a player decides to attack the ruck and gets the decision wrong, there can be a big price to pay. Joe Launchbury outlines the consequences, 'If you stick your head into a ruck in which you aren't needed,

the opposition can score a try out wide where you should be standing.'

There are cues that the defensive team can look for to decide when to contest the ruck. When the ball carrier is tackled and brought to ground, their aim is to look after the ball and ensure they protect the ball for their team. The way in which they present the ball and the speed of their support ultimately decide whether the defence should contest the ball. If the ball carrier doesn't present the ball correctly, is slow to do it, or his support is slow to arrive and clear out the defender there is an opportunity for the defensive team to poach or jackal the ball.

Contesting the ruck

Players should maintain their defensive shape and wait for the optimal opportunity to go for the turnover. If you decide to vacate your position in the defensive wall due to the identification of a possible turnover, always tell your teammates in your chain of three, as you may leave a hole in the defence for the attack to exploit.

England's back row Tom Wood discusses some of the rules in a defensive system for when to attack the ball. First up is which side to attack from, 'We don't want people coming in from the outside because it shortens your defensive line-up, and if they get quick ball and get round the corners it's very difficult for your players to fold around the back of the breakdown and realign. We attack the ball from the inside.'

When the player next to you makes a good low tackle and gets the ball carrier on the floor very quickly, you have a small window of opportunity to get on to the ball and contest possession. 'It's your reaction time and your technique that are crucial. You have to recognise that opportunity and get into a good strong position,' explains Wood. 'Shorter back rows and centres are very good at it, they leech over the ball like limpets, head low in a very low squat position and either win the ball very quickly or ride the first contact and stay on the ball and almost use the force of clear out to rip the ball free. '

There are variations in the defender's technique for regaining possession that are based on how the attacker presents the ball. Tom Wood outlines the options, 'If he presents it long – chase your feet through the ruck and get into the heart of the ruck and rip it off the floor. If he hides it under his body – go fishing for it; often he will try to squeeze it out like he's laying an egg. Go for the ball not the body. People can be too concerned with their position over the ball and they forget to try to rip it away and win it.'

Not everyone who goes into a ruck has the intent of winning the ball, however. 'Some people are just happy to get [their hands] on the ball because if they are on the ball and if the opponent doesn't let go of it they'll probably win the penalty,' explains Scotland back row **Kelly Brown**. 'Whereas if you really want a turnover you have to get low, get your hands on the ball and "rip and twist" at the same time, that's the best way to break the opponent's grip on the ball.'

Springboks No. 8 **Duane Vermeulen** keeps it simple, 'Stick to the laws of the game, stay on your feet, ensure your entry is correct and get your hands on the ball as soon as possible and keep them there.'

Like tackling, contesting the ruck is about attitude and having the right mindset to fight for the ball, says England's Tom Wood. 'You can't be worried about people coming in to clear you out or the moment will be gone. You have to take the opportunity and recognise it, be brave enough to put your head where it hurts, get in that strong position and search for the ball.'

❛ **For me it's easy** because I am so short! Finding that position where your quads are tense, your toes are pushing into the ground and grab hold of the guy and don't let go for any reason. The best position over the ball is to imagine you are doing a squat face down. When you reach the bottom of the squat you have all that weight on top of your shoulders. That is where the power is and that is the strongest position you can get into.

'Improve your technique by doing squats in training; just hold it for two seconds at the bottom before coming back up. That is the position you are always in when you go into a ruck. Then it all comes down to practice. Get one of your friends to do 10 minutes of drills after training – such as wrestling and putting them on the floor then getting back up as quickly as you can and getting over the ball.

'The ball carrier has just been tackled so I grab hold of his shirt and get one hand on the ball. I know if someone is going to hit me I'm going to go back but I'm also going to be dragging the guy and the ball. It's about being smart. ❜

Steffon ARMITAGE, England & Toulon

Defending the maul

It is important to remember that mauls can be set up by any player, anywhere on the field of play and at any time. The vast majority of mauls tend to be formed from lineouts as they provide the ideal platform to create one.

Once they are formed mauls can be very difficult to stop. It is important that defending teams work hard to ensure that the attacking team cannot set up a maul and react as quickly as possible to counter the attempt. There is no magic formula to halting a maul. Defenders must 'attack' the maul as low and as hard as possible by targeting the binds of the front players within the maul, with the hope of fracturing it and isolating the ball carrier.

We talk about defending mauls in this section based on the presumption that they have been formed from lineouts.

Prop **Dan Cole** advocates the direct approach, going low and hitting the maul as soon as the jumper lands, to try and force the opposition backwards before they have time to set up, 'Get between the holes and stay low and drive as hard as you can to get the opposition to move backwards or at least to a stalemate because the ball has to be played.'

Cole reinforces his point about body height and its importance at the maul, 'If you have a pushing contest between a guy who is upright and a guy who is bent over, they guy who is bent over will win. Best way to stop a maul is to stand the guys up and stop their momentum so you can get underneath them.'

'In defence it's probably not as tactical as it seems,' explains lock Joe Launchbury. 'It's a case of getting your head in where it hurts and try and effect that maul as best you can and split it up.'

Defence is all about reacting quickly and for

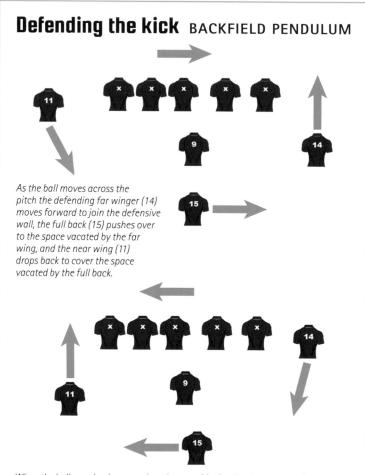

Defending the kick BACKFIELD PENDULUM

As the ball moves across the pitch the defending far winger (14) moves forward to join the defensive wall, the full back (15) pushes over to the space vacated by the far wing, and the near wing (11) drops back to cover the space vacated by the full back.

When the ball goes back across the other way it's simply roles reversed. The near winger goes back up into the defensive line, the full back goes over and covers the space behind him, the far winger will comes across and cover the full back position.

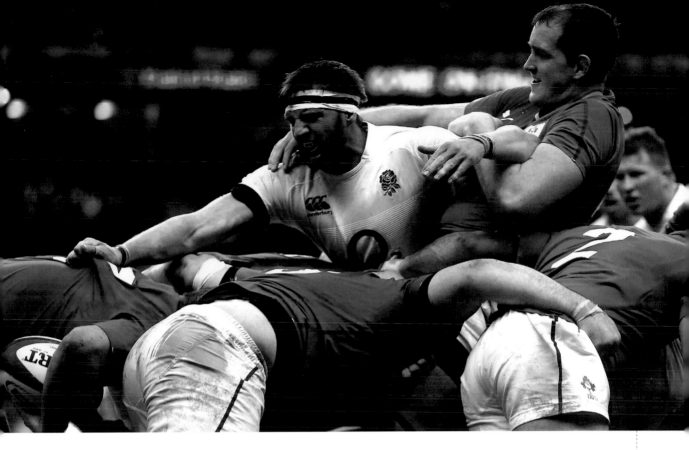

flanker Tom Wood the first two seconds are the most important because once the maul is set and the attacking team are in a strong position it is very difficult to legally stop the maul, 'From the time the opposition win the lineout ball and land on the ground, you've got to try to get into the spaces. Because it's a dynamic movement and it's flowing, you have to find a way to get in between their arms, their binds and disrupt their maul set-up.'

Set piece coach **Nick White** explains that if you want to destroy the maul, the first three players into contact need to do their jobs and stop its formation, '[You] need the two blockers [lifters] to be separated [from the jumper] and the jumper needs to be put on the deck or separated from his two lifters.'

Lock **Marco Bortolami** suggests you do this by 'gently pushing or pulling the jumper while he is landing on the ground', while Tom Wood says 'get a hold of the guy on the ball so

↑ There were 135 mauls in the 2015 RBS Six Nations Championship @AccentureRugby

he panics and tries to break out or tackle him to the floor if you can get to him.'

It is inadvisable to commit too many defenders to the maul, as this will leave holes in the defensive wall. At the same time, it is imperative to stop the maul from moving forward so there is a decision to be made. Usually the openside flanker will stay out of the maul to protect the channel inside the out half. Flanker Steffon Armitage tends to hold his ground and wait to see if the backs need him before he commits to defending the maul, 'If it's necessary for you to go in then go in, but most of the time you need someone out there protecting the 10. If you go in that's the perfect opportunity for the attacking team to break off because you are a defender down.'

While the frontline integrity is crucial, Rob Hoadley stresses that you cannot underestimate the value of backfield positioning. If the frontline defenders do a good job of containing the attack, the attack may look for kicking options, 'A well-constructed backfield has the 11, 14 and 15 working together to try and claim all kicks before they hit the ground, which if successful can lead to great counter attacking opportunities.

'The work of these players is often described as a pendulum system as they move across the pitch to cover frontline running options and backfield kicking options. The scrum half also plays a key role, following the ball behind the frontline defenders to cover any attacking short chip kicks,' explains Hoadley.

Catching the high ball

If the defensive wall does an effective job of quelling the attack, the attacking team may decide to kick the ball. They will do this either for a territorial gain or with the aim of reclaiming possession with a high kick. A high kick gives both teams a 50/50 chance of winning possession, so it can be the preferred method of unlocking a stubborn defence. For the defending team, there are steps you can take to improve your chances of claiming possession of the ball.

COMMUNICATE, COMMIT AND EXECUTE

Communicate: declare your intention of catching the kick as early as possible to your teammates. It is always advisable to move forward to catch the ball as opposed to moving backwards to attempt a catch. So, if you are in position to move forward on to the ball as it is in the air, let your teammates know that you intend to attempt to catch it.

Commit: once you have communicated your intentions of catching the ball, you must fully commit to the challenge. The only excuse for backing away from the task is if a teammate from behind overrules your decision and calls that he intends to catch the ball as he feels he is in a better position then you are. Otherwise, you must try to anticipate the flight of the ball, time your movement and 'attack' it.

Execute: it is essential that you block out all distractions from your mind and from your peripheral vision and focus exclusively on the ball. The first job is to catch it. Keep your eyes on the ball, and 'attack' it in the air by jumping with your hands either above your head, with the intention of catching the ball in your fingertips, or by creating a 'basket' with your arms and pull the ball into your chest.

HOW TO CATCH A HIGH BALL UNDER PRESSURE

USA's **Chris Wyles** loves the challenge of the high ball, which he sees as a mixture of bravery and skill, 'My biggest tip would be you've got to attack the high ball, relish it and see it as a challenge. When you see the ball in the air you've got to go and meet it rather than have the ball come down to you. The way you jump into a high ball is to have your leading knee on one side and your hands up to the sky to take the ball.'

Marland Yarde advised young players to work hard to get to the space before the opposition, 'It's about owning the space, getting off the floor, keeping your eyes on the ball and not being too worried about what's in front of you. Owning the space in the air and that last metre, the final two or three steps before you get in the air.'

← Tommy Bowe reaches for the high ball against Italy. It is a skill all wingers need to master

Communication is vital if you want to win the ball so full back **Andrea Masi** keeps his focus on the ball at all times. He relies on others to tell him what is happening on the ground, 'If you are under pressure, you'll have your wing or No. 8 stay at the back with you; they have to communicate whether to jump or stay on the floor.'

Todd Clever gives the No. 8's perspective, 'You have to listen to whoever is back there with you, letting you know if you have time or not.'

HOW TO IMPROVE CATCHING THE HIGH BALL

Players stress the need to get a sound foundation in technique and then try to replicate the noise and distractions of catching in a game to help build confidence and focus under pressure. Springboks full back **Willie le Roux** explains this common technique, 'We have a drill where someone would put a couple of balls high up in the air (usually a fly half or scrum half), and then we would have someone with a hit shield 'attacking' us as we go up to catch the ball. In a match, you will mostly have to catch under pressure, so it helps to have someone who can provide a bit of hindrance in that regard.'

At Saracens they also have an unusual way of distracting jumpers, as full back **Chris Wyles** describes, 'When we put high balls up we will ask each other questions on literally anything – could be mathematic equations, capital cities, anything – so you have to be thinking at the same time and that's an added element to it.'

USA winger **Brett Thompson** advises young players to practise their ability to get up in the air and train their explosiveness with a simple drill, 'Get up in the air and try to touch the crossbar. This gives you a target and you can see if you are making progress.'

Catching the high ball

ADVICE FOR COACHES

FORMER FULL BACK now Leicester Tigers coach **Geordan Murphy** outlines the elements of the process of catching the high ball a young player should work on:

■ An understanding of where the ball is going to land.
■ Working to create space so you can accelerate into the contact area.
■ The strength and conditioning work and the explosive work the guys do is important.
■ The technique of leading with one leg or with your knee to give yourself a little extra propulsion off the opposition player.

■ Work on getting your hands high, and the process of the catch down before you start in the air.
■ Work from very low level catching, making a basket with your hands in the air.
■ Different types of catches – catching overhead with your hands in the air, one handed catching, catching two handed, catching without any hands and just using your elbows.

✢ Counter-attack

Counter-attacking through turnovers or misplaced kicks provide optimal attacking opportunities, as the team who lost possession of the ball may not have time to organise the defensive wall so there may be holes for the attack to exploit.

How to launch a counter-attack

Players have to be able to scan, analyse and make a quick decision based on where their support is and any obvious weaknesses in the opposition defensive line in front of them.

Full back **Rob Kearney** outlines the likely options for a counter-attack based on where you win the ball and highlights how the opposition's strengths also play a part in the decisions he makes, 'If you are in your own 22, generally, unless it's really on, you'll be kicking to go long and find touch depending on the type of plan you have implemented for the team you are playing against. If you get some counter attacking ball in the opposition 22, the chances are you're not going to kick.

'It depends on how organised the opposition kick chase is. If you are running back into a wall of 10, 12 guys you are going to have to try and vary the point of contact, be it a pass or kick.'

For **Ian Madigan**, the main indicator for counter attack is the quality of the kick, 'If the opposing team has kicked the ball poorly to you, it immediately triggers in the minds of the wing and full back that they are going to counter-attack because they have won the ball back off those kicks. If the kick is executed very well, you are more likely to kick it back and that's where you see the kicking "ping pong."'

The Leinster player also rates support as a factor when deciding to launch an attack, 'If your players work back very quickly to assist you, it gives you the confidence that if you do get tackled you'd win that ruck ball back. You'll be less inclined to counter-attack if it's just you and one other player because if you get tackled there's more chance you'll get turned over.'

Defence should always look to apply pressure on attack by maintaining shape and discipline with a view of winning the ball back. This is either by identifying a turnover opportunity at the set piece or in a ruck or by remaining intact as a defensive wall and forcing the opposition to kick the ball away.

ATTACK

↑ Beauden Barrett runs through Leigh Halfpenny's tackle in a Wales v New Zealand match

The aim of rugby is to score, so possession is the key to success. However, turning that possession into points is ultimately what makes a team's attack strategy a winning one.

▶▶ Attack philosophy

How your team attacks is based on your team's strengths. It's important to identify whether you have big forwards with a successful set piece, an astute No. 9 and 10 or barrelling centres who will get you over the gain line or elusive wide backs. This will dictate the style of rugby that your team plays.

Counter the defensive threats

For an attacking move to succeed it has to outwit the defensive strategy of the opponent. There has been more emphasis on defence in recent years and therefore 'the biggest evolution in rugby in the last ten years is the advancement and organisation of defences from both set piece and phase play', suggests Waratahs coach **Daryl Gibson**.

However, he argues that the fundamentals still apply, 'What hasn't changed is that a well-executed move will always be dangerous and threatening if the participants all understand their roles and the keys to executing the move effectively'.

Play your own game

While you should focus on what the opposition can do in defence, it should not be at the expense of ignoring your own team's strengths. Leicester Tigers coach **Geordan Murphy** highlights the importance of knowing and exploiting your strengths if you want to be successful, 'Every team is different so one of the things a team needs to do is really create its own identity by knowing how it wants to play and playing to its strengths'. It's all about playing your own game. 'If a team has very good forwards then the backs upskill themselves to play around that, but then you don't want to play a loose, fast game if you've got a very good set of forwards', he continues. 'The team's identity has to come from within the team, then the coach has to build an attack philosophy around that'.

There is an ever-increasing demand on attack to be smarter, more precise and clinical in all areas of the game.

Les KISS, Ireland Defence Coach

›› Reading the defence

'Play what you see' is a theme that repeats throughout this book, but how do you 'see' the options? From set piece play when the forwards are getting ready to execute their set piece, the 9 and 10 should be scanning the field looking for space to attack.

'Scanning is reading what is in front of us', explains coach **Alex Magleby**. 'You see the whole field in a snapshot and realise that the snapshot isn't fixed; it is going to change.

'The better athletes are the ones who slow the game down by scanning before they have to make decisions. They understand what is out there and know their options. They take a snapshot and they've seen that snapshot multiple times before, like a chess master, so they know there are two or three alternatives of what could happen. Then they rescan, so they continually make these decisions before they get to the action point'.

Wales backs coach **Rob Howley** reminds players that sharing what you see is an important aspect of scanning. 'Once they have scanned and taken in the information, it is important they communicate what they have seen. This information must be clear, precise and loud'.

Howley explains what to look for in the defensive line and what are the best options,

'Low numbers in the defensive line suggests a team is narrow, so the attacking team should attack wide. High numbers in the defensive line indicates a well organised defence, so attack should be through the middle in an attempt to suck in multiple defenders and create space in the next phase of play.'

Spacing in the defensive line also offers some clues. 'Wide spacing suggests you should attack through the spaces, close spacing you should attack wide.'

►► Decision making in attack

In each phase of attack decision making is going to be based on your team's strengths, potential weaknesses in the opposition defence, where you are on the pitch and the time left on the clock. Coach **Paul Burke** is spot on when he says, 'Knowledge is king when it comes to decision making.'

'Decision making is the hardest part of rugby,' explains Sharks Technical Director **Brendan Venter**. 'I believe that your brain makes good decisions because it has been in certain situations many times. Older players are normally better decision makers. That is the challenge at the junior level.'

Leicester Tigers coach **Aaron Mauger** lists the headline information players need to be aware of before and during a game:

■ Your own game plan and the strengths of your team e.g. personnel or style of play.
■ Pre-game analysis of potential opportunities – what you know about the way your opposition defends and whether there any weak links.
■ How your opposition is set up – where is the best opportunity?
■ What you are learning about the way your opposition is defending in the game. It is critical that all players are aware of what their defence is doing, as this will tell you where the opportunities are.

The following six factors help explain the coaches' and players' perspective on decision making:

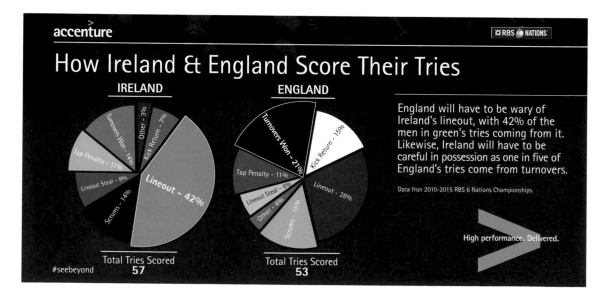

1 PLAY WHAT YOU SEE

Players should make decisions based on what is in front of them in that moment. The game plan gives you options to choose from but making good decisions is about picking the most appropriate play for the specific situation. Northampton Saints coach **Alex King** gives the example of a fly half reading the opposition, 'As a 10 when you see a defence set in front of you, your thought goes to where is the natural space to attack. Is it the seam inside the 10 and the scrum/lineout or is it outside the 13 channel because the winger is hanging back for the kick?'

2 PLAY TO YOUR STRENGTHS

This should be the aim of every team. Great decisions can only become a reality if you have the players with the skills to deliver on them, so be sure to take this into consideration. Alex King lists just some of the questions you might ask yourself when choosing which call to make, 'All the time you are taking into consideration the natural space that is available and you're also thinking of the strengths of your backline. Are you capable of attacking those spaces that you've got? Are you a quick team? Do you have pace or power? Are you looking to get across the gain line straight away? Are you looking to go round them? So you need to understand your strengths and if you have a midfield that doesn't have great distribution skills then you're going to struggle to get the ball wide, so you need to be able to adapt.'

3 WEATHER CONDITIONS

Wind that affects your kicking game, rain that makes the ball slippery and the ground heavy underfoot, or extreme energy sapping heat can all impact the decisions in a game. 'Playing conditions on the night will dictate,' explains Ireland's No. 10 **Johnny Sexton**. 'Often you'll have to kick when normally you'd run.'

4 TIME IN THE GAME OR POINTS ON THE BOARD

Is it the start of the half or are you trying to run down the clock? As a player you don't approach a match-winning kick differently to the first kick of the game, but decision making has to factor in the time left in the game and the scoreboard, 'If you are six points up with minutes left, what option you take is important,' says Johnny Sexton.

5 ANALYSE YOUR OPPONENTS

It's important to study the opposition ahead of the game and see if there are any clues to the type of defence they use or how they position their players on the field. This helps you read them in the game and call plays that exploit their flaws. 'You have to take into account the strengths and weaknesses of the opposition,' explains Alex King. 'Have they got big guys that are not very mobile in the midfield or are they fast and agile players? How quick is the line speed of the defence opposite are they rushing up or drifting in defence?'

6 COMMUNICATION

The best decisions are informed decisions so everyone on the team has to be alert and say what they see. 'If everyone is on the same page and you're getting feedback from your backline, it makes your job as a decision-maker a lot easier,' explains Alex King. 'There is an onus on the backline to scan; look up, see what's occurring and get information to 9 and 10.'

Fly half **Ruaridh Jackson** agrees that the outside backs are a massive influence on the 10 and his decision making, 'The centres and back three are the 10's eyes. The 10 has to look at the ruck, the spaces, listen to the centres, listen to the forwards and organise them. As fly half you've got a lot going on. Your outside backs can feed you information so you don't have to look.'

How do you prioritise these factors?

The list of factors can seem extensive, however, a player's experience of the game teaches them how to prioritise the decision-making process. Eventually experienced players, like fly half Johnny Sexton, get to a point where prioritising comes down to instinct in the moment, 'There are lots of factors so it's very difficult to pinpoint your exact decision-making process, so often you play what you feel.'

However, for young players learning the game, the amount of information they must process in a short space of time can be overwhelming. Alex King offers this advice, 'For a young player the three main considerations would be: the space available for attack, understanding your team and their strengths, and the quality of ball from the scrum and lineout.'

HOW TO IMPROVE YOUR DECISION MAKING IN ATTACK

'Playing conditioned games is the best way to learn/improve', advises Glasgow Warriors head coach **Gregor Townsend**. It's important that these games are relevant and reflect match situations to help 'young players to understand how to play against different types of defence and learn the tactics of the game', suggests Alex King.

There can be a temptation to use a move you have practised in training, but if the game scenario is different don't try to fit it in. Gregor Townsend reminds players to play what is in front of them and 'react to what a defence offers you during the play.' Alex King suggests teams 'use a move that has a few options so that you can adapt and take advantage of opportunities presented to you in attack.'

Video analysis can help you learn about opponents, learn about your own performance

> *Be a massive rugby fan [...] and then try to bring that knowledge into your own game.*
> **George FORD, England & Bath**

and it can also help you learn the game. 'Be a student of the game, watch as much rugby as possible, and educate yourself', advises Paul Burke. 'As a 10 I would watch the top teams and see how Dan Carter and Johnny Sexton manage a game.' Not only is it important to watch what world-class players do on the pitch and observe the decisions they come to, it's also important as an aspiring player to ask yourself *why* they make those decisions. This will help you grow as a player and improve your own decision-making skills.

England's No. 10 **George Ford** explains the benefits for players in his position, 'Watch as many games as you can and see how the fly half copes with conditions and decision making. Just be a massive rugby fan in terms of watching games because a fly half has to run the game, and then try to bring that knowledge into your own game.'

Getting better at making decisions is something that takes game time. With more than 16 years as a professional rugby player at fly half, **Andy Goode** speaks from experience when he says 'game management becomes slightly easier with age, but because the game is constantly evolving, there are always new ways of doing things.'

‣‣ Attack at set piece

Set piece offers great attacking opportunities for the team who wins the ball because there is ample space on the field to attack as a consequence of the grouping of the players participating in the set piece.

'The aim is to maximise possession', explains Blues coach **Nick White**. 'The team need a stable platform for the backs to exit their red zone or to be able to launch their back moves or attacking moves.'

The Sharks director of rugby **Gary Gold** suggests ways in which a team might achieve a solid platform that gives it the ability to strike on the front foot, 'You might choose to get your forward pack to drive and get you forward and

force the defensive line to retreat and then attack off that. Or you may want to win ball off the back of the lineout and deliver it off the top, which would allow your big physical backline to strike against the opposition.'

A team has to have balance so a good backline has to be matched by a strong forwards pack. 'It is great having backs that can finish off any launch ball that you create, but they cannot operate if they don't have something to launch off', explains Crusaders coach **Dave Hewett**.

↑ In poor weather conditions the set piece can be even more critical in helping a team gain momentum

Passes from the scrum at different positions on the field

DIAGRAM 1
Lineout on the
left-hand side

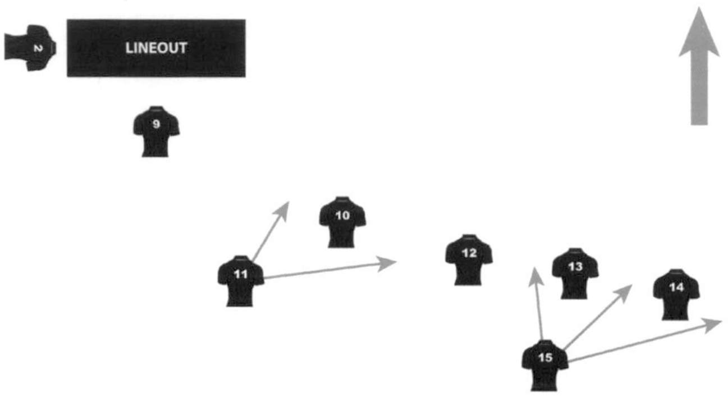

DIAGRAM 2
Scrum on the
right-hand side

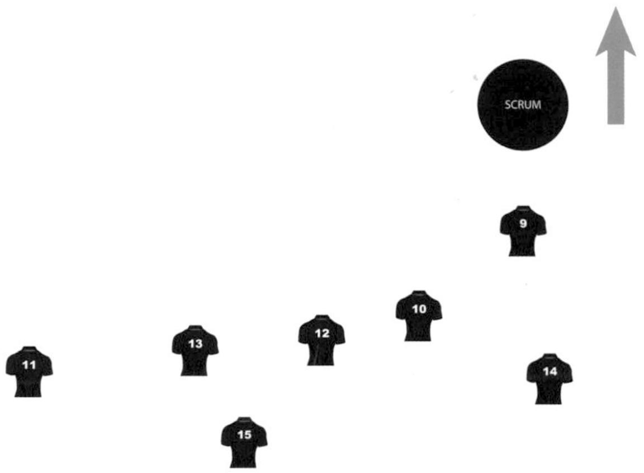

DIAGRAM 3
Midfield scrum

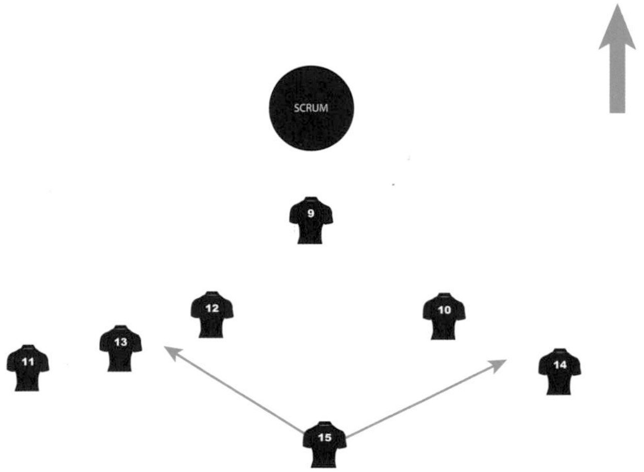

The forwards' role in attack

While ensuring possession of the ball from the set piece is the primary job of the majority of the forwards, the modern game dictates that all forwards must contribute to the overall attacking prowess of the team. The forwards' duties on attack include but are not limited to: winning the ball at the set piece, running with the ball, providing support to the ball carrier, clearing rucks and forming mauls. Ensuring the forwards have a clear understanding of their duties will maximise their individual and collective contribution to the team.

Nick White outlines the way he approaches each game, 'By having a very simple game plan, simple lineouts, simple structures the forwards can run off because if they are worrying about where they should be or where they should run they are never going to be able to express themselves. They need the head-space to dominate. Keep it simple so they can run with the ball, clean rucks and tackle. It'll give them confidence so they back your coaching and back what you are trying to do with them. They'll get a lot of confidence and trust not just with the coaching but also with each other. If all of them know their roles within the unit at the end of the day it's keeping things really simple so they don't overthink, they just go out and play.'

What do backs want from the set piece?

It depends on where the team is on the pitch. The backs may want the forwards to form a maul from the lineout to force the defence on to the back foot and to tie defenders into the maul and then launch an attack from a stable attacking platform. Alternatively, the backs may want quick ball off the top of the lineout because they think there is an attacking opportunity up the middle of the pitch or out wide off first phase.

From scrums the backs may want the forwards to wheel to a certain side so, if it's a far left-hand side scrum, it will be a tight-head wheel on the scrum to tie in the opposition back row to the scrum and allow the backs to attack to the openside. If it's a scrum on the right-hand side of the pitch, the backs will want a loose-head wheel for the same reason, so that the opposition back row will be further away from play. For a midfield scrum, the backs will want the forwards to drive straight, so they can attack from either side of the scrum. This is why the midfield scrum is the hardest set piece to read and defend against.

As a scrum half, South Africa's **Ruan Pienaar** wants his forwards to provide him with clean ball to provide service to his teammates, 'Good clean ball from the lineout and clean ball at the base of the scrum which puts the opposition under pressure and give the backs space to attack. We really need the forwards to fire and give you good front football.'

Former Leicester Tigers teammates **Manu Tuilagi** and **Horacio Agulla** add to the players' perspective, 'I love the set piece game, the scrum and lineouts,' says Tuilagi. 'As a back you get the opportunity to run the plays you've been doing all week. I prepare myself for the game so I know how many plays we've got, know my role and on which line I run.' Wing Horacio Agulla adds 'if the forwards put the ball on the front foot it makes our job much easier and we can play all day long.'

Finding space to attack

There is always space to attack and that is what the scrum half and fly half are constantly looking for. Are the wingers back covering the kick? If

❝ There is a very rigid structured game plan but at the same time I know I have freedom if I see something is on. That was some of the best advice I got from Joe Schmidt, [he told me to] play to the space wherever it is and he'd back me to go there.

'You've got space everywhere in a match. You've got to be able to look into the backfield, you've got to be able to look in front of you and try to spot the mismatches [faster attacking players against slower defenders]. Keep an eye on their forwards and where they are on the pitch. There's a lot to look at and process.

'The defence really tells you if you can run, kick or pass. If they play four up [out half, two centres, wing] there will be space in the backfield. If the full back is closing quickly [shallow in the defensive line] you might kick the ball in behind the 15. If the full back is not closing and the winger is hanging off a bit you might attack wide.

'Often you are attacking weak links as well. If their 10 is not a good defender you will attack him. If you target the 13 and he turns his hips inwards, you try to attack him.

'The opposition show you a picture and it's about trying to manipulate them as best you can and make them go the way you want them to go. ❞

Johnny SEXTON, Ireland & Leinster

they are, then the best option may be to run the ball and attack out wide. Is the full back in position? Is it a short man lineout? Decisions are made based on these types of cues and the coach's and team's playbook. That is the attacking approach New Zealand No. 10 **Beauden Barrett** describes with the All Blacks, 'The way we plan our strikes is to look for feedback. What is the opposition doing? Where are the holes?'

It is important to do your homework in advance so you can recognise your opponents' cues in the game. England's fly half **George Ford** analyses the opposition during the week to see what defensive systems they use to help him build an attacking strategy, 'For example, if they are in a blitz defence set-up, we have to use plays that involve short passes. It's important that all the players around you communicate what's in front of them on the field and decide what is the best play to use based on that information.'

While knowing your opponents' game ahead of a match is important, ultimately you look up and play what's in front of you. The term 'heads-up rugby' means players should be constantly scanning and looking for space. George Ford describes this approach as follows, 'You are checking what the backfield is like in defence to see if there is a corner you can put the ball into or to see if they have three in the backfield and you have to run the ball to the edge to try and manipulate space elsewhere. You are constantly looking for space, so keep looking up and making as many decisions as you can based on what's on in front of you.'

Argentina's fly half, **Felipe Contepomi**, reminds players that the element of surprise can be effective, 'If you're in your 22 and everyone is expecting you to kick, there might be an opportunity to run the ball because no one is expecting it. Having said this, your teammates must understand this and be alert, because if they don't you will not only surprise your opponents but your own players too.'

Attack from the maul

Any player can set up a maul, anywhere on the pitch, at any time. As long as there are two attackers and one defender on their feet it's a maul. However, it's usually constructed from a lineout and is a potent attacking option as it is very difficult to stop legally.

If a maul is going forward, the laws of the game dictate that the defence has to retreat to behind the hindmost foot. The maul has to go forward or else the ball has to be played, so defences have to retreat the whole time so the attack is on the front foot and the defence is on the back foot.

For coach **Ben Herring**, 'Successful mauls are about speed to position, togetherness and understanding how we are all working together, single bloody mindedness!' While **Joe Launchbury** sees it from the players' point of view, 'We try to set up a maul off attacking lineouts, if you get moving on the ball at the back it's an extremely powerful weapon so we use it a lot.'

ROLES AT THE MAUL
Each player has a specific responsibility at the maul. Blues coach Nick White takes us through the different roles, 'It's about the ball carrier or the jumper landing in a balanced and strong position and setting a good height for a maul. Then it's like a scrum: the lifters or the two guys at the front of the maul need to be strong and connected with their shoulders and their binds (the whole surface area of their arm) to the jumper so they can actually lay a platform for the guys coming in from behind to get into a good strong pushing position. They can then generate power straight through the maul.'

FORMATION OF THE MAUL

The front three are the jumper and the two lifters; these players are the foundations of a successful maul. They are the most important players as they give the maul its stability. England back row **Tom Wood** explains 'the pod of three have to get tight, low and strong as they are the foundations of the maul.' 'Two players should bind the lifters before the jumper is on the ground to apply stability to the jumping pod,' suggests Italy's second row **Marco Bortolami**.

A maul is about getting everyone in place binding tight and it's about body height. You want the maul to be long and narrow so the opposition don't have the opportunity to reach the ball or the ball carrier. Tom Wood describes the process, 'Keep the ball away from the opposition, keep the maul at least three men deep so no one reaching can lean over. The challenge is to stay low and in a strong position while the opposition are trying to get under you, pivot and spin you round and disrupt you as much as possible.'

'In attack you want to be in a low enough position,' stresses prop **Dan Cole**. 'If you are a lifter, you are bound on to the guy who is jumping with the ball so you want to get tight to him as soon as possible so there are no gaps for the opposition to get through and no one can get underneath you. Then it's about channelling the power from behind. If you are low to the ground, the harder it is for the opposition to get underneath you and stand you up.'

→ Scrum half Mike Blair gets his team moving forward with a pass from the ruck

BALL TRANSFER

When the maul is formed you want to move the ball back, both to protect it from the over-reaching hands of the opposition and to launch an attack. Normally the ball carrier goes in first and then you 'swim' the player back. Like an overarm stroke you put your hand on his shoulder and pull him back. He latches on to you and you take his place. Everyone goes over him, maintaining low body height. Tom Wood explains that you can opt to transfer the ball rather than disrupt the players, 'Some teams will choose to get someone on the ball initially, get in a good position at the heart of the maul and transfer the

ball back to somebody tagging on the back.'

If you do go with moving the player back to get the ball into position, Nick White offers a word of caution. Swimming someone back should not mean players do not push, 'If you have a guy sliding back through the maul with the ball, you still like him to push and have the other guys work themselves in front of him, rather than him pulling back. Instead of having guys not push and getting into a bad body position it's about putting emphasis on other guys working harder to get in front of him. You want your guys to work their way past him rather than have him slide back. If this doesn't happen, you can lose your connections and the maul can end up very weak and separating.'

The reason why the player moving – as opposed to the ball being passed back – is optimal is because there is less chance of the ball being dropped.

DIRECTING THE MAUL

Someone needs to be marshalling the maul, and for Toulon that is flanker **Steffon Armitage's** role, 'I'm the driver [ball carrier at the back], looking up to make sure everyone is onside and just waiting until the scrum halt says give me the ball. If not, I'm directing the maul where I want it to go.'

‣‣ Attack from phase play

The aim of the attacking team is to build momentum by getting over the gain line, while maintaining possession of the ball. This places pressure on the defence and forces them on to the back foot. The longer a team can continue to build phases and pressurise a defence the more likelihood the attacking team will find weaknesses in the defence to exploit.

'A lot of teams now have set calls for the first three phases and then you go into your general attack and that is where your instinct kicks in. It is very important to scan and see what is happening even before you get to the ruck so you can make the decision even before you get the ball into your hands', explains out Ruan Pienaar.

The key for successful attacking phase play is the attack's ability to commit multiple defenders to the breakdown while ensuring they get quick ruck ball. This means that the ball carrier must get over the gain line with his support players clearing out any defensive threats, while the ball carrier presents the ball cleanly for his scrum half to move it away from the breakdown quickly. The speed at which this is executed will determine the effectiveness of the attack.

Passing from the ruck

The scrum half is responsible for providing the pass from the breakdown [tackle area] to the out half or forward runner for each phase of play. He is dependent on the ball carrier to present the ball cleanly and the support player to clear out defenders accurately, so he can pass the ball away from the point of contact. These factors will influence the scrum half's ability to quickly pass the ball to the next ball receiver. The amount of pressure on the scrum half will also determine the quality and speed of his next pass.

There are a number of factors which go into selecting which pass to use when you are under opposition pressure like speed of ball, weather, distance to receiver, and bodies on the ground. Scotland scrum half **Mike Blair** describes how to adapt your technique to suit the different scenarios:

■ **Quick ball, on a plate, no legs in the way**
'Rear foot next to ball, leading foot pointing to target, low body position through the pass, sweep the ball from ground, hands to target, body through the line of pass.'
■ **Bodies in the way, no pressure**
'Rear foot next to ball, straddle bodies, leading foot to target, low body position, up and over pass to avoid bodies but maintain hands to target and body weight through the line of pass.'
■ **Bodies in the way, pressure coming through the ruck**
'If passing to the right – left leg beside ball, right leg stretched out behind you as far as possible. Move left leg back behind right leg while quickly bringing the ball into your left hip/thigh, right leg then comes out to the right, pointing towards your intended target, staying low all the time. Transfer weight with ball on left hip through to intended target with hands and momentum all going in that direction.'

HOW TO IMPROVE YOUR PASSING FROM THE RUCK
Distribution is a key part of the No. 9's role and passing from the ruck is a specialist skill that players have to work on.

England scrum half **Ben Youngs** focuses on where he puts his feet, 'I need my foot close to the ball before going into a split position and sinking down with my bum, then tilting over with my chest. Hands go around the ball, my weight transfers from my back leg all the way through the ball and my hand. I flick my wrist, which makes the ball spin, and finish with my hands pointing towards the target.'

Mike Blair advises young players try to test their skills by adding pressure in training, 'Too often you see 9s who have an incredible training ground pass but can't develop it into game play, as it has always been practised in unpressured, unrealistic situations. Make sure you have a blueprint of the technique that you want, then build it up through unpressured situations into game-like situations.'

Concentration plays a great role in consistent passing for France's No. 9 **Rory Kockott** so he advocates practising 'accuracy and not always quantity' if you want to improve.

Running lines

This refers to any or all players at any stage of attack. It could be first phase, predominantly centres and wings who run planned attacking moves with the aim of unlocking the defence through intricate or delayed running lines. It could also be forwards running off backs to get over the gain line. It's about timing, depth and spacing, which are all integral components of optimal running lines.

Centre **Jamie Roberts** believes it's all about body shapes and coming on to the ball late, 'I tend to run an out-to-in line, coming in late on those under lines, looking to attack the inside shoulder of a defender. A lot of teams use the drift defence so if you can step inside and on to their inside shoulder you can attack their

weakest spot.'

Reading body shapes and attacking the weak spots of defenders is something Roberts has done more as his career has developed, 'There are going to be times when you have to run straight at defenders and I am fortunate that my weight and size helps me win that battle more often than not. It is about creating weak body shapes in the opposition and that is where decoy runners in the backline become more important.'

The Welsh centre believes young players in his position should take pride in their decoy lines as much as their ball carrying, as both are parts of the job as a centre, 'If you can get one player in the opposition backline to check because of a decoy runner, that can create half a shoulder for the ball carrier to run at.'

Fellow centre Manu Tuilagi agrees that decoy lines are important, not only to draw in the defence but also to give his team more potential attacking options, 'The boys always laugh when I say "all options" because they just think I want the ball,' he says. 'I mean run as if you're going to get the ball every time. Know that if you are going to run as a decoy, you are still running as if you'll get the ball. "All options" is about giving the fly half options, not just one. Give him at least three options to make his job easier.'

Manu Tuilagi's former teammate at Leicester Tigers and now his coach **Geordan Murphy** believes that in order to create space you have to break the line at every available opportunity, 'Go for the line with deception. Have decoy runners who are running with a real purpose, who are not just decoy runners but are genuine options on the play. Maintaining space is probably similar to how you create space. Someone always has to run effective lines to create holes for other people and then after that everyone has to work off the ball.'

HOW TO DEVELOP WELL TIMED RUNNING LINES

Spatial awareness at training and learning where and when you are meant to be are all key to running successful running lines. 'Good centres have often played with other good centres,' explains All Black **Conrad Smith**. 'When I started I played with Tana Umaga and you can learn from guys like that. It also comes from watching rugby and giving yourself time to think why something has happened rather than looking at something and saying that's good, you've got to go a little bit deeper.'

For Manu Tuilagi, 'players definitely improve through practice at training and doing extras after training. Grab a teammate and say we'll go through that one again just to make sure.

'You do your work through the week, looking at the opposition defensive system as well as their individual defenders. Some players like to come up hard and shut down your space and others like to sit back and wait for you to attack. You look at all these little things through the week and prepare yourself.'

'There are times when you need to tread water and get the ball through your hands but, if you are really attacking the line, the timing of your run is important and the changing of angles of your running lines as well. You can't be predictable with your running lines and need to be able to change angle off both feet quite late,' explains Jamie Roberts.

'We talk about dominating the defender and getting past the defensive line,' explains the Welsh centre. 'That is far easier to do when you are coming from depth as opposed to being flat. If you are flat, you don't get any momentum and that makes you easy to defend against by coming off the line and winning that battle. You can be too deep at times but it is about finding that balance and that becomes easier with experience.'

For **Rene Ranger**, patience is also a useful asset, 'Your attacking running lines will depend a lot on the defence you are faced with. I would rather leave later then earlier. So, if you are running a strike move, you don't want to start running once the half back passes the ball. You want to delay your runs for as long as you can and ideally wait until the man inside you runs before you do. That is what I usually try to do.'

Improve decision making

Decision making is an all-encompassing term and is a requirement in every facet of the game. It is a very difficult skill to improve by any other means than understanding and realising the other options you had at your disposal, apart from the option you took. The best way to see all your options is by reviewing the play after training or the game. It is only with awareness of all the options that you will be able to learn which option may have been the best to take. This is why better decision making usually comes with experience. Having been in numerous situations where you had multiple options, and reviewing those options, enables you to learn and grow as a player. The best way to speed up this process is by closely analysing your decision making process with the use of video.

Ireland's **Gordon D'Arcy** believes that nothing beats repetition in improving decision making. Practise until it becomes instinctive, 'Picking up drills, doing drills and getting better at them. If you have to carry the ball give yourself 5 metres, then cut it down to 4, 3, 2 and then it becomes a split-second decision. That's what a game is, a split-second decision, you have a split second to make a decision and you have to make the right one.'

He explains how decisions can be impacted by doubts about your own abilities, 'In games you see lads just bottle it and not pass the ball. Then everyone looks at the video and goes "Ah, if you'd only passed that!" When the real reason he didn't pass it was he wasn't comfortable on the ball.'

Changing how you view decision making can help, as centre Rene Ranger experienced with the All Blacks, 'The coaches were looking at me as a 3/1 man, which meant that for every one good thing I did, I did three not-so-good things. They told me to switch that around, so that for every three good things I did, maybe I could get away with doing one not-so-good thing. That made me think a bit more about my decision making. When it's not on to pass, the best thing to do is just hold on to the ball, build pressure and help the team out.'

How to use space

There is space all around a defender. Trying to manipulate a defender into thinking you intend to run one way and then changing direction using footwork is a way of making the defender plant his feet, which allows the ball carrier to attack the space to the side of the defender and maintain forward momentum in the hope of breaking through the tackle.

Utilising the space around the defender does not necessarily mean that the ball carrier must beat the defender one-on-one. By forcing the defender to turn his hips towards the ball carrier, the player in possession of the ball can pass to a support player who runs a line at the space the defender previously occupied. Once a defender turns his hips towards the ball carrier, it is very difficult for him to change direction and make an effective tackle on a support player.

There are numerous ways to use space but it is very important to remember that you are trying to manipulate a defender by having him 'engage' [turn his hips towards you] on you as the ball carrier, which will open up space for your support player.

Head coach **Mark McCall** explains the thinking at Saracens, 'We try not to talk about space and depth, we talk about managing the distance between you and the defender so you can have an effect on that defender. First thing is to see the picture early and the only way to do that is not to focus on the ball but on the defensive line in front of you. After that, you put pace on or take pace off your run depending on the situation you are in. That allows you to vary your depth according to what's required.

'The most important thing is: are you having an effect on the individual defenders to get the outcome you want?

'The change in language is because "depth" isn't always the right thing to have because if you are too deep you might not have an effect on the defender in front of you. We talk about managing that distance to make sure you have that effect. It's about knowing when to put pace onto your run or take pace off your run, which New Zealand often do, to suck a defender towards you.'

For **Alex Magleby**, 'Deciding which space can be manufactured is important. It could be on the outside or the inside of the defender. If we are looking at the defender's eyes he is now thinking we are going to run at him or we could run around him. What is he going to do? The defender is now put into a moment of hesitation. What happens with the defender's hips? Are they now changing back to the inside to follow ball carrier's angle change? Now we have the defender where we want him – not knowing where we are going to go and he is held in the one channel.'

Contact on your terms

You are driving down the road in your beautiful Ferrari. Suddenly a tree appears in the middle of the road and a collision is inevitable. Do you drive straight at the trunk and destroy the car or do you do your best to minimise the damage and swerve, clipping some branches? As a ball carrier, it is not advisable to run straight into a defender, as that is where he is at his strongest. Instead, attack the space on either side of him with the aim of breaking a weak arm tackle.

Rugby is a contact sport but that does not mean you seek contact. Evading your opponent by attacking space or making contact on your terms are ways that players can retain possession, get over the gain line and build momentum for the team.

While you can't control how hard someone hits you, as the ball carrier you can control your actions in the lead up to contact and manipulate your body position to minimise the chances of a turnover.

Experienced centre Gordon D'Arcy makes an important point when he says 'people say rugby is a collision game but you know how to take contact'. As a No. 12 for Ireland and Leinster he has had his share of contact and he explains the process for young players, 'You feel someone coming, use your peripheral vision to see an opponent closing in on you. Your first priority is to look after the ball, next it's to get the ball away, then you let the man hit you, dust yourself off and get on with it. If you can get the ball in your hands, how you want it, you can control the contact as much as the guy hitting you.'

→ Ireland's Gordon D'Arcy attempts to 'run through traffic' against England

How to take contact on your terms

1 RUN AT THE SPACE AND NOT THE DEFENDER

If the ball carrier runs straight at an opponent they are likely to come off second best in the tackle, lose momentum and more than likely lose the ball. Players should run at the space around the defender, particularly at his inside shoulder. 'Having the right depth and width gives you more time,' advises Wales' Jamie Roberts. 'If you are too narrow and flat, there is really only one way you can run and that is very easy to defend. You ask any centre about defending and they will you that it is much harder to defend a ball carrier coming from depth because they can attack both your inside and outside shoulder and they gather far more momentum as well.'

It is a challenge to always find space, but as Sharks' **Gary Gold** points out, 'The field is 70 metres wide and there are 15 opposition players who have to fill that 70 metres. In a relatively congested area or even with slow ball there is space.' He believes players can think 'if contact is inevitable you will just concede and go to ground and that's not correct. Even in the most tight-knit situations there is a reasonable opportunity for you to fight incredibly hard and speed up the ball that extra little bit.'

He doesn't underestimate how hard that can be, 'It requires an incredible fight. That could mean you have to find the space between two defenders who are only a metre apart. If that is the case, it's about the body position and the height at which you go into the contact area and the dominant intent that you have to be able to exploit in that small space. That has to get you as far over the advantage line as possible while still being able to present the ball in the most optimal way.'

2 DON'T GET ISOLATED

Going too far forward in attack could mean getting isolated from your support players and being targeted by defenders looking to jackal the ball or create a maul. This is where communication is crucial. Support players need to let the ball carrier know where they are, if possible for an offload, or else to clear out the threat at the tackle area. If your support players tell you to go down, you should fight to get to ground and allow your support to clear out the contact area. Toulon's Steffon Armitage agrees, 'Once your support tells you to go down, you go down but until then you keep driving the legs'.

3 USE YOUR WEAPONS

As a ball carrier, you want to try to get the tackler off balance by squaring up their hips and planting their feet so they lose momentum. Then you want to attack their inside shoulder, ball transfer away from contact and use your weapons. If your footwork is good enough, you may not need to use your hand-off. Speed of footwork and changing angles is what makes a potent and dangerous attacker.

For New Zealand's Rene Ranger 'the first thing to do is to avoid contact. If I have to take contact, it's about looking after the ball and a leg drive. You have to keep moving, which makes

it hard for the defender'. While Mark McCall advises players to, 'Fight on your feet, using your weapons as that gives you the opportunity to keep the ball alive'.

Wing **Horacio Agulla** uses his lack of height to good effect in contact, 'The best thing for small guys like me is to get really low. You feel strongest in the upper part of your body so if you go low the tackler has to go higher on your body'. Back row Steffon Armitage has similar advice as he describes how he builds momentum as a ball carrier going into contact, 'Once I see the 9 has picked the ball up, my hands are up and I'm calling for it. I want to get as low as I can because I know it will be hard for anyone to get lower than me. My job is get lower than them and go forward, if I go high, I'm just going to get bumped back. That's the last thing you want, you want to build momentum and keep going forward'.

His advice to young players is to get a 'good ball position, ball in two hands, get it really tight so no one can rip it out and then get your legs driving'.

▶▶ Support in attack

The most important thing is to maintain possession for the team at the contact area. If there is an offload possible, then momentum continues. If it becomes a ruck situation, the attacking team wants to commit as few players as possible to secure position as this allows more players to be involved in the next phase of attack. Conversely, it is vital that the attacking team commits enough players to the ruck to ensure possession is won. It is better to commit too many attackers as opposed to too few and risk losing possession.

You have to quickly analyse the ruck situation and decide if you are needed in the ruck or not. There is one simple rule for both attackers and defenders:

IF THE BALL IS WON OR LOST – DO NOT GO INTO THE RUCK

As a support player, you will be more useful somewhere else for your team and in attack that means getting yourself into position for the next phase within the team's attacking system.

Role of the support player

The support player has multiple roles based on the actions of the ball carrier. While the support player can try to predict what the ball carrier intends to do, he will ultimately have to react to the ball carrier's actions. If the ball carrier can pass the ball, the support player must be vocal in his support and get close enough to the ball carrier to allow for an offload. The support player should be aware of any threats in front of the ball carrier as well as the threats in front of him and in the backfield. Ideally, the ball carrier changes his angle of running based on what is in front of him as this is likely to provide him with a passing option to continue the forward momentum of the attack.

1 SCAN FOR OPTIONS

Support players should be constantly scanning for options. Mark McCall lists a few ways in which a support player being alert helps the ball carrier, 'If it's obvious the ball carrier is going into a contact that he can't control, you have to read that situation and be effective at the breakdown. Get there early and affect it early. If there is an opportunity to keep the ball alive, you've got to work your way into position to maximise that offload opportunity.'

2 BE VOCAL
Communication is especially important in a support role. You need to keep your teammates informed of where you are and what you see. 'You need to be a loud voice for the ball carrier. If he needs to keep fighting – tell him; if he needs to go to deck for a quick clean – tell him; if he needs to find you in support – tell him; advises coach Ben Herring.

3 KEEP YOUR DISTANCE
As a support player it's your job to give the ball carrier options, so don't get caught up in the action and lose your position. Mark McCall reminds players to 'always ensure you have the appropriate depth or width to be an option.'

Irish flanker **Sean O'Brien** shares his thought process in support, 'If it's tight, I'll look to target someone straight away and if it's open play and he looks to make a line break I'm looking for space ahead of me. I'm not looking to run towards him, I'm going to read off him and make my decision based on what he does. I'm looking at where the space is ahead of me and trying to pre-empt where the ball carrier might go.

'If it's close I'm either trying to get a latch on or I'm trying to attack anybody who could potentially be a tackler or somebody at the ruck.'

Support at the ruck

If the ball carrier is tackled, the support player must ensure he is close enough to the ball carrier to clear out any defensive threats before the tackler or a defender can contest for the ball and possibly turn it over. It is the support player's job to be very accurate in his clearing out at the ruck and neutralise any threats to the ball.

The support player must target the threats to the ball by coming through the gate of the ruck, getting over the ball with a low body profile, hips down and eyes up and clear out any defenders past the ruck.

England forwards coach **Graham Rowntree** explains that 'forwards approaching the ruck should be thinking where's the ball? Where's the threat? The ball is the threat.'

He talks through what he looks for from his players at the ruck, 'I see a lot guys run to a breakdown, see a body from the opposition and just clear them out of the way and leave the ball exposed. I want my guys as they arrive to clear the ball. If there is no one around they might be okay to park themselves over it, not to slow it down but to protect it for the 9. If that ball is available, I might want my guys to bounce out to the side of the ruck to be in motion for the next breakdown. Or, if he's late arriving, he can pull out and be a carrier.'

Speed is a major factor for coach Ben Herring, 'Arriving fast can drastically change the options the opposition are likely to see; it will also give you fast ball. Success for the support player should always be "quick ball" and all decisions and consequential actions should have that in mind.'

Alex Magleby explains his thinking in the following scenario, 'I have possession of the ball; I decide to pass to you because that is where the space is. You are in a better position than I was. Now I'm the support player. What do I do to help continue our forward progression? It doesn't matter what the system is, the best position typically is between 3 and 5 metres behind the ball carrier so we have all options available. We now have every option – pass left or right or else drive over his hips if he is tackled.'

How to present the ball

The ball carrier wants to present the ball as far from the tackle as possible, and in a manner that allows the support players to get over it, clear the threats from the ruck and allow the 9 to get the ball away quickly. The quicker this can be done, the less time the opposition defence has to get organised and the more attacking opportunities there will be.

The ideal position is the 'long body' ball placement position, as it creates a narrow gate and keeps the ball the maximum distance from opponents:

- Body parallel to the touchline
- Feet toward tryline, arms at full stretch towards your defending tryline
- Ensure head tucked down for safety
- Keep hands on ball until 9 moves it from the contact area

↓ The aim of the player on the ground is to get the ball as far from the opposition as possible

'Usually the defensive threat will come from the same side as you have received the pass', explains Sharks' Gary Gold. 'If you work hard to present the ball away from where you received it, which is also where the defensive traffic is coming from, you put your body between yourself and the defender. It gives your support an opportunity to win the race to get over you, to bridge, to clean, whatever he has to do and for you to be able to present your ball "on a platter" for your 9 to get it away.'

Presentation will depend on how you take contact, but the aim is to reach back as far as you can towards your own teammates. This is known as 'fighting on the ground' or 'fighting on the floor'. Mark McCall explains that this 'allows you to control space between you and the defender and present the ball in a manner which keeps your team on the front foot.'

'The ball is the ball carrier's responsibility', says Ben Herring. 'Your job is not finished until the ball is smoothly back in the 9s hands. Consistent factors are strength and speed of ball presentation. It's the ball carrier's responsibility to look after ball and the cleaner's job to remove threats. Quick ball is the desired outcome.'

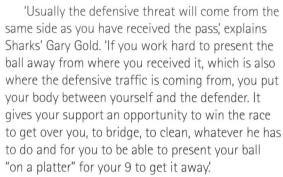

Back row Sean O'Brien shares his thought process as he goes to ground, 'If I've been tackled, I'm [already] thinking of fighting with the ball. When I'm in a vulnerable position where I'm going to be choked up or held up, I try to fight and pull back as best I can. When you hit the ground you should be fighting on the ground the whole way to the finish and thinking of keeping both hands on the ball.'

Gary Gold recommends that young players looking to improve this skill 'do work on the floor on your dynamic ability to snap your body to be able to get the ball away from where the ensuing threat is coming from.'

Clearing the ruck

All the players on the team must be capable of clearing out a ruck and ensuring their team maintain possession of the ball. The term 'one bullet, one kill' refers to the accuracy of clearing out a ruck. If there is a defensive threat, the player clearing out the ruck must be accurate and neutralise the defensive threat. It is vital to 'attack' the ruck with low body height, as the player in the lower position will usually win the physical encounter. The support player who is clearing out the ruck should have his hips low, his eyes up to see the target and make sure his shoulders are lower than the opposing player. Never have your head or shoulders lower then your hips, as you will be in an ineffective clearing position. That is why it is important to ensure your hips are low. Emulate an airplane taking off and remember to keep your eyes up. If you look down, you are going down.

Tight-head prop **Marcos Ayerza** explains why, for his position, attitude is a major part of the ruck, 'Clearing rucks is a very important aspect of mainly the tight five who set the tone and give the personality of the team. The prop has to be efficient and have that breakdown intelligence, but has to show his character, his personality and nastiness in the ruck.'

'Body position is vital and you have to make your decision really early,' advises flanker Sean O'Brien. 'If you think about it, it's too late and you won't get into an effective position. Make your decision and back yourself. Body height should be low, shoulders down, head up, wrap someone. Don't just bounce off an opponent, you are looking to take someone to ground and make sure he stays there.'

›› Kicking for territory

Kicking is a tactical decision because it usually means you are going to risk giving up possession of the ball. You are hoping either to put the ball into touch and allow your team to reorganise and compete at the lineout, or else you are trying to reclaim possession from the kick. It will depend on what type of kick you use. For Northampton Saints coach Alex King, kicking is a crucial part of getting momentum, 'A player's kicking game is vital, whether that's kicking to touch from penalties or out of hand in general play (both feet). With defences so organised in the modern game good attacking kicking is hugely important. If you are a young player with an attacking mindset looking to attack space, kicking is one of those areas in which you can get real success.'

Decision making when kicking

Kicking can also be used to relieve pressure, gain territory, turn a defence, or for a wide man to attack in the air. When deciding which option to go with, a kicker will ask a number of questions.

Irish fly half and kicker **Ian Madigan** talks us through a few points he suggests young players should consider:

WHAT ARE YOUR TEAM'S STRENGTHS?

If you want to build momentum and confidence it's always important to choose plays that your team has the ability to complete. 'If you have wingers or full backs who are very good at jumping in the air or very good catchers that are particularly tall, you have a strategy to kick the

ball contestable so that their player and your player are competing for it in the air'.

WHAT ARE YOUR OPPONENT'S STRENGTHS?

You never want to make the other team's job easier so avoid options where you feel the opponent has the advantage or where your team is under-performing. 'If the other team are particularly strong in the air, you wouldn't go for a strategy like that, you might decide to kick long but if the team has a good counter-attack you wouldn't because they are very likely to run it back. Similarly, if we have a strong lineout, you'd be inclined to kick off the field, but if the lineout is struggling, you be more inclined to keep the ball on the field'.

WHAT IS THE SCORE? HOW LONG IS LEFT IN THE GAME?

The most obvious factors to consider are the clock and the scoreboard. This will often make decision making obvious, 'If you are ahead as a team you might want to kick the ball off the pitch because it will wind down the clock and pin them back in their half. If you are chasing the game, you'd be more likely to kick the ball so it's contestable right away'.

Kicking options

■ Kick to touch

Executed inside the attacking team's own 22-metre line, kicks to touch are used to relieve pressure and gain distance from your defending tryline. You want to kick as far as possible while

→ Rob Kearney practices his kicking, a skill he has used to good effect for Leinster, Ireland and the British & Irish Lions

ensuring the ball goes into touch to buy your team some time to reorganise, take a breather and compete at the lineout to reclaim possession again.

To help explain kicks to touch, experienced fly half **Andy Goode** compares it to a situation in American football, 'If a team is on their fourth down and deep inside their own half, they need to tactically kick the ball away and more than likely turn over possession. That is just the same for us in rugby if we are deep inside our own 22 and need to kick the ball away to relieve the pressure.'

■ Box kick

The box kick is used outside your 22 because you can't kick the ball directly into touch. It is a high kick by the 9 at a ruck or a maul with a strong chase, usually by a wing or centres, to try to regain possession. You want as much hang time/air time as possible to allow your players to get a good chase under the ball and compete when it comes down. France's **Rory Kockott** suggests using it 'when you want to transfer pressure on the other team and preferably not inside your own 40-metre line.'

'It's important to take your time to get set and get a good base,' explains No. 9 **Ruan Pienaar**. 'I normally put my right foot out and work backwards with my left foot and then get into a good position to execute the box kick.' The Springboks scrum half advises players that 'the drop of the ball is very important as well as the follow-through, making sure you are not stabbing at the ball but kicking through the target. If you are kicking from the ground, you will have less time, so it is key to get your blockers in place.'

■ Up and under, 'Garryowen'

This is similar to a box kick but executed by a No. 10 or back three. Put as much pressure as possible on the catcher with a very strong kick chase to try to regain possession.

accenture   ☼ RBS NATIONS

Less Is More For Ireland's Kickers

● Ireland   ● England

35m
Avg Distance of Kick

48m
Avg Distance of Kick

Ireland's tactical kicking was shorter than England's, meaning that the ball was contestable more often. As a result Ireland regained 6 kicks, and turned England over on another 13 occasions.

0 Turnovers Conceded
From Kick Returns

13

High performance. Delivered.

#seebeyond

Full-Time
Ireland **19 – 9** England

■ Chip and chase

If you are facing a very aggressive blitz defence, you want to just chip the ball over them. The defence is running very hard forward so the kicker wants to turn the defenders while his players are still going forward. It's a tactic to quell the aggressive defensive blitz line; if you do it a couple of times the defence has to just check a little bit so usually it lands just behind the defensive line but well in front of the full back where there is usually space. The No. 9 for the defence should cover that area but, if he isn't there, there can be room to put in a little chip and chase with the objective of winning possession, turning the defence or at least slowing them down.

'When you put a high ball up it's a case of reading the backfield', advises USA full back **Chris Wyles**, 'If you aren't able to find space (grass) in the backfield, then try to turn it into a 50/50 competition with the ultimate aim of regaining the ball. Kicking into the backfield you're typically trying to find grass and roll it into touch or put the opposing team under more stress.'

↓ Ben Youngs practicing his kicking with England's Attacking Skills Coach Mike Catt

■ Grubber kick

Back three and centres use this one but it's a bit of a gamble. In rugby we say never let the ball bounce, because of its shape you never know which way it is going to bounce. Even when you try to predict it you can be very wrong. A grubber can turn a defence. At best you can try to get the ball to roll end over end and reclaim possession by running on to it. Usually on the third bounce the ball will bounce up and hopefully into the arms of a player who doesn't have to slow his pace so he can open up the backfield play. Scotland's No. 10 **Ruaridh Jackson** suggests 'a little grubber kick is quite

tricky for the full back to pick up so he might spill it. That gives your chasers a chance to get up there in twos and threes and put pressure on him.'

■ Crossfield kick

Usually used in the green zone (22 metres from the try-line you are attacking), the 10 puts up a high crossfield kick with the idea of putting pressure on the opposite winger from your guys coming in to compete for the ball near the tryline. It really stretches the defence and the aim is to score a try from it.

The mechanics of the kick

As with any skill it's important to understand the basics of good technique. Coach **Dr Dave Alred** teaches some of the best players in rugby and he shares his advice for how to deliver the two styles of kick, the drop punt and the spiral.

'A drop punt encourages you to hit the ball in a straight line and to hit the ball with the right part of the foot. So it's the top of the laces, top of your foot, driving into the bottom third of the ball. You want to get backspin and, as in the goal kick, you want to get down on the kicking foot so it's the pillar shift that does the work and not the leg.

'Hold the ball upright, if you are a right footed kicker have your right hand on the bottom third of the right side because you want to control the impact position so you want your hand close to the bit of the ball you are going to kick. It just helps to close that circle tighter so when you are under pressure you'll know exactly where the right part of the ball is to kick. The other hand is a guide hand. Make sure you align it so the middle of the ball drops virtually in line with your kneecap as you look down at your leg.

Then it's hit and go through. Point your toe so much your foot gets hard, think that you are going to punch the ball with your foot. You don't need a back swing or follow-through but you do need to follow along the line of the ball and that encourages you to use the pillar rather than just quit.

↓ Andy Goode practices the drop punt technique in training

'The spiral is exactly the same kick as the drop punt but you hold the ball in the middle, your right hand underneath the ball and the ball lying flat. If you are looking at a clock face the point of the ball is pointing to 11 and your chest is ever so slightly pointing to 1 o'clock. You just run through the kick, punching the fat part of the ball and if those angles are right the

↓ Johnny Sexton mastering his spiral kick technique while with the British and Irish Lions

For a drop punt the ball must be dropped vertically and kicked after it has hit the ground.

For a spiral kick the ball is dropped parallel to the ground.

Kicking

AS A FORMER FULL BACK FOR IRELAND, coach Geordan Murphy believes kicking is an area that can be improved a lot, especially for young players fresh to the game, 'In terms of the execution of the kick, the grubber kick is probably the easiest to master – just dropping the ball on to your foot and grubbing it on the ground – though it's a difficult skill to do at pace and on the move. Try to isolate each kick – the chip kick, grubber kick, the long-range kick that is going to bounce once into touch or just the out-and-out punt for territory. Work on all of them.'

Conor O'Shea also wore the No. 15 shirt for Ireland but now, as Harlequins director of rugby, has a more unusual suggestion for helping young players to improve kicking from their weaker foot, 'If you are practising your kicking, why not have a game where you can only kick with your wrong foot? You did that for weeks on end a player would develop and you should do that when you are younger.'

ball will find its nose and spiral.'

Dr Alred explains the benefits a player like Ireland's Johnny Sexton gets when he does a spiral kick properly, 'People think they have to kick across the ball to get a spiral and that's where they lose so much power and that's why a lot of people have given up spiral kicking because they can't do it. Really that is why **Johnny Sexton** is standing head and shoulders above the others when it comes to the length he gets, but he works long and hard on drop punts, then spirals then back to drop punts to make sure that his line is right through the ball.'

HOW TO IMPROVE YOUR KICKING SKILLS

Target drills are a very good way of measuring your kicking skills, suggests coach Paul Burke, 'By mapping out various squares on the field you can vary each type of kick depending on where you are on the field.'

As with passing from both hands, kicking with both feet is an important skill to develop. Working on weaknesses should always be a focus for a player looking to improve and it's something you can do at any stage of your career, as fly half Johnny Sexton explains from his own recent experience, 'I've started to do a lot of work on my left foot in the last four or five years. It was Dave Alred who made me believe I could take it up at a later age. I'd never really practised on my wrong foot when I was younger, I was too obsessed with getting good with my good foot and perfecting that.'

SCORING

↑ Of the 50 tries in the 2014 Rugby Championship, 35 were scored by backs and 14 by forwards with one penalty try awarded. 16 of the 50 tries were scored by wings, with back rows the second highest contributors with 13.
Super Rugby and Opta Sports

The aim of rugby is to score more points than the opposition. Points can be scored through tries, conversions, penalty kicks and dropped goals. The more points a team can score, the more likely they are to win the game. To score points, a team needs possession of the ball. To ensure possession of the ball, every player within the team, must perform their duties and roles to the utmost of their ability. **Eddie Jones** outlines how each position contributes towards a team scoring, 'The front five must work out the opposition 9 and dent the gain line. The back row must support the ball carriers and execute their running roles. The 9 and 10 must create space for the centres, who must run straight and preserve space for the back three to score tries.'

Alex Magleby reminds players that scoring is a team effort, 'Everybody has a job. If the wing scores, it means 14 other people have done their jobs correctly.'

✛ Tries

A try is scored when the ball is grounded [touched down] on the tryline, against the base of the goalposts, or anywhere in the in-goal area. A try is worth five points. The referee will not award a try if any part of the ball or the player is in touch when the ball is grounded. The player must be in control of the ball and apply downward pressure on it for a try to be scored.

✛ Conversions & penalties

Teams can attempt a kick at goal [kick the ball over the crossbar and between the posts] after a try has been scored. This is known as a conversion and is worth two points. If a team is awarded a penalty, they can elect to kick at goal. If they score the penalty kick, this is worth three points. Attempted kicks at goal are one of the few times in rugby that all responsibility rests on a single player, so the pressure is on the team's designated kicker to score the kick and keep the scoreboard ticking over.

Johnny Sexton enjoys the pressure, 'As much as there is pressure and you'd feel your life would be a lot easier without goal kicking, it's something that I've done forever and I don't think I could go without doing it.'

Goal kicking

Conversions and penalties are usually kicked from a kicking tee. The kick is taken on a direct line from where the ball was grounded for the try or on the spot where the penalty infringement occurred.

Kickers have a routine they go through ahead of each kick. This starts with the placement of the ball on the tee and ends after the ball has been kicked. This process is something that kickers develop and refine over time through practice. Experienced kickers reach a point where they know as soon as the ball has left their foot if it's a good kick or not. Every kick counts in a game, so it has to count in practice too if you are to become proficient in this skill as **Andy Goode** explains, 'There is not much point in placing the ball on the tee at training and just booting it over without thought. That's how bad habits creep in.'

The detail of a kicking routine differs from player to player but the fundamental elements are the same:

PLACING THE BALL

The placement of the ball determines the part of the ball the foot comes into contact with but it can also impact on how the player gets their alignment for the kick, as Ireland's **Ian Madigan** describes, 'I line up the seam of the ball with the posts where I want the ball to go then I get my alignment from the ball, not the posts. That makes the routine I have very simple because every kick is a straight kick for me. I always come into the ball at a 45-degree angle, which is the most natural position for your leg to swing through on a pendulum.'

The size of the kicking tee can affect your technique. **Dr Dave Alred** explains that for a young player a high tee encourages an impact position beyond your centre of gravity, so your body position is wrong at point of contact, 'Initially it might work but if you really want to hit the ball hard it encourages you to lean back and over recruit.'

WALKING BACK TO START YOUR RUN UP

Consistency is everything when it comes to developing a kicking routine. If you vary the position from which you start your run up, it can affect where you are when you make contact with the ball. A hurdler has a set number of strides between hurdles so they can optimise their speed and technique. If this changes, they usually hit a hurdle. It is the same for a goal kicker in rugby. If you change your stride pattern in the run up, it can affect the outcome of the kick.

Johnny Sexton outlines his walk back, 'In terms of routine you need to do the same thing every time – how many steps you go back, how many steps to the side – because that puts you in the same position you've been in when you've been practising all week. That way if you do what you are meant to do the ball will go over when the pressure comes on.'

Stepping back and to the side is one way to find your spot but your relationship to the ball is also critical. In his routine, Ireland's Ian Madigan uses angles to find his starting position, 'If the ball to the posts is 180 degrees, I want to come in at 45 degrees. If the ball is placed on the 22, 15 metres in from the left-hand-side, my alignment would be to run across the field touchline to touchline. On the right-hand-side, I would be running up the field, tryline to tryline, because I am a right-footed kicker.'

PREPARING TO KICK

A kicker prepares to take the kick by focusing on where they want the ball to go between the posts. While some players imagine a line running from the ball to a point between the posts, Dr Dave Alred describes a visualisation process that you can go through as you prepare to kick, 'You take a photograph of the target in your mind and turn back to the ball and concentrate on the exact impact position. While still looking at the impact position you let your mind move towards the target but you don't take your eyes off the ball. Your awareness goes back to the target. What you have drawn is a mental channel to the target. The phrase I use is that the target should be in your mind's eye once you have fixed it and then you are back looking at the ball.'

There is a 90-second time limit on the placement to contact process but not every kicker needs the full minute and a half to go through their routine. Ian Madigan is one of the quickest players to go through his routine and that's all down to how he trains, 'I go through the routine quicker than other kickers because at practice I go through kicks quickly. I do a lot of practice and obviously I don't want to be on my feet too long so I probably take two or three kicks in the time it takes other kickers to practise one kick. In matches I do slow the process down, but I feel comfortable kicking within 30 seconds.'

Concentration in your kicking process is an important part of kicking accurately, so ensure you are fully focused on the task. 'Clear the mind of any thoughts other than head down, follow through,' advises **Gregor Townsend**.

MAKING CONTACT WITH THE BALL

As the kicker commences his kick process, his body position as he makes contact with the ball is critical. It's important that you focus on where your plant foot is in relation to the ball, and where your chest is over your plant foot if you want to kick accurately and consistently.

Ruaridh Jackson explains why it's important to be light on your planting leg so you don't get stuck on the ball, 'Your kicking leg goes right through to the target, your planting foot should just lift off the floor easily and you should be able to move forward right away. If you come in too hard and plant your foot, you'll get stuck on the ball and that's when you lose power and accuracy'.

For **Mick Byrne**, a player's chest needs to be over the plant foot to make a good kick, 'That powerful position should be maintained through that step into contact, plant at contact, and step after contact. Bring that chest into a strong position over the feet'.

Dr Dave Alred highlights how poor technique can lead to persistent injury problems. To avoid this he stresses that young players should pay particular attention to their body position at point of contact, 'It's absolutely crucial that very young kids kicking size three or size four balls learn to kick with their bodies. Their leg should be an afterthought. If they mimic somebody they have seen and try to copy their technique they won't be strong enough and this is where a lot of injury problems actually start. This leads to all sorts of strain and will eventually lead to recurring injury down the track'.

HOW TO IMPROVE YOUR GOAL KICKING

Creating pressure in training helps a player prepare for the game. England fly half **George Ford** advocates reducing the number of practice kicks at goal in training, 'For example, take 12 kicks but concentrate on nailing each one of them, rather than taking 30 kicks and not really concentrating on every kick'.

↓ Ian Madigan lines up a kick while on Ireland duty

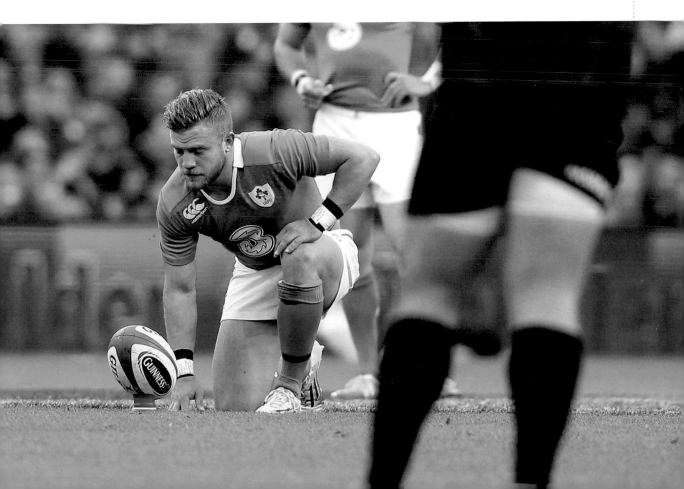

Northampton Saints coach **Alex King** promotes kicking at goal when you are fatigued, to replicate game-like situations, 'Put yourself under pressure in training by taking kicks when you've worked hard so your heart rate is up. Try to replicate that sensation where you are tired and you have to switch on to 'goal kicking mode', so come Saturday you are prepared to deal with that situation and you have trained for it.'

HOW TO ALLOW FOR WINDY CONDITIONS

Weather conditions play a big part in kicking at goal but players often overcompensate for the wind, as Dr Dave Alred explains, 'it is only when a ball decelerates that the wind can affect its flight.' Dr Alred compares goal kicking in windy conditions to 'putting a golf ball which goes straight initially but takes the borrow of the green when it slows down.'

When kickers miss kicks in the wind, they usually think they have to adjust their target, 'Kickers get it in their heads that the ball bends from the tee in windy conditions. Players think they need to kick it outside the right post with a right-to-left wind. If they hit it well it stays out there because it goes straight.'

↓ Fly half George Ford takes on the kicking duties for England

Dr Alred advises finding out your 'straight kick length' (length at which the ball is still accelerating) and use that as a guide as to when to adjust for the wind, 'If you are 20 yards from the post and kicking into a crosswind and you are a powerful kicker with a 30-yard straight kick, you aim for the middle of the middle because the wind won't affect it until its 10 yards beyond the posts. As long as you hit the right part of the ball you should be able to "drive a line."'

HOW TO FOCUS MENTALLY FOR A KICK

Kicking for points can be stressful. The clock, crowd, scoreboard and weather conditions all add to the pressure on a single player. How do the professionals tune out these pressures and focus on the task in hand? Johnny Sexton explains, 'sometimes when you kick really well you don't know where you've gone mentally because you are fully concentrating on the routine and process. Times when you are not kicking so well you are thinking about stuff you shouldn't be thinking about. I find myself lining up a kick and falling into the trap of thinking about what I'm going to do after the kick, where I'm going to put my next territorial kick. It's just about staying in the moment, but it's easier said than done.'

HOW TO APPROACH A MATCH-WINNING KICK

Kicking to win a match or a championship in the last play of the game can be extremely stressful. It is very important that kickers approach every kick in the same way, regardless of the situation. Ireland's Johnny Sexton explains that it's about focusing on your process, 'I feel every kick has the same amount of pressure, as it is going to have an impact on the scoreline. Even your first kick is a pressure kick because you've been building up to it all week and you are the most nervous before that kick.'

While this may sound simple, even the top players can lose their focus in a game, but that's part of the job description for Sexton, 'I've had easy kicks which I've taken for granted and you think about what you'll do at the kick-off and you miss it. That's just part and parcel of being a kicker. England's Jonny Wilkinson is the best there ever was in terms of kicking and we've seen him miss a few sitters but he is still the best. Kicking can be a fickle enough thing.'

Try not to focus on what might happen, focus on the process of the kick and doing your job. For a kicker that is kicking the ball between the posts and scoring points for your team. Mick Byrne

For kicking in stadiums with 70–80,000 fans the technique I use is to imagine that I'm back where I practised as a kid, my hometown of Gorseinon. I put myself there, where it's quiet and there's no one around; it's just me, the ball and a set of posts. I'm imagining a third post going in the middle of the posts, that's where I'm going to aim to hit. The ball is attached to a piece of string that goes right up to the third post.

'You want your plant foot, your left foot, right up alongside the ball, you don't want it too far back because your body turns in and rotates. Go with feet a shoulder width apart, left shoulder tight over your left leg.

'Once you make contact you take your weight right through the ball so you finish beyond the kicking tee, shoulders facing the posts. You are always keeping your head down. Not trying to get your head up too early.'

Leigh HALFPENNY, Wales & Toulon. Ambassador for Lucozade Sport.

emphasises this, 'A young player who has to kick the goal to win the game shouldn't be thinking, "if I kick this goal, I'm going to win the game" or "if I miss this goal, I'm the worst guy on this team". He should go back to his normal process and take his steps back, look at the bottom of the ball, focus on the line he's kicking, find his target, kick the ball - and when it goes through they win the game.'

It is important not to alter your technique for a pressure kick. Andy Goode stresses the importance of consistently preparing mentally for a kick for a successful outcome, 'Kickers need the same mental preparation during a kick no matter if it is the easiest kick in the world or a difficult last-minute potential game-winning kick. If you are consistent in what you do there is less margin of error.'

Kicking

ALL BLACKS SKILLS COACH MICK BYRNE and Dr Dave Alred, kicking coach for Jonny Wilkinson and Johnny Sexton among others, share their methods for developing a kicker's technique, improving their ability to handle pressure and remain focused, as well as getting the most from practice.

1 STAND OVER THE KICK AND NO STEPS

Mick Byrne starts with a simple practice drill that helps a player improve their body position when kicking. This exercise helps to build positive habits when kicking from the tee, 'Stand and get into the kicking position so your heel is back and towards your backside ready to kick, get your chest in that strong position over your plant foot and then learn to kick through the ball while keeping your chest stable in the same spot.

'What we are trying to do is get the player to kick the ball while their upper body remains stable rather than trying to generate the power in the backswing. They have to maintain balance and then after the kick they have to be able to come back to the starting position without the kick having rocked them off their plant foot.

'It helps create a habit of having your chest over your foot, but it also helps the body feel comfortable generating power in that position rather than swinging the upper body. It's similar to a golf swing when you look at a player who doesn't play a lot of golf. When he sets the ball down on to the tee, he swings a club and finishes on his back foot. When you watch a pro golfer he finishes on his front foot. That is how we want our kickers to be able to transfer their weight through the kick so they need to feel comfortable with their chest over their feet when they kick the ball.

'They are in a boxer's stance so their chest is over their plant foot with a slight bend forward and they stay in that position right through the kick. After the kick they follow through and bring their foot back. Their left foot should never leave the ground. If they can do 10 or 12 of those every day before they practise their goal kicking, they'll develop a good habit of being strong over the ball.'

HOW TO DEAL WITH A MISSED KICK

Things can and do go wrong. For kickers having a bad day means there really is nowhere to hide. You build confidence through your practice and routine, but how do you put a missed kick behind you in a game? It is vitally important that kickers wipe a poor kick from memory and move on to the next task at hand. Do not dwell on the past. Trust your routine and go through your kicking process when the next goal kicking opportunity arises. England's No. 10 **George Ford** shares his advice, 'Remember you don't become a bad kicker overnight, so when you miss a kick it's about making that next kick. During the game I also concentrate on the next play and making that as good as can be'. Ireland's Johnny Sexton takes the same approach, 'Different times in your career you miss for different reasons. You just go back into your routine, it's tried and trusted and you've worked on it all week.'

2 THE SEA OF SUCCESS

There's nothing like seeing the ball going over the posts to boost a player's confidence. Dave Alred outlines a way to help goal kickers become accustomed to success, 'I put a line of five balls 15 yards in front of the posts, with the third ball directly aimed at the middle of the crossbar. Then I move back 3 yards and place another line of five balls in front of the posts, but space each ball slightly wider than the previous line of balls. I add another three lines of five balls, each with progressively wider spaces between each ball.

'There are a total of 25 balls (five lines of five balls), and what you have to do is kick 25 out of 25. The last line of balls is on the 22-metre line, so they are all very easy kicks. What you try to do is get the kicker to target the middle of the middle between the posts each time.

'You are working within the "sea of success" because you have to kick pretty badly to miss one. If the player does miss it, it will only be a mental error. It will only be because you haven't thought through your routine. It's a tough thing to do mentally. Very few kickers, even international kickers, get 25 out of 25, because it is mentally draining. What it does is reinforce your routine. You see the ball go over, you see the ball go over, you see the ball go over. Then you get more fussy and think, "I don't want it to just go over, I want it in the middle". You can now get quite harsh on yourself because you are within success. Whereas, if you are missing kicks, that tends to beat you up.'

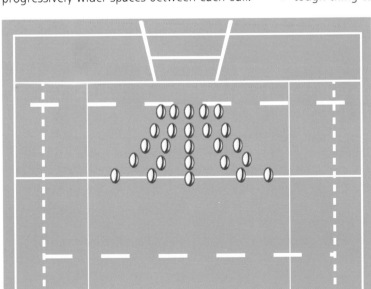

Continues overleaf →

3 GOAL KICKING CHALLENGE

Mick Byrne has a similar challenge for goal kickers and explains how to create a safe environment for players to learn about the pressures of a game without the consequences, 'We don't want to expose goal kickers to traumas. We want kickers to experience what happens to their mental preparation when they are challenged.

'Have seven kicks at goal in a row, one on the 5m, 15m, 22m – have a shot from one post, one from the other post and one from the other 15m line then one for the 40m line directly in front.

'Start on your 5m lines and, when you get one, move on to the next, but as soon as you miss one, go back and start again.'

'Players will kick the 5m because they concentrate hard, then the 15m because they want to get off to a good start. Then they get in front of the posts, relax a little bit, switch off and they'll spray a kick. That's lack of focus so it teaches them they have to be focused on every kick. Then a player gets to the other 15m they think, "God, if I miss this I've got to go back and start again"; these are thoughts that come into their heads that can distract them away from what they are trying to do. So just a little bit of pressure has come on and straight away they are changing mindset, so it's helping them identify with that.'

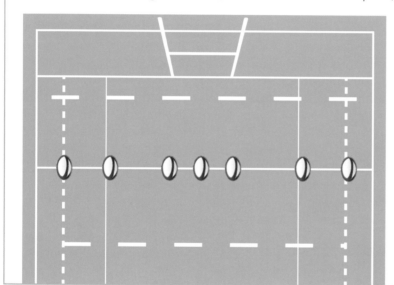

►► Dropped goals

A dropped goal is a kick at goal in open play and can be taken from anywhere on the pitch and by any player within the team. The ball must be dropped on to the ground before being kicked over the crossbar and between the posts. A dropped goal is worth three points and is a tactically astute play, particularly against a stubborn defence.

The mechanics of the kick itself are the same as a penalty kick or conversion. There are variations, however, as the dropped goal occurs in open play rather than from the kicking tee. Practice and timing are required to develop confidence in attempting dropped goals. In a game, the kicker will be under immense pressure from the opposition team, who will attempt to block down the dropped goal effort. For Dr Dave Alred the only real difference comes in the kicker's set-up, 'A drop goal is live so once you have the ball it's automatic pilot and it's how you set yourself up and keep your awareness of where the posts are. The catch is separate, but once you

4 LITTLE AND OFTEN

A challenge for players and coaches is to recreate match-day pressure during training. The consequence of missing a kick at goal during training does not have the same impact as missing a kick during a game. It is very important that goal kickers practise their kicking routine. Taking kicks at goal, one after the other, develops consistency in the kicker's technique and builds confidence, but it does not replicate game situations. During a game, the opportunity to kick at goal comes at random times and it is often the first kick at goal during a game that can set the trend for the rest of the day's kicking.

Dr Dave Alred outlines how to make practice more efficient for kickers to give them that 'first kick' practice they need, '[Practising] your first kick is the most relevant practice you can have. The more times you have to reset yourself to practise, the more times you are coming to the kick cold. It's no good if you are doing goal kicking, get thoroughly warmed up then miss the first five kicks every session and then hit the next 50. If you always miss the first five you'll be 0-5, then 1-6. You must get your brain and your pre-shot routine to work with one-offs.

'In an ideal world the goal kickers would come out 20 minutes early and work on drop punts or goal kicks. Then after the session the backs would stay behind and be kicking spirals, out-of-hands, grubs, worms, etc.

'In the afternoon I'd reverse it so the principle kickers were kicking four times a day but maybe only for 20 minutes. This makes the learning curve more steep and solid because they've had to reset every time. That's four sets of resetting; if it's one long session it's only one set. If you multiply that by four days a week, look at the gain you would have.'

have possession the kicking process can begin.' **Geordan Murphy** has more practical advice, 'Most kickers will kick a drop goal off the instep of their boot. Just on the sweet spot, between the big toe and halfway down the foot. The mechanics are similar to a golf swing – you want to get the ball out, in front of you and give yourself room for your leg to swing through the ball.'

How you drop the ball, the timing of the drop and the speed with which your foot makes contact with the ball are critical. Geordan Murphy offers this advice, 'You want to give the ball time to move because the consistency of the strike is important. Drop the ball on to the ground and let it bounce with the point of the ball coming back towards you. As the ball bounces from the ground, swing your leg through it. The consistency of that is something you can practise.'

Dr Dave Alred has a simple drill to help a player build momentum and mimic the game, 'For a right-footed goal kicker I have a sequence of one left-footed drop goal, one right-footed drop goal, and one kick off the tee straight away.'

TEN WAYS RUGBY

TO BE A BETTER PLAYER

1 FIND YOUR POSITION

Most players who contributed to this book acknowledged they didn't start playing rugby in the same position they now play in. Physical changes, injuries, opportunities, skills and abilities all combined to lead our contributors to their true positions. Time spent in other roles gave the players an understanding of what their teammates require from them and an insight into their view of the action. 'To have played second row, flanker and No. 8 helps me understand what to expect from these players not only in the scrum but also other aspects of the game,' explains Argentina's **Marcos Ayerza**.

Flanker **Tom Wood** believes a young player shouldn't limit his experience on the team to just one position, 'Having an appreciation for what a 9 or centre does will make you a better back-row player in the long run. You don't know how your body will develop so keep your options open and develop your skills so if you have to move position you can bring something to your new role.'

Playing other sports can also help you develop relevant skills and build an understanding of your physical capabilities. Tom Wood's father told him to stay open minded about other sports, 'Playing basketball has transferable skills, like hand-eye co-ordination and spatial awareness. Golf helps with discipline and concentration. All sports will have skills you can use in rugby.'

Marcos Ayerza firmly believes that 'playing football or tennis and using your body in

different sports will help make you a better rugby player, a better runner.'

So how do you know which position is best for you? Your physical attributes might guide you, or a particular strength in your game. Rugby is a game for everyone so you will find a place in the team that lets you use both to best effect.

As a young player it's important to view all your time on the rugby field as valuable experience, so don't worry too much if your heart says centre but your coach says No. 8.

2 KNOW YOUR STRENGTHS

Understand what made you the player you are and maximise the advantage it gives you. You should develop these strengths in tandem with the weaker elements of your game to make you a more balanced, confident and valuable member of the team. 'It will be your strengths that define you as a player and be your point of difference', says Glasgow Warriors head coach **Gregor Townsend**, 'Eliminating or reducing weaknesses is important, but it's not necessary to turn these into strengths.'

'Everyone can be in your face about what you are not good at rather than what you are good at but that's what will make you the player you are. Focus on your strengths and see how you can better those to your advantage', suggests England winger **Marland Yarde**.

How do you know who to listen to and how can you tell if you are improving? South African hooker **Bismarck du Plessis** shares this advice: 'Pick certain influential people and listen to them and only them. If they praise you, appreciate it and if they criticise you, listen to them and take it on board.'

Often being told you can't do something is just the motivation you need. For Harlequins lock **George Robson** that moment was 'being told I'm not tall enough to play second row, I really enjoy saying "I told you I could."' Cheetahs full back **Willie le Roux** encourages young players 'never to let anyone tell you that you can't do something', while Toulon's flanker **Steffon Armitage** says 'don't worry about the doubters, you are the only one who can judge yourself. Follow your heart.'

It's important to take confidence from your abilities and whatever the challenge play to your strengths. French scrum half **Rory Kockott** has a reminder for young players, 'Believe in the type of player you are, don't try be like another 9 in the world. They all have different and greater qualities, so keep doing what you are good at.'

In England's centre **Manu Tuilagi**'s experience, even the most talented players can feel the pressure, 'Before my first game for England I was nervous and I rang my brothers and family. They said just play your usual game; play like you do for Leicester. So no matter who you play for, focus on your own game.'

3 HAVE A MOTIVATED MINDSET

No coach expects a player to be the finished article. Of course, coaches assess a player's physical, technical and mental strengths. However, what a coach is really looking for from a player is a constant hunger to improve and a drive to challenge themselves. Waratahs' assistant coach **Daryl Gibson** believes 'talent will get you so far but good character traits combined with hard work will get you all the way to being your best and maximising your talent'. For Gibson's former centre partner for the All Blacks, **Aaron Mauger**, the answer to being a better rugby player is 'dedication to being the best you can be every time you step foot on the grass'.

Time and again the contributors to this book highlight how they witnessed potentially more talented players than themselves squander that potential through lack of effort. In many cases the X-factor that made good players was hard work, plain and simple. **Mike Cron** works with the All Blacks pack in his role as forwards coach and is familiar with the team captain's approach to training, 'Richie McCaw is never satisfied with his performance and is always trying to improve and to be the best he can be. His ability to perform at a very high standard in every game over such a long period of time makes him one the greatest of all time'.

It's not just about attitude, as a player you want to keep ahead of the opposition by constantly adapting your game, as Richie McCaw has, which can give you that edge. 'The day you stop looking to improve is the day you become a worse player because you stop evolving with the game', believes hooker **Schalk Brits**. 'If you start working hard from an early age that will take you a lot further than talent can'.

A coach can tell you how to improve but ultimately it's up to the player to take ownership of their development and put the work in to get it done. Performance coach at Blues, **Isa Nacewa**, explains how lack of motivation limits a player's potential, 'If your intrinsic motivator is to live by those standards, then you are going to go far. If you have to have standards discussed with you by a coach two or three years into your professional career then I don't think you are going to be in that elite percentage that is going to make it or that elite percentage that makes a difference'.

A competitive nature is about more than winning the game and beating an opponent, it's also about maximising your potential and, in that battle, the real competition is with yourself. 'Some call it mental toughness or grit, but the most difficult opponent we have is ourselves', agrees USA flanker **Scott LaValla**.

'You have to fight against yourself to know you are trying your best', advises Puma prop Marcos Ayerza. 'How much effort you are really putting in is something only you can know, deep inside yourself'.

> ❛ *What makes a good player a great player? Dedication to being the best you can every time you step foot on the grass.*
> **Aaron MAUGER, Leicester Tigers coach** ❜

SET GOALS

Whatever your ambitions in the game, you need to set milestones to get there. These allow you to keep focused on your ultimate goal and measure your progress. USA captain **Todd Clever** advocates setting 'both long-term and short-term goals and apply these to the calendar year, the next few weeks or the next training session.'

To explain his views Crusaders assistant forwards coach **Dave Hewett** likens practising without a goal to going on holiday without knowing your destination. 'Where are you going to buy your ticket to? How are you going to get there? People set goals around what they are going to achieve in a year but actually you need to know where you are going and what you want to achieve too. While going along that path your goal may change or, you may need to change your position, so you need to know where you are heading.'

Your plans shouldn't be so rigid that you cannot take advantage of any unexpected chances when they come along. Leicester Tigers coach Aaron Mauger believes many players miss these opportunities as they are relying on somebody else to point them out, 'The most dedicated players are aware of every opportunity in front of them and this is why they often accelerate their learning at a much quicker rate than others. Ultimately, it is you, the individual, that will decide how high you can climb.'

If you focus on the right process of being a better player, the outcome will take care of itself, as Japan's head coach **Eddie Jones** explains, 'Young players should develop their core skills, their work ethic and love of the game. Being a professional is a consequence of developing those traits.'

BUILD STRENGTH

Working on your physical abilities is not about looking the part but being physically prepared by building the strength and flexibility you need to do your job for the team. Strength and conditioning coach **Ollie Richardson**, encourages players not to 'get caught in the trap of thinking the gym will provide all the answers; no one is going to contract you because of your bench press numbers. Concentrate on all aspects of physical preparation: strength, mobility, speed and conditioning.'

For Stormers kicking coach **Greg Hechter** the message for young players is simple 'you don't do rugby in the gym. Be patient, focus on technique.'

An early focus on physical development can help to shape a career. Irish prop **Cian Healy** says he was able to make early strides because he came into the professional game very strong, 'Throughout school and club rugby, one of my main focuses was to be as strong as possible, so, when I got into the Leinster set-up, I was already ahead of the guys in gym work. This helped me fit in quickly and the physical side of training didn't phase me. It was more a case of getting on with my knowledge of the game.'

Correct technique and tailored programmes are important to help prevent injury, believes All Blacks prop **Owen Franks**, 'If you've been doing your training correctly for a long time it can make your joints strong so that you can take those knocks that might cause some people to get injured easily. It makes your body resilient and gives you that extra hardness.'

'Be very careful with quantity and intensity in the developing biological years,' advises **Felipe Contepomi**, Argentina's former No. 10 who is now a doctor. 'Young players in developing years shouldn't be treated as adults and we should respect their physical and psychological development.'

Video can help you develop good technique, as flanker Scott LaValla explains. 'Videoing yourself when trying to master a new technique on the field or when lifting in the gym helps with efficiency, mastery, safety and self-improvement.'

With all aspects of player development, however, strength comes down to hard work. In his role Ollie Richardson works daily with top international players so he knows first-hand the work it takes, 'There are very few talented players with a poor work ethic that make it to the top and stay there. You've got to want to work and you have to become accustomed to being uncomfortable.'

> *Concentrate on all aspects of physical preparation: strength, mobility, speed and conditioning.'*
> **Ollie RICHARDSON, S&C coach**

6 REMEMBER RECOVERY

'Sleep, nutrition and hydration' are the cornerstones of good recovery, according to Northampton Saints coach **Alex King**, 'If you want to progress as a player, the importance of recovery cannot be stressed enough. Small things like drinking enough water or getting enough sleep can have a big impact on match day.'

'Tools like ice baths, hot tubs and compression foam rolling used in conjunction with a strong diet and a good night's sleep, allow an athlete to recover properly,' is USA winger **Blaine Scully**'s opinion. For coach **Paul Burke** the message is simple, 'How you look after yourself off the training field will determine how well you perform on it.'

What you do to your body, like stretching and rest, needs to be matched by what you put into it. You wouldn't put diesel in a petrol car and expect it to perform. The same can be said for an athlete's body if they eat the wrong foods. Stormers strength and conditioning coach **Stephan Du Toit** explains, 'Player discipline, especially in times when they are on their own, is where the secret lies. They need to do at home what they do at work. To follow the correct diet is one of the biggest challenges a professional athlete will face.'

During a game players need to keep hydration levels topped up to avoid a drop in performance. However, it's equally important to keep properly hydrated off the field.

Players who cut corners on their recovery regime often see an immediate impact on their performance but it can also have longer term implications. Ollie Richardson believes that most aspiring rugby players rarely address their flexibility, mobility and regeneration, 'I refer to this as the injury bank. Every time a player skips out of recovery, stretching, etc., it gets logged in the bank and later on in their careers, once the blessings of youth start to disappear, the bank wants its money back and comes to collect and players miss large parts of the season through injury.'

7 FOCUS ON YOUR SKILLS

Core skills are something that players and coaches emphasise again and again, stressing the importance of a strong foundation in the basics. These are skills that should be worked on continually in practice to keep you sharp in a game, and it's 'the application of those skills within a game,' says Harlequins director of rugby **Conor O'Shea** that 'sets people apart'.

'You watch the All Blacks and it's their core skills that are winning them games,' believes coach **Billy Millard**. 'The ability to pass and catch 1–15, knowing when to offload, knowing when to hold the ball, the 1 on 1 tackle technique, breakdown efficiency. There is nothing fancy there. Without core skills you can have the best game plan in the world but it's not going to get you far at all.'

Mike Ford, Bath's director of rugby, makes it clear that he believes without that foundation in your make-up, even with the best attitude you would struggle, 'You spend a lot of time practising even when you become a professional to keep on top of the core skills. There is a saying that "you never lose it," but that's just a myth. You do lose it.'

England winger Marland Yarde's advice was 'nothing comes easy' and he's right. There is no substitute for hard work and no shortcut to the results it brings. Most players would say they'd have been better players if they'd worked harder on certain aspects of their game. Ireland and

> **"** *Without core skills you can have the best game plan in the world but it's not going to get you far at all.* **"**
> **Billy MILLARD, coach**

Leinster centre **Gordon D'Arcy** certainly believes that doing the extra reps really does pay off in a big way, 'I know if I'd worked harder 15 years ago I'd definitely be a better passer or decision maker. What sets you apart is your skill levels at the crucial moments and at international and Lions level you can see those who have worked hard on their skills.'

Talent levels may vary but every player is capable of working hard if they choose to. So take every opportunity on offer to improve as a player. Stephan Du Toit highlights the benefits that focusing on skills can bring, 'I have seen many "not so talented" players make it after they get a small opportunity due to the hard work they put in to master a skill that the talented player takes for granted.'

'You don't have to be the best player, the most skilful, or the most talented to work hard,' says Ireland and Leinster back row **Sean O'Brien**. 'If you work hard enough at any area of the game you become very efficient and very good at it.'

8 PUT THE EFFORT IN AT TRAINING

At Leicester Tigers, training ground they have a sign to make sure the players get the message: 'Welcome to Work'. Training is meant to be challenging so you grow technically, physically and mentally as a player. You need to get the most out of every session if you are going to improve.

England No. 10 **George Ford** describes training as his job and says that players 'need to be able to switch on straight away in training'. Performance coach Isa Nacewa agrees, 'You have to get out of the mindset that you just have to turn it on for game day; it's about turning on from day one in your training week'.

Springboks scrum half **Ruan Pienaar** explains some of the benefits that hard work in training gives you in the game, 'The way you train is what you will take to the pitch, so training under pressure and putting yourself in game situations will lead to good decision-making and accurate execution'.

Understanding what the aim of a training session is will help you get more from the experience. Setting small personal goals can also help with focus. Prop **Dan Cole** describes the mental preparation his team go through ahead of training, 'Before every session we run through a mental checklist of what we are trying to achieve from the day because you want to come off the field feeling better than when you went on it'.

Fly half **Ruaridh Jackson** sets himself a couple of goals before he steps on to the field, 'Really simple things like if I'm not on the line in phase play. Little things to focus the mind so I don't just float through a session'.

Practice sessions also give a chance to impress and claim your place in the starting XV, as Isa Nacewa explains, 'There are 20 games [a season] yet there are 200 hours of training, so why not use that to show the coaches what you're doing right'.

Remember, though, it's not just about the quality of training, it's the quantity too, and again the motivation to learn. Clermont hooker **Benjamin Kayser** advises young players that, due to the amount of training you need to do, 'you need to love training otherwise you have no place in the sport'.

9 BE PREPARED

As a young player, you never know when your opportunity may arise, but it is essential that you are as well prepared as possible to maximise any opportunities that come your way. 'It is all about doing the work on the training pitch, doing your homework on the opposition and getting your body and mind right', says Todd Clever. His fellow back row Sean O'Brien agrees, 'Be the best prepared possible: eating during the week, sleeping enough, everything that – come the weekend – will make you better.'

If your preparation has gone well, then game day shouldn't be about nerves. It's about staying calm and keeping your excitement in check so you don't play the game before it starts. For some players they find their focus by going through the plays, for others it's by listening to music.

It's a personal thing, as Leicester Tigers' Manu Tuilagi's pre-match routine proves, 'I cook chicken soup with noodles, vegetables and taro, a sweet potato popular with islanders.' Fellow Tiger Dan Cole's recipe for success for beating pre-match nerves is more straightforward, 'Before a game it's too late to learn anything new so you try to settle the mind and enjoy it.'

To play a contact sport you need to go on to the field animated and ready to go, as Clermont's Benjamin Kayser explains, 'An hour before – game face on, get passion in your heart and leave everything on the pitch.' However, it can be tough to get the right level of intensity of aggression while still maintaining the ability to make decisions. The balance is something that comes with experience, explains Harlequins, George Robson, 'It's no coincidence that young guys get penalised a lot. That's how you learn your limits and stop giving away needless penalties.'

When the action finally gets underway it can be overwhelming trying to cope with the pace and physical challenges rugby presents, especially as a young player learning the game. Finding ways to overcome this is important, Edinburgh's **David Denton** offers this solution, 'At age levels the game is essentially broken down into 30-second segments, as there's a break in play for a lineout or a scrum. I knew I could give it everything for between 30 seconds and a minute and then I'd have time to recuperate.'

My advice to players before a game is to know your role and do your job. Do that and you won't go wrong. For coach and former full back **Geordan Murphy** it's about playing your part for the team, 'Rugby is an out-and-out team sport and you have to rely on other people to do their jobs in order for you to do well, as a result you don't want to let the team down. It's important that you fulfil your role and do what you say.'

> ❝ *It's all about doing the work on the training pitch, doing your homework on the opposition and getting your body and mind right.* ❞
>
> Todd CLEVER, USA & OMBAC

10 ENJOY YOURSELF

You and your rugby will benefit from having balance in your life and doing other things you enjoy. It's possible to achieve success both on and off the pitch, as Welsh centre **Jamie Roberts** proved when he completed his medical degree while collecting Six Nations winners' medals and competing in Lions Tests, 'Having something outside of rugby that allowed me to switch off from the game helped me become a better thinker, which, in turn, allowed me to analyse and problem solve on the rugby pitch. I am a better rugby player because of my study. I believe that better people off the pitch make better people on the pitch.'

The game of rugby stirs such passions because of what it can offer in helping to shape lives. For me, my role as coach is to help young men maximise their potential and give them all the tools to be confident, skilful decision makers and not just on a rugby field. If I have just 0.01 per cent influence on these players as young men, then that is immensely satisfying and rewarding.

Former All Black centre Aaron Mauger echoes what a lot of the players and coaches feel rugby offers beyond the pitch, 'Rugby teaches you to take full responsibility and ownership of your actions and subsequent performance with anything that you do. It teaches you that it is OK to make mistakes if there is learning to be had at the other end, and to be proud when you've achieved what you set out to achieve.'

Enjoyment is one of rugby's core values and ultimately it's what makes you want to play this crazy game, to pick up the ball and run and tackle, kick and ruck and maul. More than anything else 'it's great fun to get out there and play rugby with your mates', says Wasps, **Andy Goode**.

Love of the game and the challenges it presents is also a key motivator for those who want to reach their potential as Welsh wing **George North** explains, 'Enjoying it will make sure you push yourself as hard as possible. You won't move to the next level if you don't enjoy it. Enjoyment means you will stay after training and do the extras required to improve.'

The final line in the book is probably the most important. It echoes the last thing I say to my players before they go on to the field and it's something every player should remember:

> *Enjoy every moment! What a game.*
> Jacques BURGER, Namibia & Saracens

CREDITS

The authors are grateful for the generosity of the rugby analytics experts who have helped to bring the game to life through their statistics.

Accenture, the RBS 6 Nations Official Technology Partner, helping to create an enhanced digital experience for fans. See beyond-the-match data @accenturerugby; www.accenture-rugby.com.

Data and insights supplied by Opta Sports. Further insights can be found following @OptaJonny on Twitter.

Southern hemisphere stats courtesy of Super Rugby and Opta Sports.

All images © Getty Images, with the exception of the following pages:

9 © Tiger Images
21, 96, 133, 126, 141 © INPHO/Billy Stickland
116 © INPHO/Nando Vescusio
146 © INPHO/Colm O'Neill
166 © INPHO/James Crombie
176 © INPHO/Cathal Noonan

ACKNOWLEDGEMENTS

Thank you to all the players, coaches and friends who gave up their free time in an effort to help our project. The worldwide rugby community has been incredibly generous and supportive. Eilidh and I are indebted to you. You gave life to our vision. Thank you.

To Kirsty Schaper and all the team at Bloomsbury London and New York, Eilidh and I would like to say thank you very much for giving us this wonderful opportunity and for all your hard work behind the scenes.

My sincere gratitude to Dartmouth Rugby Football Club, and our wonderful rugby alumni, in particular, Alex Magleby. Coach Mags, thank you for affording me the opportunity to develop as a coach and person at Dartmouth College. I am grateful for the trust and belief you have shown in me and because of this, I aspire to be the best I can be, to fulfil my own potential, every day with the DRFC Thank you.

Go raibh míle maith agaibh to my family in Ireland, my parents, Irene and Denis, and my sister, Leanne, for your infinite love and encouragement. Dad, you have always been and continue to be my inspiration on and off the rugby pitch.

To my friend and co-author, Eilidh, I will forever be in your debt. Your thoughtfulness, support, passion, and outstanding work ethic have been the driving force behind this book. Thank you for everything.

A loving thank you to my wife, Jessica, for your seemingly endless love, belief, support and patience. I am in awe of everything you continue to achieve and how easy you make it look. You inspire me on a daily basis to be a better person. I love you. Never a dull moment!
–Gavin Hickie

Thank you to the following for their assistance throughout this project, for opening doors and providing a sounding board. De Jong Borchardt, Seb Lauzier, Luke Broadley, Angus McNab, Iain Young, David Lindgren, Rick Evans, Ray Nolan.

Eilidh's back room team, without your support this book would not have happened. Kevin Farquharson, Betty Tully, Varrie Mayhew, Rachael Howlett, Helen Leng, Susan Stuart, Alison Honeyford, Debbie Willis, Maire Mooney, and the Sporting Chance Initiative team of Sue Hamilton, Wendy Inglis Humphrey, Kevin McCluskie, Ryan Carenduff & David Sherman. Oh and Murphy.

Gav, it's been one crazy journey and it isn't over yet. Thank you for your love and support, you are my rugby inspiration. #shine
–Eilidh Donaldson